A Million
Fragile Bones

Twisted Road Publications LLC

Copyright © 2017 by Connie May Fowler
All rights reserved
ISBN: 978-1-940189-18-5
Library of Congress Control Number: 2016959744

www.twistedroadpublications.com

For the eleven who perished, and millions more,
nature's children all.

"When the last tree is cut down, the last fish eaten,
and the last stream poisoned, you will realize
you cannot eat money."—Cree Prophecy

A Million Fragile Bones

A Memoir

Connie May Fowler

PREFACE

Consider *A Million Fragile Bones* my Book of Psalms, my Song of Solomon, my sacramental moment of bearing witness, my altar box of memories.

My life has been marked by moments of profound loss, but in the midst of pain and bewilderment, eventually I insist on hope.

The first great loss was the death of my father when I was six, and in the writing of this book I realize that over a half-century into my life, I am still searching for him. My method? Immerse myself in nature because my fondest childhood memories, those untainted by violence, arise from his love of the natural world. It's as if I'm trying to provide what eluded him in life: a happy home filled with found objects that, by their very existence, signal we are part of something larger than ourselves. We are seashells. We are feathers. We are bones. We are what cannot be named.

My quest led to a rare life. For twenty years my days were filled with bears and bobcats, dolphins and snakes, turtles and birds, sea and sky. It was an ecstatic journey, a hermitage well chosen. And then that too was blown asunder by human greed and ineptitude.

But I refuse to see this as a fatal blow. I am still standing, still searching.

A Million Fragile Bones is built of memories that out of the volition of cause and effect paint the canvas of my life. Each memory leads me to the next crucial moment. And every moment is my attempt to find my place in the world as a daughter, a wife, a friend, a keeper of dogs, a writer.

The story begins in the middle, when I am at peace. But we all know the middle is simply the beginning of stepping backward and flowing forward. After all, every creature on this good earth lives out her days in the ebb and flow of life's mysterious currents.

"He pleaded so much that he lost his voice. His bones began to fill with words."
— Gabriel García Márquez, *One Hundred Years of Solitude*

Paradise, Part One
How I Got Here

I live on the edge of the world, alone except for the occasional boyfriend or husband, always in the company of pets, books, art, friends, sundry wildlife. Only part-time neighbors inhabit the houses closest to me. There are no stores, unless you count the ship's store, which is rarely open and where a carton of milk will cost you five times what it costs in town. The only real commerce that occurs is illegal, and no one speaks of it, so it might as well not happen. Though I have less money than anyone I know, I rarely wake up depressed and often feel inappropriately rich. I suppose it's all this beauty: dunes, water, sky, and wildflowers whose lives are so temporary even the gentlest of rains fall in the silence between life and death.

Here on the sandbar animal talismans abound. Creatures soar and scuttle, slither and lope, swim and sleep, their existence seen and unseen, their lives forever unfurling, individual threads woven and rewoven into nature's ancient sutra.

Amid the bustling rhythms of the natural world, time is not an abstraction. Rather it is visible, amorphous, revealed in tumbling swaths of sunlight, stardust, cloud shadow, and fog.

At dawn, amid the chime of first birdsong, I throw back my bed covers, walk across worn pine planks, and step into a waking world. The sky's canvas is full. A rising sun. A sinking moon. An insistent, bright planet. Hungry seabirds cutting dark and fast against blooming white clouds.

On earth, sand gathers around the edges of my bare feet, warming them. I close my eyes, knowing below, hidden from view, silent to my ear, limestone mazes shift and crack. Subterranean tangles of tender roots attached to salt impervious plants curl through these mazes with a natural ease I will probably never possess, tethering the dunes to this ever-changing world. Perhaps they tether me, too.

To linger here, a woman must get her bearings.

The wide sweep of the northern Gulf of Mexico and Apalachee Bay is in perpetual motion, reshaping, and at times, reclaiming my front yard. Alligator Harbor, with its clear shallows and deceptive currents—pulled by the moon, the sun, the trickster we call weather—defines and sculpts my backyard, revising boundaries and property lines, confounding appraisers and owners alike. Sometimes, when under the influence of hurricane or winter gales, I watch, awed, as this usually placid bay boils forth—white caps and all—pushing unmoored boats, wayward crab traps, and lost life jackets to within a few feet of my shack.

Butterflies, neo-tropical birds, songbirds, snow birds, sea turtles, sea horses, seashells: everything in flux, everything in a state of rebirth, which means death is ever present. Ants swarm a nest of black-capped chickadees, stinging to death the baby birds and then devouring their warm, swollen bodies. In turn, a blue jay eats the ants, ingesting the chickadee-rich nutrition. Whoever coined the phrase cycle of life was clearly an optimist.

At its zenith, this peninsular sandbar rises only thirteen feet above sea level. That's where my old wooden bird of a sea shack is perched—as if it is its own weather vane—wind-blown, crooked, stubborn, and sweetly tattered at the diminutive apogee of a comma-shaped barrier island known as Alligator Point, a semi-wilderness scarred with too many vacation homes and attached by an umbilical cord of piney woods to the far larger island of St. James.

The configuration of its sugar sand shores and wind-ribbed dunes are, like the living human body, never static. And also like the human body, complexity is its strength; fragility in the face of sudden change, its greatest weakness.

Amid this burgeoning sunlight, I am pelted by shadows. To be exact: shadows cast by great wings. I look to the sky and count. Twenty-seven brown pelicans race in a straight line from the west, moving southeastward, out into the open blue eye of the Gulf.

Like me, these birds are survivors. Like me, their survival depends on the kindness of strangers.

On December 31, 1972, the EPA made the pesticide DDT illegal in the United States. Without that legislation—and without Rachel Carson's environmental masterwork *Silent Spring* changing the mood of the country—these twenty-seven birds would not exist.

On December 31, 1972, my father was long dead, my sister was out of the house, making her own way in the world, and my mother and I were living a tremulous existence in a roach-infested cottage in Tampa. Blooming into a teenager, I was afforded small but significant freedoms. On New Year's Eve morning, Mother dropped me off at my friend's house—a trailer at the edge of town—so I could spend the day with him and his family. Four hours later, she phoned, her voice wavering as she said, "Don't come home tonight. The house is crawling with goddamned demons."

The next day, we—my mother and I—abandoned everything we owned. Every shoe, every blouse, every skirt, every dress, every scarf, every pair of underwear, every earring, every pillow, every book, every juice glass, every dish, every music album, every scrap of paper, every Christmas card, every towel, every spoon, every knife, every photo, every mirror great or small. Everything.

We took only my dog and the clothes on our backs. As we drove around town on New Year's Day, looking for a place to live, and as my mother spoke in detail about the knives that flew through the air all night, and the Bible the demons hurled at her before ripping it into holy confetti, and the rosary that levitated right before her eyes, I held Tiny close to my chest, running my hand down her spine, my fingertip pausing at each vertebra, knowing the sole thing saving me at that moment was the unwitting love of a castaway dog.

The thing about memory is this: It's who we are. We define ourselves by memories, however shape shifting they may be. Without them, we possess no narrative, no history, no *if this or that had happened, I'd be a different person.* If I hadn't ferried into adulthood the memory of Tiny being the one constant in my life that exhibited what I interpreted as unconditional love, I don't think I would have had the strength of mind to discover the sandbar. Love counts, wherever we find it, even if it dwells solely in the hazy lens of recall.

In his journals, Gauguin wrote, "Painting is the most beautiful of all arts. In it, all sensations are condensed; contemplating it, everyone can create a story at the will of his imagination and—with a single glance—have his soul invaded by the most profound recollections; no effort of memory, everything is summed up in one instant."

Ignoring Gauguin's conceit that only painting stirs the soul with such profound sense of recall, the Old Master is approaching something quite important: the power of a single image and how it can reveal an entire life or a person's vast emotional landscape—as large as a continent yet as intangible as air—within the divine territory of a canvas, a poem, a dancer's gesture.

My father's smile. My father surf fishing at "the rocks," a brief spit of coquina sand, orange like my hair. My father relaxed and in his element, his eyes crinkled with mirth, his white hair blown by the breeze—a crooked crown.

A happy daddy immersed in nature—always larger than life; always rabidly cursed or hysterically praised by my mother—his masculinity and gentle humor on display amid salt air and the Atlantic surf and the rare coquina outcroppings: that single image remains my mandala, prompting me to spend days, weeks, months sifting through the windowpanes of my childhood.

From my front yard, I look toward the sea and will my mind to close the windowpanes, to avert my gaze, to forget remembering. Perhaps it's the sandbar's silence or the infinite sky or the fact that at this moment I do not see another human being—there is no one and nothing to staunch the flow. The memories insist on their due. Their weight is enormous. They are a floodtide. There I go.

Before Tampa there was St. Augustine, the nation's oldest city, the place I lived when my father, Henry May, was alive. That mandala image of a happy daddy—the sea, the sky, the coquina, his hair, his smile—might be why I keep insisting on love, why when I feel divorced from nature, I tumble: a grown woman in free fall and who fears a hard landing.

In St. Augustine, I was my father's reflection. He fished, so I fished. He cast nets, so I cast nets. He loved little dogs, so I loved little dogs. He gazed at the big blue sky and smiled, so I gazed at the big blue sky and smiled. In St. Augustine, I knew he loved me and my goal was to never abandon him.

But there is no talking to death. Or to a woman shattered from the loss of the complicated man she loved and hated with an intensity few mortals could sustain over a lifetime. He died when I was six and, unable to withstand the memories that crowded in on her no matter the time of day, the angle of light, my mother whisked my sister and me out of St. Augustine, out of the lives of our half siblings and our aunts and uncles and nieces, away from everyone who knew and loved my father, away from everyone who knew and loved us, away from every kernel of family history, away from every familiar bone, away from the sea that even on the most violent days offered me glimpses of hope.

First my father dies. Then my mother rips us from the familiar. Maybe those two historical markers are not wholly bad. Maybe they prepared me for the losses to come.

Decades later, even in the salt air of Alligator Point, this memory clings to me:

As Mother slipped behind the steering wheel of our black Rambler—her cigarette a determined white bird clamped between ruby red wings—in her usual bent for drama, she issued a final edict before heading to Tampa: "None of us will ever hear the sound of the surf again. That's for damned sure. Not one whoosh. So get used to it. Because it goddamn isn't going to change."

But change is constant. My mother should have known that. Her life was rarely stable. I have no idea if the madness that gripped her as an adult was also present when she was a child. And does it matter? Does the moment my mother lost her mind mean anything? I don't know.

I walk toward the sea. In moments, I will pass over sand dunes whose history I chart in small, spiral bound notebooks. I will pause at a clump of sea oats and notice their circumference grows slowly, but with imperative, as they send out new, tentative roots, unsettling yet strengthening the sand they grow in. I will look up at the sky and ponder the notion of something creating upheaval and strength simultaneously. I will understand that there are holes in my family history I will never fill.

But, still, I will try.

My father grew up among Florida's oldest houses, its deepest history, and earliest tourist traps. He was a street urchin dancing and singing for tourists who tossed coins at his bare feet. It's where, I believe, my mother and father met. If there was a stable home among our people, it was my grandmother's house—filled with glinting glass trinkets she stole from the tourist shops—in the African American neighborhood called West Augustine. The fact that we lived in West Augustine, which was located on the wrong side of the tracks, west of the San Sebastian River and the more affluent African American neighborhood of Lincolnville, the fact that my parents explained in smoky, shifting abstractions that grandmother—who unlike me was dark-skinned and black-eyed—wasn't allowed to live in a white neighborhood, the fact that each time I asked about the grandfather I'd never met I was summarily told he'd joined the circus, the fact that my parents explained almost all of my early questions about identity with the vulgar, dismissive quip that there was a "nigger in the woodpile"—all these clues, many designed to hush a too curious child—were scraps, faint proof, of a complex lineage the adults refused to discuss.

Grandmama May died when I was five and was buried in West Augustine, across the street from the St. Luke A.M.E. Church, her headstone the size of a baby's pillow. A year later, my father died of a massive coronary suffered at home and was buried under the pink blossoms of a crepe myrtle tree in Jacksonville Beach. In the springtime, you have to brush away the petals to see his headstone.

I believe in the first few weeks after his death, I transferred much of what I felt for my father to his hometown. Thinking about him could be a perilous venture, but if I poured it all into his beloved St. Augustine, I could focus on memories that did not hurt: the old town's ancient Spanish houses, the sea oats and palm fronds that rustled with what my grandmother said were the voices of our ancestors even though who those ancestors were remained a mystery, the pin oaks sculpted into a resolute tilt by the near-constant westerly wind, the jewel-toned coquina we gathered at dawn and ate in a chowder at dusk, the moment in first grade when I was lifted off the ground by a nor'easter's abundant gale.

My fetishized notions of St. Augustine were fed by mental movie reels flickering through my mind—I could not stop them—and that was okay because by and large, they were benign: Mother and Father barreling down the coastal highway, A1A, amid the glory of the palmetto hammock and the primal perfection of the Guana River, the nights we were a happy family as we traveled through the pungent marshlands bordering Vilano Beach, the nightly brawls my parents seemed unable to avoid—brawls made only slightly tolerable thanks to nature's beauty balm, the comfort of books, the lessons taught to me by stray dogs, lost cats, caged birds—my father's ghost who rambled through our beach house in the weeks following his death, his ghost that through no fault of his own seized my mother's fevered mind once we'd fled St. Augustine to what she hoped would be a more bountiful life in Tampa, triggering in her a temper that would know fewer and fewer boundaries.

Within a year of my father's death, my corporal self could not contain all these memories. I had to put them somewhere or, I thought, my veins might burst. What did that first time look like? That moment a child, me, wrapped her fingers around a pencil and pressed it to paper? *This is my story. This is how it goes. This is exactly what happened. Let me whisper my truth.*

I possess no recall of the exactitudes, only the impression that I was awash in my own private tsunami. Memories flooded the page—poems and stories and novel fragments. I wrote on anything I could find. Notebook paper was reserved for school projects. We—my mother, my sister, and me—were a government check family living in vermin-infested hovels that seemed to grow humbler with each gleaming rise in Tampa's skyline. Everything was a luxury. So I began scribbling on grocery bags.

"I want to be a writer," I announced to my mother when I was twelve. This after I gave up my goal to be a marine biologist, bowing to the irrefutable fact that science required something I was incapable of grasping: math.

Mother laughed and, after taking a deep draw on her Salem, said, "You stupid little fool. Stenographer. Airline reservationist. Typist. Jesus! Do something that will give you a goddamned future."

But with my father dead and buried, it was the past I craved. I wanted to know who those mystery people were in that mythic woodpile. I wanted a living daddy. I wanted his ghost to wither and die. I wanted his flesh, blood, and bone to be made manifest. I wanted resurrection to no longer be reserved for the anointed. I couldn't remember for sure, but I didn't think Mother beat me when he was alive. She slapped and spanked and called me names glittering with expletives, but she saved the worst for after he was gone. Perhaps she had been too preoccupied pointing out to him his sins and indiscretions to bother much with mine.

Why was I so insistent on writing down everything I could remember, laying bare even the most horrible moments? Because, I think, creating images that crystallized my past so that I could look at my life, contemplate the love that grew like weeds in the face of my family's hell bent violence, was my attempt to impose order and beauty on chaos and ugliness.

These are the things I learned living in poverty. Roaches can eat through anything: plastic hair clips, textbook covers given out on the first day of school, homework, paperbacks and hardcovers, the glitter card I made for my teacher, the Almond Joy bar I didn't eat fast enough, the dirty clothes I left too long in the hamper, plastic fruit, my skin. Do not stomp on that giant spider lumbering across the floor because she might be pregnant, like the one I smashed in a fit of hysteria when I was eight and living in a broken-down blister of a travel trailer, breaking open her belly's dome, sending her premature, motherless, head-of-a-pin-sized babies scurrying in surprised panic from the destroyed womb. Ignore the landlord protestations and keep the stray cat happy because she kills the rats that dart through the darkness. A dog, despite how much it eats and how many pairs of shoes it chews and how much it poops and pees, is worth the trouble. The alternative—life without a dog—is the bleakest of songs. No matter the violence or ridicule, write everything down because even at six, seven, eight, nine, ten, twelve, a child knows the power of words.

Yes. Unending avalanche. Worlds spawned from consonants and vowels, syllables and phrases. Words upon words—prayers for the hopeless, prayers for the beaten, prayers for the poor, prayers for the fatherless, prayers for two girls who wished their mother dead, prayers for a mother whose Appalachian childhood had been so flamed with cruelty, rising from the ashes was never an option—piled up all around me, but I kept writing.

I scribbled in the darkness and the light. And when my mother wasn't home, every word I wrote, I burned. I planned ahead, stealing matches from her tobacco flaked, roach-riddled pocketbook and then—alone except for the rats and roaches that fed on each other's droppings (roaches sought me out at night, feeding on my skin as I slept; Mother's uncharacteristic, tender response? "They're just nibbling a little")—I torched the stories and poems in the kitchen sink. If I wrapped the charred remains just right in toilet paper, I only had to flush once.

And if Mother returned home before I had time to air out whatever rental trailer or termite-gnawed bungalow or flea-bag motel we found ourselves in, I would lie, saying I had burned toast. The lie was a much safer choice than the truth because when she beat me, it was with abandon. And although I will never know for sure, I remain convinced that if she had read my scribbles, I never would have survived her leather belt fury.

I pass over the dunes and in my mind's eye I see the belt. It slices the air before striking me across my mouth. And though the violence occurred years ago, I still taste the blood. This is not a memory I want. So I push it away by envisioning my sea shack filled with impromptu altars cluttered with sacred found objects—feathers and bones, seashells and sea glass, collars belonging to dead pets, and black and white photos of long departed parents. As I dig my toes into the sand, I wonder, is this why I write? To bear witness amid the silent void of my mother and father's absence? If it weren't for this life built of words, would I even exist? Or would I simply be a spectral presence chasing an idea of me?

My skirt hitched up, I stand knee-deep in the Gulf. The surf is calm today, the water clear with vast stretches of turquoise and teal. The twenty-seven brown pelicans have flown beyond my line of sight. Four American oystercatchers glide by and land onshore, searching for a meal … limpets, crabs, clams. About two yards away, a mullet jumps three times. Beyond the languid breakers, a dolphin and her calf meander westward. Their pace is slow, casual, as if this is a day free of tribulations. Something rubs against my leg, catlike, and moves on. Nurse shark? Maybe. I do not bolt. In fact, I will it to return.

It was 1987. By now both parents were out of my life. My mother had died nearly ten years prior, and in the time between my father's death and hers, I had become a quiet over-achiever, socially awkward but academically driven, getting straight A's, editing my junior high and high school newspapers, winning awards and scholarships. No one knew how poor we truly were.

No one knew of the violence. Bruises could be mottled over, explained away. Thanks to an uncanny ability to be attracted to bad men, through the years my personal life remained in flames, but I was putting one foot in front of the other: going to college with the aid of academic scholarships, working as an editor, paying my rent (barely). I was still in my twenties in 1987. Ronald Reagan was president. James Baldwin would be dead before the end of the year. And I was a newlywed. The day after I married my first husband, we left Tampa and headed to Lawrence, Kansas—a college town that interrupts only briefly the vast prairie, a cacophonous crossroads of cultures and ideas pinned to the geographical center of the contiguous United States—where I would begin my graduate school studies.

On the surface I was living my dream: a grad student studying literature and writing, a young woman with every reason to believe the future would be much kinder than the past, a poet whose professors were forging her into a novelist. And though I had remained a good daughter in the years since my father's death—staying true to him by fiercely loving Florida's rivers and streams, marshes and oceans, birds of the sky and fish of the sea—this devotion left me ill-suited for other climes.

Heading into Lawrence from the east, travelers must cross the Kansas River, a body of water that was, in my estimation, nothing more than a dirty brown vein cutting through hard soil—soil that had almost nothing in common with sand but suggested, instead, the resolute pessimism of stone.

Yes, I was a walking, talking sack of bad attitude. Aesthetically and internally, I couldn't embrace Lawrence's Bowersock Dam or the graceless river it harnessed. Where were the cypress knees, the moss draped oaks, the jungle that cocooned southern rivers and provided habitat to gators, snakes, birds, erstwhile lovers?

The Kansas River and its rocky shores possessed a beige, muted beauty I seemed molecularly incapable of grasping.

As I toiled over my first novel and graded student essays and tried to acclimate to the lovely colossus that was the University of Kansas, I often found myself wondering where was the real Kansas, the Kansas that existed prior to the arrival of the well-intended New England progressives who wandered out into the prairie with guns, Bibles, and messianic zeal. I'd seen scant evidence of it. Thanks to agribusiness and the pesticide manufacturing and use that fueled industrialized farming, the bucolic Kansas countryside was as toxic as a Florida golf course.

In my discontent, when I had a few hours of free time, I explored. One morning, preferring off-the-beaten-path routes, I meandered westward and, without premeditation, stumbled upon a place I believe is holy, an expanse of land unsullied by human greed: The Konza Prairie. Located in the Flint Hills, it is the largest area of unplowed tallgrass prairie in North America. During my nearly three years in Kansas, I had somehow managed to avoid the state's greatest treasure: a pristine, untouched rumble of land that evoked the devout beauty of what had become myth: the prairie pre-white-settlement.

Driving along the two-lane country road, the rigid geometry of modern farming gave way, supplanted by an ancient, untamed place. Stupefied, I steered the car to the shoulder, got out, and turned a full 360. A sea of golden prairie grass surrounded me. As far as the eye could behold, the grass undulated—rising and falling, pushed by the wind—just like the ocean. Something sweet and hopeful broke apart inside me. I tasted notes of home. This was the prairie where reality and myth were one, where the grass grew so tall it tickled a horse's belly. This was part of the prairie Indians' Godhead—sustenance, Mother Earth, home. This was nature abundant, a land that supported bison, bobcat, coyote, badger, and copperhead snake. Birds flourished. The sky: infinite. Fourteen hundred miles away from the swamp and sea and once more the memory of my father flashed through my mind. His hair: a crazy crown of thorns. His hope: the deep, cobalt sea. He would have liked it here. But he would have returned home. He was a fisherman. Not a farmer. And so was I. And that was okay.

Standing in the middle of the Konza Prairie, I made peace with Kansas. And I would like to think Kansas made peace with me. Oddly enough, I felt I needed the prairie's permission to go home.

By the time I graduated in August of 1990, I had to admit the landlocked state that seemed so foreign three years prior had been very good to me. The only person in my family to ever attend graduate school and only the second to finish college, my first manuscript was sitting on a New York agent's desk. I had reasons to be proud, reasons to celebrate, reasons to go home. But home was not Tampa. Though I had lived there for two decades, home to me was largely defined by my loss and longing for my long-dead father.

So, with that mandala image of him by the sea flashing in my memory—a beacon inviting me to a far and better shore—I circled back around, returning to the place he loved, the place my mother took us from in the wake of his death. A place that, I would learn, markets its ghosts with the same savvy other cities market their art galleries or mountain ranges.

I hitch my skirt a little higher—the tide is coming in—and knot the hem in two big bunches in order to keep it dry. A plover torpedoes into the water and snags a shiner. The bird is white and no larger than my hand. Plovers lay their eggs on the beach, the shells exquisitely camouflaged in order to trick raccoons and other marauders. But this evolutionary mode of survival is no match for the biggest problem plovers possess: humans, humans who don't see the eggs and largely don't care if they avoid them or not. They stomp right through the clutches, breaking open the shells, hell-bent to stake out whatever bit of real estate they can in order to sunbathe: manifest destiny reduced to weekend drinkers intent on having their way.

I close my eyes against the strengthening sun and a recently acquired memory blooms: a plover looking out to sea with a single chick beside her. The baby bird, like all baby birds, was a marvel of down fluff and wings not yet able or sure. The baby stayed close to its mom, taking in the world and its new home, the sandbar, and I wanted to know if it felt the absence of its siblings, the ones whose shells were crushed under the feet of unaware beachgoers.

The plover flies westward, toward the end of the Point. A pod of dolphin cruises ever closer to shore. An incoming tide, with all the fish that ride in on it, means its mealtime for the dolphins. And just like that, there it is again: life and death in a single pulse beat. I shade my eyes and watch. A dolphin tosses a mullet into the air and catches it in its beak. Dolphins possess extremely sharp teeth. This gives me hope, hope that the fish is already dead. The whole suffering paradigm seems totally unnecessary to me, cruel and unfortunately not unusual, like a really big mistake God made.

But there are so many mistakes, so many memories sliced and diced, borrowed and earned, born in childhood, repeated in adulthood, remembrances made dynamic if only because I fear they will never end:

My much older half-brother, my mother's son, never speaks to me without mentioning how many times he believes my father cheated on our mother, how many times my father beat our mother, how many times my half-brother interrupted their fights, how our mother's nose was broken at the hands of my father, how our mother's teeth were knocked out by my father's fists, which is why my mother, a former Catholic nun, kept a ready supply of paraffin Gulf Wax and penitently—at least every three days—ran a nub of wax under hot tap water, ignoring the scald, fashioning a fake tooth. When the wax was shaped just so, while still incandescent and malleable, she affixed the newly fashioned temporary tooth to her gum line and the teeth on either side of the gap.

My half-brother obsessively repeats, as if he is his own stuck record, details that suggest I was brought into the world in a whirlwind of regret and violence. Our mother was pregnant with me, a situation that was not a cause for celebration because she had convinced everyone but her doctor she was going to die giving birth. My half-brother is not the only person in my family who behaves as if this story was a cause for familial pride. Mother often told versions of it during Thanksgiving and Christmas dinners. "You were the last thing on this planet I wanted," she would say, studying her cigarette as if it offered answers to long-held quandaries. According to her and my half-brother, deep into the pregnancy Mother and Father got into a shouting match, which was quickly threatening to escalate into a physical altercation. In every rendition I have ever heard, my half-brother is a hero, saving the lives of my mother and her unwelcomed, unborn child: *I beat that son-of-a-bitch down. I told him next time I would kill him. It was the last time he ever laid a hand on her.*

To this day, I haven't a clue what to do with that information.

My horror regarding my father's treatment of my mother is shot through with confusion. He was always kind, indulgent even, with me. He was my go-to person. My memories are of my mother raging against him the moment he walked through our front door at the end of each day. And when he didn't come home, my memory is this: the three of us—my sister, my mother, and me—getting in the car at twilight and cruising local bars, searching for his car. When we found it, my sister or I or both would wander in and retrieve him.

And this memory: Mother and Father giggling, drinking, dancing in the living room.

And this memory: The golden brooch studded with pretty faceted stones—a bird in flight—my father gave my mother, which she wore with all the preening coquettishness of an in love schoolgirl.

And this memory: Mother screaming at my father, hurtling cuss words like they were Mardi Gras beads, telling him what a worthless, useless, piece of shit he was.

And this memory: Mother ordering my sister and me into the hallway to witness our father—drunk, naked, swaying, and giggling—as he reached into the hall closet for a towel, unaware of our presence or the words my mother uttered in a calm, acid-laced voice: *Look at him, girls. Look hard. This is who your father is. Nothing but a goddamned drunk.*

Yes, my memories are wholly different than my half-brother's. My sister, who is also older than me, says she retains no memories.

There was a time—say for almost my entire adult life—I would occasionally reach out to other half-siblings, my father's children, but their recitation of my father's antics—rarely home, other women, my mother as The Other Woman—eventually became too painful. I cannot fix my parents. I cannot heal my siblings. I cannot change their memories. I cannot jibe my memories with theirs. Some days, I am the baby who needs to be held.

I have stopped reaching out.

But I have not stopped loving my father. Should I be ashamed of this?

The incoming tide is gaining on me. My hitched skirt, despite my impromptu efforts, grows wet at the edges. I love an incoming tide almost as much as an outgoing, so I stay put as baitfish swarm my ankles. A crab skitters past, trying to hold its own against the hydraulics of the moment. For some reason, crabs remind me of spiders. And spiders remind me of fear and shame. I think about the enormous spider I squashed when I was a girl and realize I had it wrong all these years. The babies weren't in the womb. Spiders don't experience live births. They lay eggs. And in a wondrous act of nurturing, wolf spiders, which arachnologists insist are very good mothers, carry their infinitesimal babies—hundreds of spiderlings—on their abdomens. This knowledge does not help me. The fact that the spiderlings were already born—I must find a way to banish the false memory of them exploding out of the mother's battered womb—doesn't make me feel better about killing her.

Nor does knowing Lenore May was given to hyperbole and madness make me feel any better about my birth story. I could not have been older than eight or nine when she told me she drank a full bottle of castor oil in hopes of ridding her body of me. She intimated a friend gave her pills that were supposed to induce a miscarriage. She said she would have gone to a back alley doctor had she not feared death by mangled abortion.

A wave slaps my thighs, soaking my skirt, and I have a sudden urge to cry. How horrible those nine months must have been for her, carrying within her a child she did not want and going through a pregnancy she viewed as a death sentence. I wring seawater out of my skirt. I hear my mother's voice rising through a blue haze of smoke: "I have no goddamned idea how you managed to be born."

And yet, here I am.

Maybe one of the reasons I felt compelled to return to St. Augustine post-graduate school was to convince my mother's ghost that giving birth to me was actually a positive in this world, not another tragic event in her too-short life. And also, this: Before I ever knew there was a place called Alligator Point, before I was a woman determined not to repeat the sins of her parents, I believed if I could cast a brighter light on my familial history, all of my questions about identity, love, and madness would be answered.

So, amid St. Augustine's thick heat, I wandered through cemeteries in search of family graves.

Because they knew my father once upon a time, I sought out old men who sat on their windy porches, knitting casting nets. When recognition struck, their eyes gleamed with the light of their own memories. *Oh my God, you're Oochie's daughter!*

At twilight, on cold winter days, I ate oysters, a faint memory pinned to my heart: my father in the backyard, roasting freshly harvested bi-valves under a wet burlap bag.

I searched for and found Grandmother's old house. The house, itself, looked good. Whoever lived in it maintained a collection of glass trinkets in the windows, just as my grandmother had done, and I wondered if theirs, too, were stolen: crystalline blue chickens, yellow unicorns, purple seahorses, sunlight refracting through them only long enough to signal the weight of invisibility.

The coquina goldfish pond—a symbol of a happier time, an oasis where I escaped the chaos of my parents' anger as I watched the fish languidly swim amid shivering lily pads and where I took solace in the murky water and the fish-dance and the secret world of survival that thrived there—was crumbling, overtaken with dirt and weeds. I pushed down a hard knot of panic (I too easily believed in signs) and told myself such is the passage of time. Things crumble. Things fall apart. Things go *whoosh*. Things evolve into new life or stubborn decay. Fashion yourself a tooth born of melting wax. It's not the end of the world.

From the perch of my car seat, I studied the house, tried to get the gumption to knock on the door. A good memory flew in through the window: Grandmother tilling her garden with bare hands, the fruit of her labor: collards and tomatoes and okra and datil peppers. She was still there, I decided, a ghost amid a fallen garden. Did she look up from her haunted toil and recognize me? Or was I just another lost, nosy tourist?

I did not turn off the car, gain the steps, and knock on the door. I did not ask to see inside. I did not say, "This was my grandmother's home." I did not spill my guts to the house's current owner, saying something pathetic such as, "I'm desperately trying to figure out who I am, who I come from."

No. I was a stranger. I belonged here and I didn't. I put the car in gear and sped down the road, a nebulous suspicion forming. Once a moment in time is relegated to the past, perhaps it no longer exists.

"That can't be," I whispered.

I lie in the shallows and let the sweet Gulf waters roll over me. I imagine the pod of dolphin growing curious and swimming closer. I imagine they sidle right up to me. I imagine I grab two of them by their dorsal fins and they swim me deep into the sea. I'm happy there.

A week ago, I began reading Gauguin's journals for the second time, not because they are well written but because there is something in the text about isolation and beauty and loss and life I need to learn. My favorite line—"I close my eyes in order to see"—seems deceptively instructive to me. So, lying in the Gulf, I try it. I close my eyes. I feel the water lapping at and over my body. At first I think I can still see the sun's rays behind my closed lids. But within seconds, everything fades to black. What am I looking for? What could Gauguin see that I can't? I hear the *keer! keer!* of a tern and the black is dispelled, replaced by a grainy, sienna-edged memory: that inerasable moment when my sister and I hid between the wall and our bed, fearing my father's guttural death moans and howls were the result of him turning into the monster our mother always claimed he was. At warp speed, we bypassed the possibility of a heart attack and dove straight into the heart of darkness. And this quick image, which I bear solely because I finally I dared to patter down the hall: Mother kneeling beside my father, screaming for him not to die as she pounded on his chest, trying to batter his motionless heart into *one more beat, just one more, please, goddamn it, dear God, Henry Jefferson May, don't do this to me!*

I open my eyes wide—maybe I'll never close them again— and struggle up and out of the water.

That can't be. As I wound my way out of my grandmother's still devoutly poor and predominately African American neighborhood, I sped toward what I hoped would be a happier cache of memories: the rocks. And rather than dwelling on the possibility that moments of our lives disappear in the scuffle forward motion, it dawned on me that when the past meets the present, the lens initially appears warped. We require seconds, minutes, hours, or entire eons—depending on our flexibility—before our vision adjusts.

I threaded my way south on A1A, eventually taking a left-hand turn toward hallowed ground, and was happily surprised to find the rocks had become a state park. Since returning to St. Augustine, I'd discovered many of my father's favorite places had been mowed down and paved over in the service of "progress." But the state had had the presence of mind to save this small stretch of coast. I paid the entrance fee, parked on the ocean-side, and climbed the steps to the boardwalk. There it was, my father's sacred place, never static, undestroyed, brilliant. I climbed atop a huge coquina rock scattered with sea urchins, starfish, anemones, and thought, At least this won't go away. Not this. Not ever.

I gazed at the breakers and listened to the surf's roar. Every time my father caught a catfish, rather than a red fish or a sheepshead or a drum, he would laugh mightily, as if the ocean was playing a game with him, one that he aimed to win. I sat down on a rock that contained depressions filled with seawater. The pools harbored tiny crabs and small darting fish. I watched their lives unfold. They were very busy … eating, hiding, swimming. The surf surged over the rock, soaking me. I didn't care. It felt baptismal. My mind bloomed: Father's smile, his white crown of hair.

And then I thought, I need to live here.

A few months later I bought some land, a little palm tree studded patch of earth five minutes from the rocks, and I built a house.

Summer Haven is a tiny hamlet located sixteen miles south of St. Augustine. Situated at the juncture of two rivers and the sea, I decided this village with its oyster middens, sand dunes, wind-tilted wooden houses, and proximity to my father's favorite beach would be the missing piece of the puzzle, the crooked edged interior piece that would finally lock into place a bird's eye view of my past, present, and future.

Nothing in this life is static. Summer Haven is no longer situated at the juncture of two rivers and the sea. In 2008, Mother Nature rearranged her living room. A tropical storm followed by a nor'easter erased Summer Haven River. A new bridge arcs gracefully across what is now a wide swath of white sand. The oyster beds and trout fishing are but a memory. Yet by the time anyone reads this, that situation might have changed. Again.

The fact that there was once a river the wind stole will be a story old-timers will tell indulgent newcomers. The story—because it sounds Biblical, outrageous, like the meandering thoughts of a great failing mind—will smell faintly of mothballs and death and predetermination and God. The story will defy what we want, what we think is real: permanence.

I walk, dripping wet, across the wide expanse of sand. When I reach the dunes I scan the area. There are no animals to be found. The sun is at its afternoon peak and everything is on siesta, hiding in the shadows but aware of my presence. I crest a high dune and the shack comes into view. It is perfect. A tiny jewel the sandbar made. I'm bashful to admit this, but the shack is my heart.

Summer Haven prepared me for what was to come next, for it was amid the island's oyster middens and rivers and inlet and sea that I became a birder, where the notion of animals as messengers took root and wouldn't let go, and where I unwittingly took my first steps toward activism.

In the Summer Haven house, I saw my first painted bunting, a glorious, nervous little bird. With violet heads, lime-green and yellow backs, jade wing bars, and red underbodies and rumps, the males startle with their beauty. Indeed, their beauty might be the cause of their apparent nervousness. John Audubon noted in 1841 that thousands of these animals were trapped and sold as ornamental caged birds, with many exported as far away as Europe. The illegal trade in these birds, which continues to this day, along with habitat loss and the thug behavior of brown-headed cowbirds that lay their eggs in the nests of painted buntings and other songbird species, contribute to this smallest of finch's dwindling numbers.

The female buntings are not as flashy, but I find them just as beautiful. Their subtle green-to-lemon-yellow coloring complements the rainbow males in much the same way female cardinals offer a subtle counterpoint to their blazing red mates.

In Summer Haven, I learned to spot the difference between a bald eagle and an osprey, and I became adept at identifying juvenile bald eagle, which is tricky because before their heads turn regal white, they look nearly identical to young vultures. I witnessed the first colony of roseate spoonbills take up residence in the Summer Haven River. Even then, before global climate change was a household term, I knew their arrival—though thrilling—was due to habit loss and a warming earth. *Peterson's Field Guide to Eastern Birds* became my constant companion and soon I could distinguish between black-crowned night heron and yellow-crowned night heron, great egret and snowy egret, orchard oriole and Baltimore oriole.

Despite becoming a passionate birder, I found myself in a constant state of low-grade worry because my schipperke, Atticus, liked to nap on the sundeck in the unfettered sun. On at least five occasions, I scared off vultures by engaging in what can best be described as an epileptic Banshee dance as the corpse-loving buzzards spiraled downward through the blue, Atticus clearly in their sights. I was positive they thought the diminutive dog was dead.

In the Summer Haven house, I experienced my first visitations. Not long after I moved in, a rufous-sided towhee began flinging himself against my studio window and continued to do so for weeks. When he wasn't flinging, he was staring at me with what I perceived to be unhealthy intensity. I would pause from my writing and place my hand on the glass pane. He would peck at it and then look at me with urgent, curious intelligence. We would stare at each other for very long moments that eventually cumulated into hours. I wasn't getting any writing done. I was as obsessed as he.

"What do you want, little bird?"

In the second month, the bird grew more frantic as did I. Finally, on a blazing, cloudless afternoon, I went outside, looked up at my window where he was perched, and said, "I have no idea what it is you need, but apparently you want to come into the house. So let's go."

I walked back inside but left open the door. I stood at the base of the stairs and waited. The bird flew from its perch, landed on the front stoop, and walked in.

"You're welcome to stay," I said.

The bird inspected the foyer, walking the length and breadth of it. He even inspected the antique walnut table, pecking its cabriole legs. He lit on the second step and studied me, his red eyes intent and searching. His movements were no longer frantic but purposeful. I stayed very still and felt oddly calm. The bird tilted his head and looked up the stairwell. I thought it might take flight and inspect the rest of the house. Instead, it hopped onto the bottom step, looked at me once more, walked back out onto the stoop, and flew away.

I never saw the bird again.

Whoosh.

The towhee, which I admit I missed, had been gone for three weeks when the second visitation occurred. It was twilight and I had just stepped outside with the trash when I saw a dark form take shape in the shadows beneath the palms. A bobcat! Local media did a good job of instilling panic over possible sightings of rabid bobcats and raccoons, which in actuality was simply a ploy to keep us glued to the news. But still, fear raced through me. I turned to reenter the house. As I walked, I glanced over my shoulder, scared the wild cat would spring from the darkness and attack me. I turned back around, scanning the entire yard. There was nothing there. Just shadow.

On three other occasions, I stood at my studio window at dusk and witnessed the animal amid the trees, staring placidly at the house. Every time I looked away and back again, the bobcat was gone. I asked my neighbors if they'd seen it.

One old-timer said, "Not in years."

Another one said, "That cat died a long time ago. You were lucky to see it."

If I was truly going to belong to this place I considered home, I decided I had to do something about what I had started calling The Destruction. Florida has long been a state that divests itself of its environmental and historical treasures with all the somnambulant ease of a molting lobster. With its abundance of natural beauty, St. Augustine was a developer's dream. I could do nothing about what was already lost but I could try to help save what remained. This plan was part of my insistence on being The Good Daughter, the one my father would be proud of were he alive. So I threw myself into the local environmental wars. My friend and neighbor, Annie Ferran, and I would watch the sunset or gaze out at the bright Atlantic and get worked up. Worked up enough that we wrote letters to elected officials to which we never received a single response.

One day over a plate of freshly steamed shrimp and vinegar coleslaw, I said, "You know what we need?"

"What?" she asked, her twinkling eyes matching the ocean's blue.

I waved a shrimp at her. "A constituency."

Her beer-reaching hand paused, as though she were stunned. And then she stated the obvious. "But it's just the two of us."

"Yes. Yes, it is." I considered the shrimp, the way it trembled on my fork, how—having been steamed—it looked nothing like its living counterparts. "But they don't know that."

After lunch, I headed into my studio, sat at my computer, and went about the business of creating letterhead. "What should we call ourselves?"

"Let's see," Annie said, squinting into the afternoon heat. "How about Not Too Bad for A Couple of Girls?"

"Nope," I said, determined that we look legit: a legion of voters. How difficult could it be to turn water into wine? I studied the pink flamingo clip art we had copped. It wasn't what I'd have chosen in a perfect world, but it looked professional enough and was free. "How about … River to Sea Civic Association? I'm president. You're vice-president. And we won't mention under any circumstances that we're a force of two."

That afternoon we mailed our letters on River to Sea Civic Association letterhead and within a few weeks, the governor, members of his cabinet, and other local, state, and federal elected officials were writing back.

"Whoa," Annie said the day I showed her the I'm-in-your-corner response from Governor Chiles, "we've got to start a membership drive."

I had no connections in St. Augustine and my childhood-inculcated distrust of people made me unsuited for the limelight. But Annie was a natural. She knew all the right people, knew the right things to say, and—sad that such a skill was needed at all—knew exactly when to bat her eyes. She enlisted the help of Pat Hamilton, a local realtor—yes, a realtor—who to this day is one of the most committed environmentalists I've ever known. As our numbers grew, we wrote more letters, signed petitions, spoke at county commission meetings and before the Governor's cabinet. We wept over and worried about all the battles we lost. We won a few but mainly we got kicked in the teeth. But then we did something huge.

Many of us thought our biggest battle would be our easiest. Who wouldn't want our river system to be studied, tested, kept relatively pristine? As it turns out, lots of people. We battled industry, business, and St. Augustine's good ole' boy body politic before successfully snagging—to the amazement of foes and friends, alike—a National Estuarine Research Reserve designation for the Guana, Tolomato, and Matanzas river systems. Two of its key provisions were funding for water quality testing (something the owner of a prominent speed boat manufacturer insisted would create unfair advantages for his competition outside the reserve because only *his* company would be fined for dumping toxic waste into the river; for the companies upstream, it would be business as usual) and kindergarten through twelfth grade environmental education in the public schools, something our foes opposed out of fear, I surmised, that, if educated, the children would grow into card carrying environmentalists.

I learned an important lesson during my early days of activism. The opposition wasn't brighter than we were. Rather, they were richer, which made them patient. They didn't have to show up at interminable meetings. They hired lawyers who did that for them.

But we had a secret weapon. A mole in county government tipped us off with only hours, sometimes minutes, to spare each time the cloud of an unannounced commission meeting mysteriously mushroomed. Out of tenacity that was often stretched thin—and with the invaluable help of the mole—we always managed to pull together a contingent in time to prevent a secret or unscheduled vote.

But we grew tired. We had children, family, lovers, blowouts, breakdowns, jobs, food poisoning, vacations, visitors, recitals, and TV shows that sometimes we simply couldn't miss. After all, we were only human. That's how the other side won almost all but that single battle: by waiting us out.

With the stakes so high, the fight was worth it. And so were the lessons I learned from seasoned environmentalists who knew how to speak truth to power, whose voices were strong and passionate, whose footsteps I longed to walk in.

Amid the environmental work, I stubbornly continued to shake the locks on my family history, but by the end of each day I had opened no doors. My father's friends were dying and in their presence—which I was grateful to be in—I learned once more the shape-shifting nature of memory and truth. Nobody's stories jibed and in the intervening time between visits, tectonic revisions took place. *Your father met your mother when he was entertaining the troops who were here at the beach for R and R. Your father entertained the troops in Europe and met your mother over there. She was an army nurse. She was on vacation in St. Augustine and joined your father's band. She had perfect pitch. That's why your father married her.*

Between the shifting memories of the dying and the wholesale destruction of places I held sacred, even in my studio filled with sweet Florida light and the scent of jasmine, I could not cut out a paper doll likeness of father and daughter.

I have no goddamned idea how you managed to be born.

Back at the shack, with the dogs gleefully jumping on me, I strip off my wet clothes and leave them in a pile on the back deck. I hose off in the outdoor shower. I walk through the house naked and dig a towel out of the clean laundry bin.

I would not say I am lonely out here. In fact, most people scare me. The fear, I understand, is a natural reaction to my upbringing. Still, there are people in this world I dearly love, people who prompt me to pick up the phone and say, "It's been a while. Why don't you come down to the coast? I'll fix supper."

My friends share a healthy sense of place. Perhaps this is why we love each other. None of them bat an eye when I gaze out at the sea and say, "This is my church."

For some reason—some cranky bout of temporary insanity—even as my first novel sold for a decent sum of money, I opened an antique shop on a cobblestoned, one-lane road named Aviles, after St. Augustine's European founder Pedro Menendez de Aviles. My stock-in-trade was fabulous 1940s jewelry—Bakelite, sterling Trifari and CoroCraft, giant Eisenberg brooches studded with exquisitely faceted crystal rhinestones, intricately beaded Miriam Haskell, extravagant and oft times surreal Schiaparelli. Evidently I had inherited my grandmother's affection for bright, shiny things. Some days I would clean each piece by hand and I'd remember my mother's beloved bird brooch, that sweet gift from my father, and I'd wonder how in the world it had become just one more lost family trinket.

Aviles is our nation's oldest street. And though old and quaint and ridiculously historic, tourists shaded their eyes, craned their necks, and gazed at us from the hubbub of the main square, the Plaza de la Constitución, but nearly none of them made the trek south to my store or any of the stores, preferring to stay in tourist central, known by locals as Tourist Hell. As Dan Holiday, the building's larger-than-life owner, was fond of saying, "We could bowl in the middle of the day right down this damn street."

As I sat there morning, noon, and night, selling almost zip, I was saved from an incurable case of *Oh my God! What have I done!* thanks to a friendship I struck up with someone who lived a block south of the shop. Flynn Bevill, the town's pharmacist, was renovating a 1700s clapboard cottage (it was rumored to have once been a slave cabin), using might and ingenuity, courage and a wing-and-a-prayer, and a well-worn copy of that classic *Time Life Books Complete Home Improvement and Renovation Manual.*

I loved so many things about Flynn. His golden red hair. The fact that he never met a stranger. The fact that he welcomed everyone into his home with warmth and brown liquor. The fact that we were on the same artistic wavelength, meaning we found humor, humanity, and grace in the ordinary and meager. The fact that he loved St. Augustine with a fierceness equal to mine. The fact that sunshine could make him cry. The fact that I'd found someone equally vulnerable, equally committed to doing no harm. The fact that even though his marriage was over and mine was experiencing ever deepening stress cracks, we *knew*, we just *knew*, everything was going to be alright.

It was the early 90s and the Summer Solstice was upon us. Flynn called the store and said we should spend the Solstice together, by the water.

"Hold on."

I checked the street. Not a soul.

"See you in ten minutes."

On the longest day of the year, I closed up the pretty shop with all its gleaming treasures and met him at the seawall.

As the sun reached its zenith, all the shadows left us. A clarion light suggestive of infinity, of affirmations gentle and otherwise, infused the air. Being alive in a shadow-free world, amid saltwater and boats and darting fish, felt exhilarating. I wanted it to always be like this: two friends sitting by the bay, chatting, at ease.

And then the only shadow in my known world at that very moment crossed Flynn's face. Sometimes when a friend is troubled, we want all the details, we want the problem pinned to a board where we can poke, prod, dissect, fix. But there are other times when, even if that were done, the problem would scramble off the board bigger and badder than ever, defying definition or resolution. This was one of those moments. Flynn explained he was leaving St. Augustine in the only way his situation would allow: in vague details. It was a spiritual crisis. A moment of *What does any of this fucking mean?* An insistence that New Mexico with its ancient indigenous cultures might heal whatever it was that was cracking him open.

"You can't leave. You'll die if you leave."

"I'll die if I stay."

I slipped my hand in his and we were silent. In tandem, our attention was drawn to the sky. A convocation of osprey was riding the thermals. Seemingly without effort, they glided up, up, up.

Icarus' wings, I thought. Flynn's melting wings, I thought. Osprey mate for life, I thought. They have reversible toes, I thought. Friendships should be so flexible, I thought.

"Wow," Flynn said.

"Yes. Oh my gosh."

The osprey continued to spiral ever higher, a ribbon of black and white unfurling until one-by-one, like stars extinguished, they were gone.

"What are we seeing?"

"I don't know."

Flynn squeezed my hand, his gaze still pegged to the disappearing birds. He closed his eyes. He lifted his face into the light. "There I go."

Whoosh.

There are animals in my shack that aren't supposed to be inside: a lizard, a frog, and a rat snake. The rat snake, to be honest, is a part-time visitor. Sometimes I find him curled up in a jeweled coil on my kitchen windowsill, getting warm.

I don't mind. But I worry about them getting enough to eat. I keep telling myself if they grow hungry, they know the way out.

Freshly showered and dressed after my sojourn in the Gulf, I sip tea and watch the brilliant green lizard I've named Ed sun himself in a circle of light on my living room floor. I wonder if it's healthy, me living with all these animals. And then I remember what Gauguin said: "Civilization is what makes you sick."

Amen.

Winter took a liking to north Florida in 1994. Summer Haven, with its promontory rising from the Atlantic, took nor'easters head on. When I wasn't being blown asunder, I felt weighted down by the gray, the fog, the lead-lined bleakness of cold. Flynn was gone. My marriage was rocky, although I told not a soul. And I was about to shut down my shop simply because every day I went there, cocooned by pretty objects and loneliness, the winter chill deepened into what my bones perceived to be rejection.

But on this particular late winter morning, I was trying not to let the weather or life's vagaries affect me because I was embarking on a road trip to the Florida panhandle, specifically Pensacola—a military town amid white sand beaches—where, under the auspices of the Florida Humanities Council, I was to speak to a group of new residents on the topic "Making Florida Home."

Still in St. Augustine, sitting at a red light at U.S. 1 on my way to I-95, I gazed out the windshield at a highway construction crew that, to ward off the cold, had donned sweatshirt hoodies and thick gloves. One guy was bent over a clanging machine, his thermal underwear blazing white. The men's breath erupted like petite Furies. The very idea of new construction in any form threatened to turn my blues into something resembling midnight. I studied a dead gnarl of jungle that had been bulldozed in service of progress. To hell with it, I thought; I'll take the back roads.

I threaded my way through two-lane black tops and villages that emerged from sand hills, pine forests, and swamps. In the pulp timber town of Perry, I headed west on Highway 98. Farmland soon emptied into jungle forest, then swamp. And I mean, unruly jungle, unspoiled swamp. Paradise untouched … how was this even possible?

I tilted my head and glimpsed the sky—cloudless and bright blue—pinched crystalline by the cold snap. Before long, the light shifted and I entered the dappled landscape of an old growth cypress forest, its canopy towering above me in a graceful arc. The air churned a few degrees cooler. The world glittered with critters on the wing, the light deepening into a meditative fugue, and my inner landscape shifted: a spry spiritual realignment, a faint recognition of something ancient regained. It was as if old waters long hidden became tidal and known. I wondered if Flynn, now gone many months, was experiencing something similar out there on the western mesa.

Just as it had in the Konza Prairie, an awareness of having entered a holy space rose within me, as did those images of my father fishing by the sea. He in his element: the salt air. He in his glory: the open sky ablaze; a canopy blooming blue and clear; his white hair shivering like a teardrop or a cloud. I slowed the car and surveyed my surroundings, recalling a fact from my art history days. At least as far back as the ancient Byzantines, religious people viewed the canopy—its shape and intent— as a place conducive to worship. They built their churches accordingly.

As I took in the beauty, I wondered if ancient civilizations with the sky their sole canopy better understood what "sacred" meant—its complexities and responsibilities—than their modern day progeny who wandered through a world divorced from nature, where living a sanctified life was defined by, and reduced to, the act of passing the collection tray. Take Abe to church and all that.

A great blue heron sliced the sky, an egret fished the tannin-rich waters (newborn mullet resembled tiny birds and I wanted to know if this bothered the egret or if its wisdom outpaced the reality imbedded in the shadow of death), and a hawk—zipping through a tangle of branches the way a dancer tumbles through the give and take of space—created a cacophonous winged-puppet show composed of shadow and sun, want and need, joy and desire.

In that moment, when all the world seemed to be engaged in some sort of flight, I felt the good parts of my past—my father's big smile when I tumbled into his arms, my mother's wobbly insistence, even amid her rage, that her children have a better life than she did—surge through me.

Without intent, when I was barely looking, I had stumbled upon a place akin to home, the Florida my father knew.

I discovered the shack because I was supposed to. Because maybe dead parents really do look after their living children from a space so great it escapes the cartographer's gaze. Because who in their right mind could not travel down a road that led to a village called Alligator Point?

Truth: When viewed from the highway, betwixt vertical columns of a piney forest, the village appeared to rise from the sea: a mirage of structures glinting in the Gulf's magnified light. Atlantis ascending. I drove until I reached a turnabout—a sandy half-circle mounded by oyster shells, felled pine trees, one white tennis shoe—and reversed my course, backpedaling until

I reached the winding road that would lead me to the shack, already knowing with a certainty born of bone I wanted to live the rest of my days in the gleaming, beating heart of that mirage.

One more beat, just one more …

For a good ten or fifteen minutes, I drove through the lake-dotted woods, which eventually led to a dogleg veer to the right and the Gulf of Mexico, its sapphire eye glinting right beyond the undulating dunes.

This was not an unspoiled sandbar. Vacation homes, modest affairs with plenty of porches, hunkered amid sand juniper and pines twisted—as if plagued with arthritis or swollen with sap—by the insistent force of gale winds. Newer stilt homes provided passersby with Gulf views through the open spaces cluttered with boats and motors and fishing nets. But there were no condos or McMansions preventing a view of the sea.

How could this be? How could there be a beach in the state of Florida not overrun with asphalt, goofy golf courses, pesticide green golf courses, Margaritaville knockoffs, drunken tourists, drunken locals, trinket shops specializing in Welcome to Florida snow globes, billboards advertising "steaks and titties," and snowbirds who preferred giant, air-conditioned mausoleums-in-waiting to the open breeze?

I kept driving, searching for something … an evocation of childhood, of belonging, of a past woven without error into my present, of a place as important as Flynn's New Mexico. *Something.* I passed the KOA and the water tower. In front of the campground, storm-beaten stilt houses wavered in the sugar-white sand and I wondered if their owners had to wade home during high tide, balancing groceries on their heads. I did not yet know that only a few years prior, two miles of beach stretched between these houses and the Gulf waters. Erosion and the sea's desire to reclaim the land was, I would learn, an ever-present reality on the sandbar.

West of the campground, the homes were simpler—weathered and mainly unoccupied—and the elevation grew slightly but I still felt an odd tug of being below sea level. As I cruised down a straight stretch of road, I spied a compound of whimsical buildings, one with a bell tower, another with an octagonal, thatch-roofed gazebo—the property stretching from the bay to the Gulf—and a sign painted with those magical words "For Sale by Owner."

I pulled over, studied one of the buildings, a wind-worn home without a stitch of plastic or paint. Hand-cut gingerbread scrollwork (fish, moon, stars: my holy trinity) trimmed the roofline. A screened-in porch ran the length of this simple wood frame house nestled amid pine, palm, and fruit trees. The house didn't assert itself on the landscape. Rather, it appeared to be an integral part of it, as if it grew from the dunes under the pine tree shade.

The front yard shimmied under the weight of the breeze. Sea oats swayed, their long reeds bowing toward the earth, the sky, the earth, the sky. Ox-eye daisies grew, as is their habit, with happy abandon, providing groundcover of deep jade jeweled with yellow petals. I took note: Sod was not welcomed here.

Tearing up, I turned off the engine and felt what I feared and hoped was the hand of providence. I tumbled out of the car and walked toward the house, the seismic rumblings of a mental earthquake fueling my journey, for in spirit and mind I recognized the complexion and extent of an overdue reckoning. I gained the front steps, pressed my head against the screened porch door, and peered in. Unlike my grandmother's house, I belonged here. My memories belonged here. My musings belonged here. My future lived here.

The full moon bathes the surface of the Gulf in a light that resembles liquid silver. I have changed back into my wet skirt, although by now it is mainly dry. Midnight approaches and the tide is out. I am barefoot and dancing in the sand. Each step I take sparkles, for we are having a bioluminescent night. The surf is full of naked-to-the-eye critters that, like fireflies, are living chemical reactors of light. As the water ebbs, these light-makers are left behind in the sand. I spin a full circle. The light chases my orbit.

Out of the corner of my eye, I see something dark and amorphous. I pause and try to interpret the shape into something familiar, but recognition eludes me. It is moving through the dunes, ignoring me, and its gait is not that of a dog.

Amid invisible creatures that cause the water and sand to pulse with light, it is easy for me to believe I am in the company of a spirit animal. Perhaps I unintentionally brought a hitchhiker or two with me from Summer Haven and they are finally making themselves known. I run along the shore—it looks like lightening is pulsing in my wake—thrilled with the insane possibility that a spectral bobcat watches over me.

I had barely put the for sale sign in the front yard of the Summer Haven house when a couple from Maine made an offer. She was an artist smitten with Florida's all-illuminating light; he was a retired physician who simply wanted to spend the rest of his days unencumbered—no more perpetual life/death tango—staring into the feral blue waves of the Atlantic.

Despite having fallen head over heels for the sea shack, I experienced moments of deep hesitation. How could I leave

St. Augustine? I had not yet uncovered my family secrets but suspected I never would. Mother, Father, and Grandmother May (the only grandparent I ever knew) had with their dying neatly cut the umbilical cords to our pasts, taking the answers I sought to their graves. I had to accept that the clues I turned over and over in my mind forever led to more questions, never answers. I envied people whose familial history and lineage was known, unchanging. They seemed to possess a confidence I lacked, as if knowing who and where they came from justified their existence, indeed magnified it. All I could do was examine rumors, fading memories, a handful of alleged facts, and guess.

My prevailing theory, eventually supported by DNA testing but unconfirmed by a single human soul, is at its crux America's story. My people were a mélange of races—Irish, Scandinavian, North African. I suspect those who were of color and light enough to pass, slipped into the landscape of the majority race, burying their history and denying whatever diverse genes had contributed to those wild, high cheekbones, that dense black hair, the nappy curls, the dark eyes. Of course, they chose their partners accordingly. The end result, after a few misses, was the bleaching of the gene pool, enabling me to emerge: red-haired, green-eyed, pigment-free lashes and brows, with skin so fair I sometimes think moonlight might burn me, a person who genetically falls within the albinism range.

This intersection of racial identity and sense of place was, I realized, one of the main factors that kept me writing, searching. The cacophony created by mingling identity and place also rendered me perpetually confused, even after discovering this word pinned repeatedly to my mother's side of the family on a 1910 census: mulatto, mulatto, mulatto.

What did mulatto mean in 1910? According to written instructions the census takers were to follow, "For census purposes, the term 'black' (B) includes all persons who are evidently full blooded negroes, while the term 'mulatto' (Mu) includes all other persons having some proportion or perceptible trace of negro blood." But people make mistakes.

And why did any of it matter? Wasn't it only Americans who possessed such a race fetish they would come up with something as bizarre and empirically suffocating as the one-drop rule? I needed to move on. After all, I was an adult doing grown up things such as building houses and buying houses, writing books and selling books. Real life decisions and conclusions about the here and now had to be made even if they were wrong.

Every condo that went up, blanking out more of the sea-sky, further separated me from the father I knew so briefly and the few images I retained of him, images I carried in my heart and mind the way other people carried photos of loved ones in their wallets. I, and my inner orphan, needed to live in a place that looked similar to the world my father had lived and died in. I needed to place my faith in the mirage I'd witnessed when gazing at Alligator Point from Highway 98.

With no possibility of answers, and with resurrection off the table, I made up my mind. I sold my house to the nice folks from Maine, packed my belongings, and with my father's crazy crown of white hair burning a tear drop in my heart, headed west to the piney woods of the Florida Panhandle and the tiny sea shack perched on the edge of the world.

And so it begins.

Paradise, Part Two
My Life in the Wild

I know this to be true: The only way to learn what the sandbar can teach me is through total immersion. I must be ever observant, vigilant. I must be silent in my wanderings. I must be up early every morning, taking it all in, jotting down details.

Just outside my door, sea oats sway to and fro—a testament to the old adage that what does not bend breaks—as cardinals, resplendent in red and orange plumage, hang on, nipping the seeds and feeding them to their partners. The wind carries scents of seaweed and salt. The Gulf rumbles with the softness of falling silk, *whoosh*, and I think, Mother, you were wrong; now and forever I will reside within earshot of the surf.

I gaze out of the living room's French doors, south, toward the dunes and beyond to shifting shades of blue and that giant bowl of saltwater lapping the shorelines of Florida, Alabama, Mississippi, Louisiana, Texas, Mexico, and Cuba. Time to roam.

Flip-flops, sunscreen, hat: check. I step into an astonishingly busy world. Gossamer sea mist spins spectral in the gaining day. Ghost crabs have dug tunnels overnight in the sandy oyster shell driveway. If it weren't for its dark bug-eyes, I probably would have missed seeing the crab that skittered right past my toes before disappearing into a hole and its underground bunker. A black snake, maybe four feet long, winds its way through a bed of California poppies and nasturtiums planted along the kitchen side of the house. Squirrels and songbirds fight for space at the platform bird feeder that stands under the mulberry. In my peripheral vision, skinks—all neon blue and deep black—zip by, crackling through dead and dry underbrush. Terns squawk like barnyard chickens that fear the fox and its desire. Across the way, poking her trowel in dirt that is black and rich and, therefore, obviously imported, is my part-time neighbor, Anne Coloney, the woman from whom I bought the shack, the woman who planted my yard in all manner of salt-hardy plants. I call her name. She looks up and waves her trowel. Pushing back what at times for me is almost paralyzing shyness, I ask, "When you get a chance, can you take me through the yard, tell me what all this stuff is?"

At first Anne demurs, but this sixty-something Florida native, I'm about to learn, is a master gardener who loves to share her secrets, her successes and lessons. Soon we are walking through my yard, which in some ways will always be her yard, arms linked, as she reveals the history of each plant: when she cultivated it, why she chose it, the surprise of this one making it and that one not. She teaches me the plants' names, their needs, their weaknesses. Ox-eye daisy. Black-eyed Susan. Rugosa rose. Confederate rose. Chinese lantern. Wild sweet pea. Wild onion. Sprawling rosemary.

The orchard is a marvel stitched from knowledge, trial, error, love, and tenacity, for such abundance normally doesn't survive in the salt-and-sun harness of the sandbar: two cultivars of persimmon (soon I will learn the fox family arrives at dusk and eats the fruit, and as summer rises, the birds feast and get drunk on the fallen fruit that has distilled in the heat, their juices fat with alcohol), tangerine, grapefruit, Myer lemon, kumquat, fig, sprawling fig, blackberry, blueberry, mulberry, pear, and most lavish of all—a cashew tree that will never bear (she warns me it might need a mate and I must cover it in cold weather) but is glorious all the same.

The fruit of pindo palms and prickly pears can be used to make jelly, she tells me with an air of such authority I decide she is sharing this information not as a suggestion but as a requirement for living. The wax myrtles, which grow at the edge of the bay, contain tallow and therefore, she explains, can be used to craft homemade candles. An image of myself sweating over a cauldron of waxy leaves wafts through my mind and, because I'm earnest to a fault, I add candle making to my mental learn-to-do list.

Anne points to the straight line of tall pine trees that is the dividing line between her property and mine. "My daddy planted those trees when we first bought the place. I still can't get over the shade."

She squeezes my shoulders and I wonder if this is what it feels like to have a mother you're unafraid of. My heart cracks the way it tends to do—always at the least convenient moments— and I bat away tears, hoping she has not noticed.

I point to a vigorous rush of dollar weeds growing at the foot of an empty trellis. Their utter abandon, the way they grow profusely in any condition—even popping their green, round heads through the stress cracks in the railroad ties that outline and define the various garden plots—sullies the image of a tidy English cottage garden I've been cultivating ever since she explained the mock orange can be sheared into whatever shape I fancy. "I have to pull those out," I say, sounding more determined than I feel.

With the broad brim of her hat eclipsing her cheekbones, she shoots me a wise, indulgent smile. "Oh, dear, I don't think so. The dollar weeds love this yard. You're just going to have to learn to love them back."

Learn to love weeds? I don't think so. As soon as she and Wayne, her husband, return to Tallahassee, I will rip out those suckers and replace them with a kitchen-cutting garden. I am tempted to tell her so, hoping she will approve of my industriousness, but she has moved on. I run to catch up as she heads to the bay-facing side of the house.

Within the fenced yard that will be the dogs' domain, we run across another anomaly: an asparagus patch.

"It has taken me four years to get it to produce," Anne says, a hint of reminiscence sweetening her voice. She runs her hand over the airy, lacey green foliage that wafts amid the arrow-straight spears. "And now there is no stopping it."

I sneak a peek at my thumbs. I spy no green whatsoever. Dear God, deliver me from ignorance, I think. If I kill her garden ... and then I stop my negative train of thought in favor of what will become a frequent, equally negative, but declarative, mantra. *I will not kill Anne's garden, I will not kill Anne's garden. I won't I won't I won't.*

Though my relationship with my sea shack and its environs is all about life—growing things, feeding things, honoring things—there was a time when my new home was bombarded with, well, bombs.

Each time Anne and Wayne come down from Tallahassee, over cocktails they fill me in on the history. And with each new nugget, I feel as if that sinkhole called my fractured past is filling up.

My sea shack is a former army barracks built on-site during World War II. Camp Gordon Johnston set up shop in Franklin County, primarily in East Point, Carrabelle, Lanark Village, Dog Island, and Alligator Point, the villages that comprise what the Chamber of Commerce has dubbed The Forgotten Coast. At one point, the camp extended across 165,000 acres and twenty miles of coastal beach. Ultimately, a quarter of a million soldiers would be trained at Camp Gordon Johnston. In 1944, the sprawling military facility also became a prisoner of war camp, housing Germans and Italians captured in Africa and Europe. For its part, the sandbar served as a bombing range and a training ground for amphibious forces made up of men born far from these shores who would venture to even further shores: Normandy and the D-Day Invasion.

Anne and Wayne claim the military bombed every shred of vegetation into oblivion and after the war, having no need to own 165,000 acres of coastal Florida, sold plots at bargain basement prices. Tallahassee families bought the bombed properties, built homes, replanted (thus Anne's amazement at the pine tree shade), and spent lazy summer afternoons discovering live ordnance.

I find these details thrilling. How lovely to live amid resurrection and danger! I run my hand along the weather-beaten edge of one of the Gulf-facing windows, a window built by a recruit whose name I will never know, a young man pulsing with dreams and aspirations. In the theater of war, did he perform with valor? Did he survive and return to a full or haunted life? Did he perish in Normandy and, if so, did he see the face of God?

The shack is a simple balloon frame structure hewn from the trees that grew where the house now stands: oak, pine, magnolia. The hallway leading to the "new" bathroom was once the latrine. I walk past a place where soldiers relieved themselves and am ever so grateful that scent is temporary and a good carpenter can erase the past.

Because some of Camp Gordon Johnston troops would serve in the Asian-Pacific theater and the army wanted them to grow accustomed to heat and mosquitoes, and because, I suppose, the army simply did not feel any compulsion to pamper its recruits with air conditioned barracks, the house is composed primarily of pocket windows. The meager walls serve one purpose: to support the weight and slide of the windows that disappear within them. The open vistas, combined with the house's diminutive size and proximity to water, allow me to pretend I live on a boat. I'm Sophia Loren chasing a bundle of kids who aren't mine and don't like me while Cary Grant can't get me out of his mind.

Quickly, I discover the preponderance of disappearing windows provides relief only when there is a cool breeze and that a hot breeze is worse than still air. The soldiers, I'm sure, were aware of this problem. In the coming months, having decided to renovate the main room, with bare hands I will tear away the old, crumbling wallboard. As the dust settles, I will trace with my index finger these anguished words scrawled by a young recruit onto a pine two-by-four weeping with resin: "This damned place is a living hell."

While unpacking a box marked "studio," I come across a raft of paper cards that measure two by three inches. I bought these years ago at an art supply store in Kansas City. Still unopened, they seem very important to me. Like, I've found a treasure. Like, I can create something wonderful out of them, something that will matter when I'm an old woman profoundly alone, sitting on my porch, staring at the Gulf, listening to its song. Maps.

I shall draw tiny renderings of my new environs. It's as if with each legend I create for each map, I will be saying, "See this, Father? See paradise? I finally found it. Aren't you proud of me?" *As it was in the beginning, is now and ever shall be, world without end* ... this doxology of faith, this attempt to both pin down and celebrate the glory of the world I find myself in, this act of gaining approval from a dead man, a dead woman, becomes my hymn, my psalm, my *hosanna!*

In my maps, I minutely detail the beach, the bay, the forest, the road, the shack.

In this way, I will never be lost.

In this way, I am a child again, discovering the good earth.

In this way, the maps are an incantation.

There is one road on and off the Point. This two-lane black top is the only thing that separates me from the Gulf and the chickee that resides at the base of the dunes.

A traditional Seminole Indian structure, the chickee is essentially an open-air pole barn built about two feet off the ground and topped with a palm thatch roof. Anne and Wayne tell me that after each hurricane, they hire several Seminole Indians who come up from the Everglades and weave new thatch for the chickee in a matter of days.

I sit in its palm-thatched shade and divine a future, something that was once impossible for me. In fact, I will sit in the chickee and gaze for years at the Gulf, dreaming, fretting, scheming. It is where I will write poetry I will never show a soul, and where on the palm of my hands I will draw the most beautiful maps of the beach that I will later wash away with Dawn and a scrub brush (the colors swirling down the drain will make me ache, but for years I won't know why), and where downward facing dogs become a special joy because the sea upside down changes a woman, and where I promise this patch of sea and sky I will never leave them, and where I will laugh and tell lies and scream the truth. It is, ultimately, where I will fall in love.

Even though I have lived on Alligator Point for only a few months, time has already become so fluid clocks and calendars and other strict measurements of our tick, tick, ticking lives make less and less sense to me.

Oddly, I do not miss St. Augustine or Summer Haven. There is no room for nostalgia in this new here and now. There are gardens to plant, birds to watch, low tides to linger in, dogs to love.

There are very few humans in my life anymore.

I wander over to the beach and am delighted to be alone. I sit on the sand and draw my sweater close because the wind off the Gulf is brisk. I dig my hands into the white crystals. I listen to the surf, the terns, the breeze.

An image of my mother and father kissing washes over me. I don't think this is a recovered memory. I think I'm making it up, creating a new them.

It is a late winter morning and the air is cold. Wrapped in my sweater, but barefoot, I walk down a broad elevated deck leading from the back porch's side door, past the louvered outdoor shower, and to the octagon-shaped gazebo that is, like the chickee, crowned with a thick thatched roof. The thatch is tight and waterproof. It is the color of the Konza prairie, though it is made from palm fronds. The gazebo, which like the shack, has bay-to-gulf views and is nestled in the shade of those towering pines, will become my writing studio.

I fling open its screen door, sit on the built-in bench, and attempt to figure out what will go where. Computer? Printer? Books? Soon enough, I'm on a tangent, trying to discern more about the future than a human has a right to know. The truth is, my world will be transformed by the endless hours I will spend in this eight-sided structure. It will take time, but this will happen: I will clutter the wall with pages from favored novels. Eventually art and book posters and photos of friends, family, mentors, pets will spiral up, up, up, as if on their own invisible thermals, until even the ceiling is decorated. Alters composed of bones, sea glass, seashells, paintings, desiccated lizards, puppy teeth, cat whiskers, and found objects will abound. The gazebo-turned-studio will be the place where, in the hours prior to a hurricane, I will watch a squirrel weave an impermeable pine needle plug. He will, with his frenetic but strong little paws, stuff the woven plug in the opening of a bluebird house that I will have nailed—Gulf-facing—to a pine tree just outside my bay-facing window. And it is where I will watch that same squirrel, hours after the hurricane has moved on and the air has been scrubbed fresh and blue by the cyclone, pull aside the woven plug, gaze out the hole, and, evidently deciding to err on the side of caution, pull it shut again, as if the pine needle cork were a great door protecting a mighty fort, his heart, his well-being, his progeny. And I will keep watch, for there isn't a lot to do on the sandbar. As a reward for my watchfulness, I will possess this morsel of sweet knowledge: He will remain in his shelter until dawn, at which time he will push out the pine needle cork and scurry into the world, bee-lining it to the bird feeder with its onyx mound of sunflower seeds.

Yes, in this gazebo that will soon have solid walls, I will write my way into a different life, isolated but abundant. I run my hand along the wooden bench, avoiding a splinter in the nick of time, and I say to the empty space, "I'm going to be somebody new."

That evening, I sit on the grand, screened-in back porch (it is at least as large as the shack) in the faint light, my old dog Katie at my feet, Atticus in my lap, my cat Abdul staring out at the bay as though in deep concentration. I watch a snowy egret fly west where it will roost in the trees that grow on protected, restricted land at the tip of the Point. As I watch the bird—a white, feathered arrow—journey toward the setting sun, I know I will insist that we keep the writing studio's thatched roof. It is a fight I will, and probably should, lose. But sitting here, amid a million shades of blue and the shushing rustle of the pine trees and the quick flash of the egret's yellow feet, all that matters to me is the ecstatic present, because in this moment I have a clearer inkling than I did this morning of what my purpose is on the sandbar: to make peace with the past, not relive it, which, I finally realize, is a necessary condition for growing up.

I bend down and pet sleeping Katie. She is a black Labrador and German shepherd mix and has seen me through the worst of times, keeping me as safe as a canine can in the midst of physical violence, fleeing with me at first light many years ago.

Abdul is her best friend. He's a big orange tabby given to me by a friend before I left Tampa for Kansas. Katie, even now in her old age, spends hours grooming him, nibbling down his spine as if he were a corncob, creating a series of great dog-spit-stiff spikes as she goes from shoulder to spine to tail.

I rescued Atticus from certain death in St. Augustine. Inexplicably, for the first six months of his life, he was imprisoned in a dark room in a metal cage. Until the afternoon I brought him home, the little dog had never seen daylight, a blade of grass, a patch of dirt.

I ushered him into the light gradually. His sense of smell developed in tandem to his strengthening eyesight. For three months he screamed as if he were on fire when I held him because any stitch of humanity and its attendant desire to lay on hands had eluded him.

Now, nearly three, he lies curled in my lap, soundly asleep, his soft snoring murmuring his contentment. But still, he is damaged. Atticus will, over the course of his seventeen-year-life, get even with his captors by biting many people, including me. As balm, I will, beginning in his third year, send to friends, families, and colleagues annoying holiday letters, listing all the people Atticus bit that year. People will call and say, "But, Connie, he bit me, too, and I'm not on the list."

With the efficiency of a chain-smoking, sexless secretary, I'll ask if he drew blood. The answer will be no, because I will keep immaculate notes on Atticus's triumphs and failings. I will calmly explain to the not-injured-enough-party that to make the annual bite list, blood must be shed. There will be something funny and invigorating about an infusion of gallows' humor amid a holiday season grown fat and meaningless with consumerism and sweet cakes.

Finally, above all else, this is true: I will protect Atticus with my last breath, for survivors recognize in one another the beauty our tormentors missed.

Soon there will be a third dog: Scout, another schipperke, who will sport the laid-back temperament of a happy, ganja-sedated surfer. Eventually, Lazarus will join the tribe, a bird dog hit by a car and left for dead at the Franklin County pound, which, in keeping with her run of bad luck, will be battling a mange outbreak. One vet will insist I amputate the poor, mange-ridden girl's broken leg. Another one will say, his fat hand resting on her rump, "Let's wait and see."

And we do. It will prove to be a just decision for Lazarus will be resplendent, running down the beach on all four beautiful long legs, the light of life and a second chance fueling her sprint.

But on this twilight evening, it is just Katie, Atticus, and Abdul. Our attention is snagged—Katie wakes and tests the wind with that expert nose and Atticus stretches, yawns—as two great blue heron sound their plaintive cries and settle into the sentinel oak at the edge of the bay. The birds fuss for a few minutes and then fall silent. Lovers, I think, suspecting we will soon have baby herons in our midst. I make a mental note to walk down to the oak in the morning in search of a nest.

When the fox slips into the fenced area, unconcerned by our presence, and checks the persimmons no one barks. We—the dogs, the cat, and I—watch in silence, amazed, as the fox sits upright and inspects the flame-glow fruit, which evidently are not yet to his liking, with expert little paws.

When I was a young girl, my mother and father took my sister and me on a weekend getaway to the Gulf of Mexico, which is shallow and calm except when stirred by gale winds, and my mother dismissed its tranquility, calling it a "pee pond." I held onto that prejudice for a very long time. The Atlantic is volatile and massive, its waves rippling like muscles. Poseidon and Neptune seem to be throwing fits out there all the time. And, yes, the Atlantic has its shallows where life is born, but I will soon learn the Gulf—my new home—is one of the most abundant marine nurseries on the planet, which makes spring special here. But I don't know that yet. All I know is winter's chill is gone, the new season is in full bloom, I have just woken up, and the air, which smells of roses and salt, is alive with bird song, surf song, wind song.

I reach for my robe. Katie and Atticus look at me with disgruntled little faces. Evidently, it's too early for them. For a sleep-addled second, I reconsider rising at dawn, but like sap, a resolve wells up within me, dispelling the dreamtime cobwebs. I will never understand my new place in this world—nor will I heal or forgive—until the sandbar reveals to me its mysteries, its wildness. I don't know exactly how this reckoning works but I'm all in. Already my life out here is a leap of faith.

After feeding my hungry trio and downing a jolt of tea, I dress quickly, remembering to slather on sunscreen but forgetting my hat.

It rained in my dreams and when I step outside, I realize the showers were real. The sand is pockmarked from raindrops and the plants look sated, ready for whatever comes next.

I make my way down to the bay and the sentinel oak. I gaze through its branches in search of the heron nest. I don't see anything I can clearly identify as such—perhaps it's that large clutch of sticks and grass up high and near the center—but I do make out three small songbird nests. I wonder if this old tree is sentient, if it knows it's essentially a wildlife condo, providing shelter and protection against the elements, its widespread limbs dappled with nests that will soon be cradling new life.

Something moves through the reeds. I spy just its tail: a black snake. I don't know if it's the same one I saw outside the kitchen or not, but I'm happy it's here because it keeps the rats in check. I follow a set of raccoon tracks along the water line. They are fresh, so the animal must be close by. Try as I might, I don't see it. Maybe it's hunkered down in the tree, safe from my prying eyes. The animals know all the hiding places. But soon, I will too.

I head to the beach, across the dunes, navigating my way through the railroad vine that seems to have grown exponentially overnight, and see that mine are not the only footprints, simply the latest. A heron must have been in search of a ghost crab midnight snack, or else it simply wanted to take in the view from on high. I follow the thick, whiplash track of a snake before the trail goes cold amid a stand of sea oats. I walk quickly, in case the snake is still there, watching me, testing my scent with its flickering forked tongue. The calligraphy of small shorebirds—pipers and plovers—stipples the sand. Great books were written overnight and soon the wind will commit a grand erasure.

I scan the sky. Anne and Wayne told me to be on watch for purple martin scouts. They say the birds first send scouts to find suitable nesting areas before the hordes descend.

"You might want to hang some gourds," Anne had said, "so they have a safe place to have their babies."

I make a mental note: Go to hardware store in Crawfordville, get martin houses, figure out a post to hang them on. She also said I might be too late, that the scouts can show up as early as January, but I am a birder of infinite hope. Besides, Johnny-come-latelies need shelter, too.

Amid the hardy evergreen growth that helps the dunes survive the wind (in this ecosystem, everything has a purpose beyond its evident beauty), thanks to the generosity of rain and warmer temperatures, wildflowers have become known and spritely, their blooms blurring the dunes in a wash of impressionist pastels—pink, blue, yellow, orange, flaming red.

As I stand here, the whisper of the surf song unfolding and refolding, I spy a ragged flotilla, colorful scraps of movement swirling along on the wind. As soon as these fragments of pigment and motion reach the dunes, they float downward, landing on the blossoms, transforming the dunes into a living kaleidoscope. At this moment, I exist inside a prism of Monarch butterflies.

I know a little bit about the migratory path of Monarchs. They winter in central Mexico, then come north through Texas and the plain states, eventually making their way to Canada. But not until this moment do I realize this is not the full story. There must be micro-migration patterns, ones perhaps not as large as the Mexico-to-Canada path. How else to explain all these Monarchs? Is this the first wave? Is this proof they actually can make the nearly 500-mile crossing over the Gulf of Mexico? Do some of them leave central Mexico, stop in the Yucatan to feed, before arriving on these shores? Or do they come up from Texas and for some reason veer east? All I know is what I see: The sandbar is their way station and the wildflower nectar is, in all likelihood, the first food they've had since leaving their wintering grounds. I kneel down and study them. Their markings remind me of stained glass windows. If I could only see through their winged panes. Imagine what mysteries exist there, beyond the transom of the ordinary.

Other types of butterflies are also feasting—gulf fritillary, zebra long wing, cloudless sulfur, and others whose names I do not yet know.

I rise and stand very still, breathing as though air is lighter than vapor, wishing my ears were superhuman so I could hear the sound of nectar being sipped. How long, I wonder, does it take for one sip to slip down a throat the length of a human eyelash? Two butterflies I cannot identify land on my left foot. Then one monarch, then three, and then more than I have the presence of mind to count, light on my arms. Before long, I am a human being dressed in a sheath of butterflies. My skin tingles under the weightless scintillation of tiny legs. Are they feeding on me, nibbling just a little as my mother said of the roaches? I extend my arms and spin a full circle. This is, I know, the closest I will ever come to flight.

During the lengthening days that pass one after the other, each distinguishable through light patterns, wildlife migrations, lone animals appearing and then disappearing, the movement of planets, the phases of the moon, the sun traveling and dragging its sunset along, I research butterfly migration. Though central Mexico is, indeed, their primary wintering ground, researchers have found the species as far south as the Yucatan, Cuba, and Venezuela. On their way north, once they reach North America, three generations will mate and die, their offspring left to continue the journey. The fourth generation will complete the circle, coming south again, and gathering in minor to great conclaves along the Gulf prior to making the big journey to Mexico. Surely, I surmise, this means my front yard will be a gathering place, a fueling stop, before they return to Mexico in the late fall. I shall be prepared. The new and improved butterfly garden is already taking shape in my brain and on my sketchpad. I will plant all the milkweed I possibly can.

I learn how very specialized monarchs are, how they are dependent on a single species of tree: *oyamel* fir trees—the *abies religiosa* or "sacred fir'—which exists solely in Mexico's transverse volcanic belt region. That all sounds exotic and magical until I learn that less than five percent of the original *oyamel* ecosystem survives.

The withering of the *oyamel* is mankind's doing, of course. Climate change and logging have devastated the sacred fir, which directly impacts the viability of the butterflies. Monarchs and *oyamels* have the exact same special needs—a winter of cool but not freezing climes and wet conditions. The butterflies, like some of my friends who possess fragile hearts, may have become dependent on a vanishing species. If the *oyamel* is pushed into extinction, the monarch will have to find a way to adapt—a new forest on which to hang its wings—or it, too, will die. Perhaps that's what the monarchs in my yard are all about: like me, they are off the beaten path in an effort to achieve long-term survival.

These studies, because they focus on migration, lead me to the hummingbird—the ruby-throated, to be exact—for that is the predominate species on the sandbar. I hang a bevy of feeders from my eaves and plant Chinese bellflower, honeysuckle, torch lilies, glory flower, cardinal flower, butterfly bush. I find myself again reading about the Yucatan where the diminutive birds gorge on spiders and garden-variety insects, fattening themselves, nearly doubling their weight, in preparation for their northern migration. The males leave the Yucatan two weeks earlier than the females and depart in successive waves over a span of three months. Survival of the species, I decide, operates with sacred intelligence.

I mull over the strength of body and mind such Herculean migrations require. I consider all the years birds and butterflies have traced and retraced paths laid down by their ancient ancestors, the mechanisms of which we still do not understand. The meticulous, clockwork beauty of their journeys inspires wonder and devotion in scientists, nature lovers, and artists, alike. Yet their fates rest in how we respond to global climate change, catastrophic development, irresponsible logging practices, and the wall-eyed worship of money.

When humans decided we were not of the animal kingdom—when we decided to translate a biblical Aramaic word as "dominion over" rather than "caretaker of"—did we seal our fate as well as that of our planet?

I gently remove the monarchs from my body, butterfly by butterfly, and transfer them to the surrounding wildflowers. When I'm done, I wander to the shore where the cold surf rushes over my feet, leaving water diamonds on my toes. I gaze across that great expanse of water and picture myself landing on the shores of the Yucatan. In my mind's eye, I fly with the hummingbirds and monarchs, our wings silent and sheer, my belly so close to the waves I glide on a mist of sea spray.

Imagine: one forest in the entire world that holds at its heart the fate of the monarchs. I try not to think of the final tree being felled or the final flight that ends with nowhere to land or a ravaged landscape peppered with wings.

And then I wonder, what is the Gulf's enemy? What could bring it to the edge of oblivion?

With the arrival of spring, a woman roams the beach at dawn. Known on the sandbar simply as The Turtle Lady, she searches every morning for turtle nests, looking for the telltale signs: the wide swaths of sand that have been moved into semi-circle shapes by the mother turtle's flipper-like legs, the large indention in the sand where she deposits anywhere from 100 to 120 eggs. The Turtle Lady marks the nests with little signs: *Do not Disturb, Sea Turtle Nest.*

I will learn a great deal from The Turtle Lady, including the fact that Alligator Point is a major nesting ground for the most endangered sea turtle of all: the diminutive Kemp's ridley. Not only is it the rarest of marine turtles, it is also among the world's smallest with a shell only about two feet long. But alongside the Kemp's ridley, the loggerhead sea turtle—one of the largest of all oceanic turtles, weighing on average nearly 300 pounds—also commonly nests on these shores. The official turtle season runs May 1 through October 31, although occasionally other types of sea turtles might nest as early as March.

Of the many hazards faced by newly hatched turtles, humans pose the greatest threats, threats which come in many shapes and sizes: trash and belongings such as chairs left on the beach become obstacles preventing the hatchlings from completing their perilous journeys across the sand to the sea. Leaving on lights at night confuses them, wreaking havoc with their navigation systems. Humans allowing their dogs to run loose and unsupervised create opportunities for nests to be trampled and eggs destroyed. Between human carelessness, land and sea animals on the prowl for food, and Mother Nature spawning cyclones during nesting season, The Turtle Lady agrees with me: It's a flat out marvel any of the babies survive into adulthood.

Other things the Turtle Lady teaches me:

Female turtles will return to these same shores throughout their lives to lay their clutches. I am awed at the thought of this circular journey having taken place for as long as the Point has existed.

Sea turtles are among the oldest inhabitants of earth, having dwelled on our planet for over a million years. The ancestors to our present-day turtles were land animals in the time of the dinosaurs but, in order to survive life amid giants, took to the sea where they became expert navigators. Like their ancestors, modern day turtles travel widely—over huge distances—and my imagination is once again pulled to the Yucatan ... butterflies, hummingbirds, sea turtles ... what else do we share?

I will learn that The Turtle Lady is stubborn and fierce and strong in the face of threats issued by a part-time resident who fills in wetlands under the dark of night for people who have no respect for the sanctity of this place. He also, on a beach that doesn't allow vehicles, rides his buggy across the dunes and through the nests, destroying them. The Turtle Lady's insistence that he keep his vehicle off the beach prompts him to threaten her with bodily harm, leading me to harden my stance: once an asshole, always an asshole. The threats will escalate and The

Turtle Lady will no longer feel safe doing her job. In fact, she will feel so threatened she will move away.

The only good thing about this story is that others will take her place. In fact, an entire organization will arise whose purpose is to mark the nests, make scientific notations in an effort to gain a more detailed picture of the turtles and their nesting habits, determine how better to protect them, and educate newcomers and old-timers.

The man who threatened and harassed The Turtle Lady will become a pariah. Many of us, including myself, will spit when we say his name. In a community as lightly populated as ours, he will learn whom to avoid.

The isolation, the time to think and read and garden, the quiet: It's working on me. People still frighten me, but not the way they once did. And I feel something else building up inside me. I can't yet name it.

In the meantime, in my new life the moon, not the clock, determines my schedule. At high tide, I write. At low tide, I walk. It's a Monday morning in mid-March and the full moon is exerting its pull, resulting in a particularly vigorous summer low tide.

Come winter, I will discover cold weather low tides are wondrous. The harbor nearly empties of water, prompting me to abandon whatever project I'm working on in order to wander across the face of the bay. Walking amid the newly exposed ribbed mud, I jot in a notebook everything I find. Starfish, crabs, and marine worms sink into the mud, hiding from birds that obviously view the vast expanse as a smorgasbord.

The Gulf, too, surrenders to the winter moon's hard tug. It's an amazing sight: normally submerged sandbars laid bare to the sun, teeming with living shells and wildlife. Every time

I'm lucky enough to experience such a tide, I walk far into the Gulf, traversing the newly revealed sea bed, out to where the water has receded—shallow and clear, dolphins ever present—and I imagine walking all the way to the Yucatan, sloshing right over, visiting the critters that descend on the Point by air and sea during their spring and fall migrations. They would not recognize me—a woman who toils in dirt enriched with horseshit to make sure they have sustenance—because their lives are full with the business of survival. Humans are a deadly distraction, a species that kills knowingly and unknowingly, our collective conscious rarely piqued, as if we're insolent gods.

On this spring morning, however, when I set out to the bay in search of life, I stumble upon a dead heron that has washed ashore and lies tangled in the marsh grass. The bird is picked clean, the bones nearly white. I check the sky. No vultures. The sand, however, is covered in coon tracks. But what leaves a skeleton intact? Not coons, not feral cats, not neighborhood dogs. Maybe baby fish. Yes, the dead bird floated to shore, providing nourishment to what would have been its prey on a better day. The heron is not one of the lovebirds that roost in the sentinel oak. I saw them ascend at dawn.

Although I have no idea who I'm praying to, I experience a moment of spontaneous supplication. My rational self knows after-the-fact prayer to an unknown deity is suspect, yet I can't stop myself. I pray the bird's demise was quick, that it did not suffer. *Rest in peace, little bird, rest in peace.*

The sun, despite the calendar, is merciless, the air still. It's as if the world is holding its breath. I look across the bay to the forest beyond. I imagine entering, wholly unafraid, its wavering shadows. Snakes look at me bemused but they do not strike. Bobcats gather in my wake: a golden, wild sea. Songbirds pause, listening to my footfalls. Spiders mend their webs with slow, deliberate movements: tiny tai chi dancers. I feel ancient in a good way, at peace. I pull my gaze from the forest, back to the present and the tangled, dead bird. I know what must be done.

I kneel down and, bone by bone, extract the heron from the marsh grass. Slowly, determined to do no harm, I stand. Its skull rests in my right hand. Its spine and legs drape across my left arm. I walk toward the shack, carrying a rosary of bones: both brittle and strong, intricate and blatant, each meticulous part—skull, neck, ribs, spine, wings, legs, feet—a holy moment in the river of time.

Rather than, out of ignorance, killing the beautiful gardens Anne planted, I decide upon a more prudent route: learn everything I can about how things grow and then expand upon her work. I phone her and inform her of my intentions. "I want to take care of the gardens you started and make the property even prettier."

The next time she comes down, she brings her notebooks, which contain meticulous records regarding everything she planted. "Reading those is like walking around in my brain," she says with a soft laugh.

For weeks, I stay up late reading her musings:

I think some salt intolerant plants might thrive on the bay side. I have discovered if a plant has glossy leaves, they can put up with the salt air.

Maybe another mulberry, for the birds.

Cut back the asparagus every winter. Mulch if a freeze threatens.

I order gardening books and read them cover-to-cover. I keep a stack of seed catalogues by my bed, circling my have-to-haves. By the time summer arrives, my backyard, the one that faces the bay, thrives: cucumbers, patty pans, okra, black beans, string beans, yellow plum tomatoes, Cherokee heirloom tomatoes, zucchini. Down by the bay, beyond the fence, a patch of corn begins to slightly obscure my view.

When I dig in the dirt, I remind myself of my grandmother. Do I possess ancestral memory? Is it her hand, mine, or both that makes the depression, drops the seed, covers it with dirt, and reaches for the hose? When I plant a colorful clutch of zinnias in the front yard, I remind myself of my mother. No matter where we lived, how awful a hovel, how wretched our lives, she planted zinnias each summer without fail. Maybe it was her way to remind herself joy was not out of reach. I shall do likewise. *Do this in remembrance of me.* Zinnias for mother, for mother and daughter, every summer. Zinnias.

What an unexpected joy: to feel connected to my mother and grandmother through the ancient act of growing things.

Amid all this planting and sowing and watering and picking pests off the tender undersides of bright green leaves, my nephew, Sean, who is on the brink of becoming a teenager, visits from Tampa.

I am delighted to spend a couple of weeks with him but also nervous. What will he do in a land of no shopping malls? No movie theaters? No fast food joints? He grew up in Tampa, an urban metropolis centered on football and consumerism and everything Cuban. I'm not knocking it. I love Tampa. Its diversity and insistence on celebrating, even maintaining, its Italian, Cuban, African, Anglo cultural mix could teach a lesson to many places. But there are things to do there that don't involve snakes and birds and fish and staring at the blue, blue sea.

My first order of business, because it feels ancestral, is to introduce Sean to this region's bivalve of choice: the Apalachicola oyster. I do so the same way my father, a man my nephew never knew, introduced it to me: steamed, with saltines and lots of cocktail sauce, lemon on the side. We stand amid the wild clutter of my kitchen. I ask about school, movies, and the perpetual nag, *What do you want to be when you grow up?*

He expertly navigates through my questions about his future, tossing in everything from actor, comedian, musician, and teacher. The fact is, he could be any or all of them. Yes, I'm a proud aunt.

As I listen to his recitation of possible careers, I pile the oysters in a colander, set it over a pot of boiling water, drape the whole thing in a wet hand towel, and top it with a lid.

After about ten minutes, I lift the towel and take a peek. Most of the shells have popped open. "Perfect," I say. Using my old, wood-handled oyster knife, I slice an oyster from its shell, squirt it with a shot of lemon juice, place it on a saltine, and dab it with heavily horseradished cocktail sauce. This is a ritual. Something tangible I received from my father. *Take this, all of you, and eat it: this is my body, which will be given up for you.*

"Here, take it. The first one."

He does but looks at me warily, holding the crowned cracker aloft as if it might poison him.

"You'll like it," I say.

He studies the oyster that is half-hidden under sauce. I can tell he's unconvinced.

"Sean, we come from a long line of oyster eaters. That's your heritage you're holding in your hand."

He starts to laugh and I realize he has taken my comment and dragged it through a dirty mind.

"Sean."

He doesn't move. I think he's wishing he never met me. I stare at him, resolute, giving him no way out: Refuse to eat it and hit the Doritos or take a chance and taste the ocean.

"What the worst that can happen, Sean?"

"I die?"

"You won't. I promise."

He scrunches up his nose, as if I'm asking him to eat dog poop, but he does it. He pops the crunch and ooze into his mouth and chews. His eyes widen. He swallows. *Do this in memory of me.* "Huh! Not so bad." And he makes himself another.

The next day we embark upon a sightseeing trip through the county. We head west off of the Alligator Point road, through the tiny hamlets of St. Teresa, Lanark Village, and Carrabelle. Tate's Hell State Forest hugs the road's right shoulder and the blue jewel called Apalachee Bay hugs the left. Soon we cross through the fishing village of East Point and over a long, winding bridge that deposits us into the heart of the county seat, Apalachicola.

Meticulously restored antebellum homes look out over the bay. Smaller houses—their yards stacked with nets, fishing boats, motors, oyster boats, oyster tongs, and other fishing paraphernalia—reinforce that Apalachicola is not simply a tourist town filled with art galleries and seafood restaurants but is an honest-to-God working fishing village. In fact, the entire county is comprised of fishing villages, tiny burgs that emerge from the shadows of the piney forest and bustle with the business of commercial oystering, shrimping, fishing, and processing plants. If it weren't for the oyster and commercial fishing industries—occupations the locals have excelled at for countless generations—the Forgotten Coast might be better dubbed the Abandoned Coast because in places like East Point, Carrabelle, and Panacea that's what people do: harvest oysters and crab and shrimp and fish, plus however else one makes a living from the sea.

"Without the seafood industry," I tell Sean, "this place would be a ghost town. That is until the developers turn it into a gated golf course community."

"Yeah," he says, "filled with people who don't care."

"About what?" I aim the car in the direction of my favorite Apalachicola eatery: Boss Oyster.

Sean gazes straight ahead, not missing a beat. "The oysters, the people, the locals."

Spoken like a true native, I think. "Yeah, we'll become quaint annoyances who carry their suitcases."

"And ask, 'Would you like fries with that?'" Sean laughs. We both do. But I know it's not really funny, that it might actually happen one day, that the bubble locals refer to—the invisible dome that protects this area from falling into the Disney-esque abyss of the rest of the state—might be a temporary condition.

As we wind through the town, I tell Sean, "The whole area is a National Estuarine Research Reserve. The people here gave us a lot of help when we worked on getting the designation for St. Augustine. The thing is, here the commercial fishermen and the environmentalists have figured out they are fighting for the same thing. Bad water means no oysters, which means no Apalachicola. Not in the way we know it, anyway."

Sean listens but says nothing. When we pass the rambling lovely Gibson Inn that sits in the center of town like an architectural *grande dame*, he breaks his silence. "Why don't you live here? Where the people are?"

"Too many people."

He shakes his head and I know, just like that, I've become The Beloved Crazy Aunt.

But The Beloved Crazy Aunt, aware again of the ticking clock the rest of the world ties its existence to, understands Sean will soon have to return home, meaning there is limited time to show him all the little wonders I've discovered.

That's why I rouse him out of bed the next morning at 7 a.m. Tossing him a bottle of sunscreen, I say, "Slather it on because we're going for a hike."

"Where to?" Sleep fogs his voice and he looks caught between worlds: childhood and adulthood. I suppose the teenage years could be defined as that, a form of purgatory wherein our loss of innocence and how we deal with that determines what kind of adult we will be.

"All the way to the end of the Point. You'll like it. I promise."

Phipps Preserve, at the western tip of the peninsular sandbar, is a largely untouched ecosystem owned by the Nature Conservancy: no houses, no trailers, no cars, no docks, no manmade anything. The preserve is accessed by boat, or—if you're willing to walk a fair distance and crawl across a rock jetty barrier—by foot. The Alligator Point road ends at the preserve and its chain link gate. Rattlesnakes, it is rumored, thrive in the preserve's interior, so the few people who venture out there stay by the water. But even along the sandy shoreline, one must walk carefully. All of Alligator Point, but Phipps Preserve in particular, is home to birds that lay their eggs in the sand: least tern, snowy plover, Wilson's plover, piping plover, American oystercatcher, and willet.

So my nephew and I walk carefully, pausing from time to time to watch osprey fish for mullet and bald eagle spiral on thermals. A large dolphin pod fishes the waters just beyond the surf break and from time to time one leaps out of the water—a silver gray arc. When one slaps it tail fin, otherwise known as a fluke, on the Gulf's surface, sending a spray of water into the air, Sean and I cheer. It's breathtaking. We wade ankle deep through clear water teeming with horseshoe crabs and baby fish and shells that suddenly stand up and move, their motility provided by their inhabitants: various species of mollusks. Stingrays breach the water and fly, and fly again. We shuffle our feet so that the rays and skates lingering just under the sand will sense our presence and move on. Young nurse sharks zip by, unconcerned with us.

This is as untouched as nature gets in the late twentieth century. My nephew asks questions. *What kind of bird is that? How come pelicans fly in a straight line? Why do people take shells with things living in them?* Some of his questions I can answer and others I can't. But I feel great—not The Beloved Crazy Aunt but The Beloved Good Aunt—for introducing him to a world his maternal grandparents understood and loved. I pick up a living sand dollar and show him the peristome, which is where the creature's mouth resides, and the periproct, located on the slim edge and is, essentially, the sand dollar's anus.

"No way!" he says.

"Way." I'm beaming. I feel as if I'm helping to continue the circle, the knowledge, the love that survives amid the ruins.

When we round the far edge of the Point and are about to trek eastward, Sean says, "Wow! Wow, wow, wow!"

He's pointing at his feet. "Oh my God!" Starfish surround us. They blanket the shallows and the sand. *A fever of starfish.* We cannot walk without stepping on them. So we don't. Rather, we stay still, taking it all in.

"How many do you think there are? Millions?"

"Nah."

"Thousands?"

"Maybe."

"It's as if all the stars ..."

I finish his sentence, " ... fell to earth."

Later that night, he and I will lie on swinging beds on the windy back porch and gaze at the celestial dome, knowing the stars are still up there. Every single one of them. The sandbar boasts almost no light pollution. And this night will be moonless.

The Milky Way will scintillate. So many stars. Such an ancient sky. For the first time in my life, I will understand why our ancestors looked up to the heavens and spun stories. Stars like these, so thick and bright you can't help but give in to the human impulse to lift a hand in order to touch the face of God, inspire.

And I will feel a broken bone heal when Sean, his face meeting the heavens, says, "This is a good place."

Three weeks later, I evacuate and head for higher ground because the first tropical cyclone of the season is upon us. I will, in subsequent months and years, come to believe the Florida panhandle attracts hurricanes the way dogs attract fleas: unwittingly and without effort. I will in equal doses grow to appreciate and fear the monster storms. And I'll become adept at keeping irreplaceable treasures in pretty wooden boxes for the inevitable grab-and-dash.

But this is my first real storm since I was a girl and my father was still alive. Hurricane Dora hit Jacksonville and St. Augustine head-on. In preparation for its arrival, my father covered the plate glass windows of his sewing machine store in Atlantic Beach with plywood. He painted across its surface, as if he were penning sheet music, the notes and words to "Hello, Dolly," changing the proper noun to "Dora." A reporter from CBS interviewed him in front of his appropriated song and we watched the segment air on the CBS Evening News with Walter Cronkite later that night—the wind howling—from our digs in downtown Jacksonville at the Roosevelt Hotel.

I thought the cigar-cigarette girls were the most beautiful women in the world, and I made a vow right there and then, at the Roosevelt Hotel's fancy restaurant, as I tried to chew a steak that was too tough for me and I was too young for: One day I would grow up and join their ranks. *Cigar? Cigarette?*

My desire to parade through smoky joints wearing almost nothing but tobacco products competed with my equally fervent desires to be a nun or a brain surgeon or Sophia Loren's prettier twin sister, and sometimes in my imagination I managed to be all four at once.

Our little blockhouse was badly flooded by the storm surge and our insurance would only cover damage if the water had invaded by means other than surge. I remember how gleefully my father took a kitchen chair to my bedroom window (the east-facing window, so it made sense Dora could have blown it out) and my mother's wild, trilling laughter that swirled into the hurricane-scrubbed air along with her cigarette smoke. I stood near him as he flung the chair, mud staining my white sneakers with the stubbornness of oozing blood, and I was confused. Why were my parents so happy? Though the word "fraud" was not yet a part of my lexicon, I knew it when I saw it. Weren't we supposed to avoid breaking the law? And if we did break it, weren't we supposed to be ashamed?

"That will teach the bastards," my mother said as she picked her way through shattered glass.

Six months later, almost to the day, my father was dead. And in that little house, until my grieving mother swept us into a whole new life in Tampa, my dead father was a near-constant spectral presence, wandering through the bedrooms, the kitchen, the living room, and down the hall. He seemed bemused, as if his new circumstances, though unexpected, weren't entirely unwelcomed. Perhaps he was simply adjusting, trying on death, figuring out what it meant for his future.

I kept a silent watch, following him from room to room. And yes, he *could* walk through walls. He didn't hug me or speak to me or in any other way acknowledge my existence. I was okay with him keeping his distance; I might have freaked out if he'd stroked my hair, squeezed my hand, tapped my nose while telling me if I counted all my freckles he would buy me a hot chocolate sundae. Were ghosts even capable of touching the living? Despite a thin veil of misgivings, mainly his presence soothed me, and because he wasn't totally gone I held out hope he would resurrect and all this nonsensical grieving—the crying, the wailing, the what-am-I-going-to-do's—would come to an end.

Apparently, I was the only one who saw him, but I was wise enough not to mention it. No telling what sort of fist-flying fury such an admission would inspire in my mother. However, when she announced several months after his death we were moving, I could remain silent no longer. We could not abandon my dead daddy. Bemusement would turn to sadness because surely he would interpret us leaving him as us no longer loving him.

He was right there, in the kitchen, standing in the corner, staring at my uneaten plate of scrambled eggs. Was he hungry? *Don't worry, Daddy, I will protect you.* I gripped my fork so tight my knuckles flamed as I screamed, my tears sudden and cold, "We can't leave. We can't leave Daddy!"

Mother slapped my face, then the back of my head. She moved fast—she should have been a prizefighter—and, while still throwing open-palmed punches, accused me of being a crazy, fat, little bitch who was bent on making her life a living hell. I scanned the room through my tears. Daddy was gone. I caught a glimpse of his shadow as he headed down the hall. I scooted back my chair, slipped my mother's grip, and ran to the doorway. He paused one second, looked over his shoulder, and disappeared through his bedroom wall, the place where he had taken his final breath. That was the last time I saw him. Ever.

I spent many nights in my bed staring at the stars through the new window, thinking he was out there amid the star shine. I prayed hard. I prayed to him and to God. *Please come back.*

Thirty years later—after ply-boarding my windows and doors, the stinging rain leaving welts on my skin—with two dogs and a cat in tow, I drive through a blinding deluge at midnight, the radio constantly buzzing warnings, and find a motel willing to take pets near 1-10. The power goes off around 2 a.m. The room has no windows that open so it quickly becomes stifling. The cat caterwauls his discontent. For hours. I do not sleep. The next morning, after putting fresh batteries in the radio, I hear the news is not good for Alligator Point and that residents are not being allowed to return.

Eventually, I decide to dump the sweltering motel room and try to talk my way back onto the sandbar. In Panacea, I spy a nest of cars at The Oaks, an old family-style restaurant. I stop in and find it full of Alligator Point folks—mostly part-timers—who are as worried as I am.

After several hours of drinking bad coffee and checking on the pets who have remained in the truck I've left wide open with my belongings, word trickles in the authorities are allowing residents to return though there is no electricity and the road at the KOA—where the homes are in the sea and some are no longer standing—is washed away. I thread my way across the back route: the ridge that marks the KOA's northern, bay side. The campground is battered but mainly intact. It looks as if storm surge breached much of the property and large ponds of seawater reflect the blue sky. I curve along the ridge and hit the main road again. Trees are down. Roofs are peeled off. The southern walls of Gulf-side block homes are obliterated but their north-facing walls appear untouched. As I approach the shack, I close my eyes, certain the U.S. Army-built structure, which wasn't supposed to last more than five years, has finally succumbed.

I close my eyes in order to see.

With one eye open, I pull into the drive. I open my other eye, and like a mother inspecting a newborn—ten toes, ten fingers—I quickly do a rundown: roof, shingles, siding, windows, doors, fence. Everything of major importance is intact. Some screens are blown out. They will be fixed by nightfall. And there will be no hurling of kitchen chairs at bedroom windows, only the occasional wordless prayer aimed at a father ensconced in eternal sleep.

This running away in the rain and returning in the brilliant light of a post-cyclone world becomes a seasonal ritual, the cost of living in paradise, a habit one must not break if one wants to survive, my own private migration, a circular journey marked by a singular hope: May the little shack by the sea abide.

The turtles did not fare as well. The storm surge inundated half-a-dozen nests. I stand on the beach, gazing at what was once an incubator made of sand and try not to let the destruction tear at me. After all, some nests survived. So I concentrate on that, on how the babies that do hatch and make it to the shoreline will by instinct—that innate knowledge of purpose—enter the open blue gate of the Gulf and then beyond to the vast pelagic prairies of the Atlantic and Caribbean, traveling along their own inscrutable silk roads composed not of stone and dust, but of water and tidal currents.

A year in and my studio has walls and a real roof. In it I produce a memory novel: *Before Women had Wings*. As inspiration, I use borrowed memories, those of my siblings who told me those horrible stories of my father beating my mother. But it is infused with plenty of my own memories, too, and in the writing of the book I struggle with my mother as if she is still alive, trying to understand her, trying to heal her, trying to win her love.

I buy more zinnias.

It is late summer and I am in my backyard garden hoeing weeds. The phone, which is on the back deck, rings. I have a phone phobia, this being a natural outgrowth of my human being phobia, so I do not want to answer. But something needles me, something whispers in my ear, "Pick it up." I do, but I don't say anything. No hello, *hola*, what's up … nothing. For all the person on the other end knows, they just dialed a heavy breather.

"Connie?"

"Yes."

"This is a friend of Bird's."

My protagonist in *Before Women had Wings* is nicknamed Bird, but the book doesn't come out for a few more weeks and I don't connect the name with the book. I am at a total loss.

"Excuse me?"

"This is a friend of Bird's."

I am convinced this is a crank call and am annoyed I interrupted my weeding to talk to a crackpot. "I'm sorry. I have no idea who this is."

"It's Oprah."

"Oprah?"

"Yes, Oprah Winfrey."

Actually, as it turns out, it really is. And once I accept this surreal reality, I begin jumping up and down, grateful she can't see how I manifest elation. She wants to make the book into a movie. Yes, she does. Am I losing my mind? Did I step into a parallel universe in which I have fantasies of grandeur and rescue?

No. This is happening. Oprah does indeed want to adapt the novel into a movie. And I will indeed make a small pot of cash off the deal. The sandbar and its creatures and its stillness has cleared out some of the noise in my brain, allowing me, I believe, to step into this good fortune with just enough confidence to keep me afloat in what will become a bright, bright media glare.

This more confident me, in a fit of optimism, actually picks up the phone and calls a well-connected acquaintance in Tallahassee. I tell her what's brewing and say I want my good fortune to extend to others. But I don't know who, what, how.

She invites four women to her house, all of whom are strangers to me, for the purpose of helping me figure out what I want. At one point in the conversation, Debbie Lightsey, a Leon County commissioner, says, "You know, Refuge House, our domestic violence facility, serves eight north Florida counties but has only three bedrooms."

As soon as she utters this sentence, I zip out of the living room and into the kitchen and do what I always do when clarity strikes: cry. Amid the woman's colorful china, as much as I might want to wiggle out of it, I know I've spied a future I cannot escape. Once I am composed again, I return to the living room and say, "Okay, that's it."

The next day, I make another phone call. I feel bold, as if my voice had never been battered into submission. I call Kelly Otte, the director of Refuge House, and say, "I'm going to start a building fund for you."

And I do. It's a fund that will, over the course of the next two years, blossom into a full-blown capital campaign. We will build a new facility with many bedrooms and transitional housing and a library full of children's books. The books, I know, will bring the battered children hope.

That build-up of energy and emotion I felt forming after living here for a few months begins to fully manifest. And I can name it. It's my voice gaining assurance. It's me stepping into the footsteps of wiser women. As a child, I was too scared to go into a Seven-Eleven alone. As a young adult, I could barely say a complete sentence when standing in front of an audience. And now? I lobby Congress to pass the Violence Against Women's Act. I make speeches across the country to conventions full of people who work in the domestic violence trenches. I go to shelters and talk to the women and children. I raise money. I create the Connie May Fowler Women with Wings Foundation. I take no salary. Every dime raised goes to meet a shelter's needs. I convince publishers to donate books so that more children in more shelters will have access to literature so that they will know a better life awaits. Helping shelters create libraries becomes an obsession because before I'd even had my first period, I knew this: When the role models in your life fail you, pick up a book.

I do all of these things in memory of my mother. I come home from Washington, D. C. or Chicago or Miami and I pause at the clutch of zinnias. I think of my mother scalding her fingers as she fashions a wax tooth. I think of her dancing with my father in the living room, gazing at him as if he were her god. I think of her pounding on his chest, trying to revive him. I think, as insane as it sounds, despite what they did to each other, they were wildly in love.

My life on the Point is quite full. I garden. I bird watch. I walk. I write. I cook. I collect bones. I zip out of town to give talks and raise money for domestic violence organizations, environmental concerns, and child abuse prevention groups. It feels as if with each passing season, my once lost voice grows stronger.

However, my greatest source of joy is not writing or advocacy work or any of the aforementioned activities. It's my pets. I am up to four dogs, plus Abdul, who remains Katie's best friend. Scout and Lazarus have joined the ranks. Katie, I think, would be happy if the other dogs wandered off and got lost in the woods. She isn't mean to them. She simply royally ignores them. Atticus and Scout try to goad her into playing. She walks away, looking disgusted. Lazarus curls up beside her and naps. Katie glares at her, and then, after a heavy sigh goes to sleep. But she still grooms Abdul into a punk rock cat. I think, even in old age, it soothes her.

Katie is seventeen-years-old. Her muzzle is white and her eyes are lightly shaded with cataracts. Some days she seems young, galloping through the yard, barking at falling leaves. But other days her senses are diminished and I fear she's completely deaf. In order to not unduly surprise her, I stand in front of her, wave my hand in her face. *Katie, it's time to eat.* Deaf or not, I sing to her a song that I've sung to her since that first day nearly two decades ago when I rescued her from a guy who clearly beat his wife. K-k-k-Katie, k-k-k-Katie, you're the only d-d-d-dog that I adore …."

It is in this era, during the time when it's impossible to look at her and not sense her mortality, that I have The Talk with her. I promise when the time comes, I will not allow her to suffer, I will be with her always, I will ferry her to the other shore, she will be forever loved.

I believe she understands.

So when I look up from my reading and watch her walk across the living room with an uneven gait, I immediately take her to the vet, the same one who rested his fat hand on Lazarus's rump and said about her leg, "Let's wait and see."

He watches Katie walk around the exam room and concludes, "There's nothing wrong. She's just old. Like me."

We go home and I try to convince myself the vet is right, but other possibilities haunt me ... brain tumor, heart murmur, cancer.

A few days later, friends from Tallahassee come down for Saturday brunch. Of the four guests, two are doctors. Peje, a physician from Sweden, standing in the living room, drinking strong coffee, listening to the John Lee Hooker CD I've got cranked too loud, says out of the blue, "I think Katie has had a stroke." He watches as she lopes heavy and uneven through the room.

Dr. Dave, a dear friend with whom I've opened a free medical clinic to serve the women and children seeking safety at Refuge House, observes Katie as she enters the kitchen. "Yep, I think so."

"It's the gait," Peje says.

"I knew it!" I say, setting aside my galette dough, trying to tamp down fear, panic, premature grief. "I'll take her back to the vet on Monday." Old age indeed! Yes, old age and a stroke! What does one do for a dog that has had a stroke? Medication? Physical therapy? I'll insist he do something. I will say, "This is not just old age!"

But by Monday, I think Katie is having a series of ministrokes. The odd, loping cadence worsens and she sometimes appears to not be present, as if her mind is slowly closing the window. I can't tell if she's in pain or not, but I know this isn't going to get any better. In fact, with every hour, her condition declines. By noon, she can't walk. And I know the decision has been made for me. I promised her: no suffering. Have I waited too long already?

I call the vet. I want him to come to the shack. I want him to euthanize her here, at her home, because she hates the vet's office and is newly frail. I do not want her last moments to be spent in a place she fears. But the receptionist tells me my vet is on vacation for the week. The other vet, someone new to the practice, refuses my request. I beg the receptionist to put her on the phone.

"I will pay you anything. Please. Please do this for me."

The vet firmly repeats her hardline stance: no house calls.

I ask her to make an exception. I tell her how many animals we have, what good customers we are. Again, I offer her whatever amount of money she needs to drive the thirty minutes to the shack. But she remains unmoved.

I carry Katie to the car. It is a long, grim drive. When I get to the vet's office, I go inside and demand Katie be euthanized right where she is, in the car, surrounded by her blanket and chew toys. The receptionist says she does not think the vet will agree to that.

I don't know what I say next. I am righteous and beyond anger. Perhaps I am grief made manifest, compassion seared with flaming swords, Joan of Arc channeled and ascending. Whatever it is I say, I get what I want. I walk back out to the car, hold my dying dog, and wait. After several minutes, the vet comes out with a single syringe. I won't know until many years later, when I have to put down Atticus, that there should have been two syringes, one to tranquilize, one to euthanize. For the rest of my life, I will wonder if the vet acted out of stupidity or revenge. Would things have been different if I'd carried my dying dog through her doors?

Katie howls as she dies. I hold her and howl, too. It is the vocalization of absolute loss. The vet is already walking back to the office. But when she hears me wail, she pauses, turns.

She appears shocked. Does my pain surprise her? As I hold my lifeless dog in my arms, I have a hateful thought. I hope my wailing haunts the vet to her dying day.

By the time I return to the shack, a light, steady rain is falling. I bury Katie underneath the tangerine tree, which was her favored spot for sunbathing.

Abdul watches from the porch. The dogs are gathered by the grave. I can tell they know. How they process death is a mystery, but they are quiet, subdued, respectful even. I pray for Katie's safe travels to wherever her soul might journey. I am confused by religious dogma, but I believe in sanctity. And if there is a ferrying of spirit, I will help Katie into the dark or light or whatever it might be. I get on the ground and whisper my prayers into the earth. Lazarus nudges my face, but it's not a joyful nudge. Maybe she thinks I'm crazy. Maybe she wants me to know I'm not alone. Maybe she's trying to convey her grief. Finally, I stand and wander up to the porch where I sit with the cat, trying to gain my bearings. Eventually, I will go inside and leave on all the lights just in case Katie needs to know where I am. Abdul will remain on the porch, staring at the newly turned earth.

The dogs will remain graveside. In the rain. All night.

K-k-k-Katie!

Less than a month later, Abdul dies. He'd lived nearly his entire life with Katie, a dog who doted on him, cleaned him, napped with him. The official cause was sudden kidney failure. But I know when Katie died, his little cat heart snapped in two.

Loss takes many forms, as does migration. The purple martins that first year did arrive, despite how late I was with their accommodations, and they've arrived every year since, setting up house in the vented plastic gourds that have bottom hatches so that when they are vacated they can be cleaned and prepped for the upcoming season. Sometimes the birds get in squabbles and I have been known to run down to the martin pole I erected near the bay and scold them. They stop fighting every time I show up. I believe they think I'm off my rocker. But I also think I might hold some sway. How else to explain their cooperation? *Please stop fighting!* And they do. *Please come back next year.* And they do. I mean, they could take up residence in another yard but they return to mine year after year even with my meddling.

Perhaps all of us exist in a perpetual migratory state. Our minds are wandering to where they need to be at any given moment—a happy memory, the right word, a daydream. Our hearts, too, surprise us with sudden love, sudden hate, needs and desires we did not know we possessed until we feel that telltale plumpness rise in our chests like fresh bread.

Amid the shifting light of changing seasons, I became a single woman. But in many ways, I have forever been alone. After all, an unloved child is single. An orphan is single. An artist who lives life in the ecstatic landscape of the imagination is by definition single.

In this world of migration, birth, death, rebirth, I continue to change. My pain is quieter. Saltwater purges my bitterness. Moonlight forces my nightmares into the open so that I can challenge their veracity. Falling leaves remind me of flight. Birdsong at dawn is a call to prayer. Wildlife is my temple. Here, amid the alpha-omega tug of the natural world, I am both chrysalis and butterfly.

I stand in my kitchen and watch the sky's darkness begin to break. It is summer again on the sandbar. As I watch a flock of ringed-neck doves light on my platform, I wonder how many summers I've spent out here? Eight? Ten? Twelve? To know, I'd have to track down a calendar and that might take days. Surely there are better ways to spend my time.

Before the heat becomes too intense, I step into the dawn-lit mist and feel myself more fully gather into wakefulness. Standing at the porch rail, I watch an osprey on the osprey pole eat a mullet. My mind swirls, jumping between memory and intent, rationality and chaos. Yesterday I saw a bumblebee die in mid-flight. It simply fell out of the sky and landed by my feet. Do bees suffer from heatstroke? Do they have teeny, terrible heart attacks? How big is a bee's heart? I should write for three hours, walk the dogs at low tide, vacuum up sand and dog hair. Maybe I should switch from Spanish lessons to Mandarin. I would look funny speaking Mandarin. Like a Dalmatian speaking Hindi. The garden needs watering. Maybe it will rain and I won't have to drag the hose from here to hell. My hair is too wild for a woman my age. I bet if I moved to Mongolia, I would be a hit, but who would take care of the dogs and the birdfeeders and the butterfly garden? Who would keep the purple martins in check? I think I'll plant corn again down by the bay in the spring. What the birds don't eat, I will.

My reverie is shattered by what sounds like a B-52 strafing my brain. I duck. What the fuck is happening? Am I having a stroke? Is this what Katie went through? Are my eardrums spontaneously combusting? Are we being bombed? Why would anyone bomb Alligator Point? Aren't they done with that? Out of the corner of my eye: a shadow, then a form. A male ruby-throated hummingbird zips from my hair to the feeder. It mistook my strawberry blond curls tied in a topknot for a flower. Jesus! It just tried to feed on my hair! This is both awesome and completely discombobulating.

To avoid a second close encounter, I step off of the deck and onto the backyard patio where within two seconds, to my everlasting horror, I trip over a dead rat. A big fucker. A big dead fucker. Fuck. A rat. It's just lying there in repose—no blood, no gaping wound—like it decided to take an early morning nap, like it's a trickster intent on ruining my day. I check my feet: no entrails, no goo. I stomp just to make sure the fucker is really dead. Yep. Goner.

What is happening?

Did the rat, like the bee, die of heatstroke or heart attack? Is there a plague?

What the hell am I going to do?

This is a far worse situation than being strafed by a confused hummingbird. The only good thing about my current predicament is the dogs are lazing about inside the house, in the air conditioning, where I'm starting to think I should be. I can't leave the dead fucker to rot under the blazing sun because eventually the dogs will wander out of their cool sanctuary. They will hone in on it like it's crack. They'll take it into the house—a gross trophy—and plop it on my pillow. But first, they'll rub themselves all over it, which has to be one of the worst instincts in the world. Ever. As I ponder my choices, I wonder two things: How does what appears to be a perfectly healthy rat simply keel over and why me, God?

I walk to my gardening bench, grab my ovaries and a long-handled spade. Oh god oh god oh god. And then I do what has to be done. I shiver the big dead fucker onto the spade. I swear, I can feel its living heft, as if it might not be totally dead but simply stunned. Praying I don't trip or run into the hummingbird or suddenly become afflicted with seizures, I carry the rat at arm's length into the driveway and then—being ever so careful to throw it away from me and not on me—heft it, as though I'm an Olympian shot putter, into the field beside the house.

Whew. I dealt with that quite nicely, even though my imagination won't let me forget the strange sensation of living warmth in a newly dead big fucker. But still, I took care of it. I wish I had empathy for the rat, but I don't. Maybe I have some buried resentment in my DNA regarding The Plague. I venture back inside the yard and head for the hose. I should clean the area where the rat died so the dogs don't get the scent and, with legs and tongues akimbo, start flailing in dead fucker residue. But I don't make it even halfway across my yard because the five-foot-long resident black snake is coiled where the rat was, its Twilight Zone eyes gleaming. I know that pose. I've seen it in books and movies and nightmares. That snake is going to strike me. I'm not stupid. I run. But the snake gives chase. As I gain the steps and fling open the back door, I think, This is the craziest fucking day of my life.

For five days, every time I go into the backyard, the snake chases me. No matter what I'm doing—writing, reading, bathing, sleeping—I know it's out there waiting for me. It wants to kill me. It wishes I had never darkened its territory. It spits mysterious, previously unknown venom every time it thinks of me. I never knew snakes could hold grudges. I didn't know they had emotions and moods. But this one sure as hell does. I might as well be married to it. During the third chase, during which it has run me out into the driveway, back into the yard, and up onto the deck, I finally realize what this is about. I interrupted the snake's meal. The heat didn't kill the rat. A bad heart didn't kill the rat. The snake killed the rat. And I mucked it all up. As I run into the house, screaming in an octave few mortals can achieve, I wonder how fast I can get to the nearest pet store.

On weekends the sandbar is about people … primarily drunk people who crowd the beach, leave their trash scattered from shore to street—even soiled baby diapers—and who seem to have zero regard for the sandbar's inhabitants, human or otherwise.

It happened all at once. For years—other than the Fourth of July holiday, which is a perennial blowout—Alligator Point's ranks swelled only modestly on weekends and the visitors tended to be quiet people in search of quiet times. But as if a floodlight switched on and God shouted, "Time to par-taay!" one weekend The Hordes arrived, leaving destruction and rubbish in their wake and—*voila!*— ever since The Hordes have returned weekend after weekend, behaving as if they are extras in *Animal House*. At first, I silently fumed. But fumed silence is bad for the heart. So I got mouthy. I figured if I could talk to a packed meeting hall about the need to stop hardening the Florida coastline or to a group of politicians about the challenges domestic violence victims face in the courts, I could go *mano a mano* with The Hordes.

The first time I asked a grown woman to take her pile of dirty diapers with her, she glared at me with what I interpreted as untainted hate. But I also knew she bore no blades, no brass knuckles, because she barely fit into her day-glow orange bikini—no place to hide weaponry. And though she told me to "Mind my own fucking business," she took the soiled diapers back to town, unless those I found strewn on the road, tossed out of a car window no doubt, was a trail she blazed. It was as if she were intent on marking the sandbar with her baby's poo.

Still, once I spoke up, I became an uncorked font of How to Behave at The Beach. Now when I go out among them, I tell their children to stop tearing the legs off starfish and tails off lizards. Sometimes I kneel so I'm at their eye-level. I smile, my eyes steady and without mirth. I order them to quit with the dismemberment as I squeeze their little hands. Hard. Normally, their eyes widen with the sudden knowledge that a reckoning has taken place and they return whatever creature they'd been torturing to the sea or sand. I ask adults to only take shells that are unoccupied, not the ones housing living creatures. I ask teenagers and grown-assed people to pick up their dogs' waste. I ask college students who are playing Frisbee to avoid running through and destroying turtle nests. I ask, "How many sand dollars do you need? And can you take only the ones that are already dead?" The Hordes look at me like I'm nuts, like everyone knows sand dollars aren't alive, that creatures dying slowly within the spiraled walls of their conch shells is the animal's problem, not theirs; that the turtles ought to be more careful where they make their nests.

"Did you know," I say, "indigenous tribes believe every animal you kill will howl on your grave for all eternity?"

A bottlenose dolphin has between nineteen and twenty-one vertebrae—seven cervical vertebrae and twelve to fourteen thoracic vertebrae. I have, during my many beach walks, collected enough washed ashore vertebrae to create three new dolphins.

The male bottlenose lifespan ranges between forty and fifty years. Females can live fifty years or more. Dolphins die of things humans die of: viruses, bacterial infections, fungal infections, skin diseases, stomach diseases, and respiratory disorders. They die of tapeworm. They die due to human carelessness, human cruelty, and human criminal behavior. They asphyxiate in fishing nets. In Japan they grace the dinner plate. Some countries make shoes, belts, and other leather goods from their skin and what's left of their corpses is churned into fertilizer. Habitat destruction kills dolphins. Manmade toxins kill dolphins. Manmade toxins that kill dolphins include agricultural runoff and industrial pollutants. Overfishing kills dolphins. Take away their food—this is usually accomplished by overfishing—and they starve. Plastic bags and other trash discarded in the sea kill dolphins. Sewage spills kill dolphins. Engine propellers kill dolphins. By-catch kills dolphins because by definition if you are by-catch you are dead. Noise pollution and Navy sonar kill dolphins. Oil spills kill dolphins.

I collect the beached vertebrae in order to remember. To honor. Sometimes all that is left is the round bone disc. Sometimes three surrounding bones are attached to the round disc, forming a shape that causes me to think of Jesus, a crucifix, a sun. I gather the bones and place them on shelves and side tables and in windowsills where they rest amid osprey feathers, eagle feathers, heron feathers. I tuck them amid rocks, quartz, raw amethyst, crystal geodes, hatched bird eggs, and shed snakeskins. On a day I can't yet imagine, a man will walk into my house and say, "Oh my God. You have little altars everywhere."

A PBS film crew is at the shack. We are in the backyard, the pissed off snake is nowhere to be seen—he must have found another delicacy to sate his hunger—and I'm being asked questions such as, "What does this place mean to you and your writing?"

I can't tell the truth—it would take too long—so I try to focus on a single aspect of love, which also is impossible. You either tell everything or you tell a lie. I'm arguing with myself, trying to pinpoint a feasible response that encompasses The Truth—place as sanctity, memory as sanctity, the keeper of bones and dead fathers as sanctity—when we're interrupted by the cacophony of barking, snarling, tooth-baring dogs. A stray mutt is under the house, placidly watching Atticus and Scout attempt to tear through the fence, presumably so they can, in redneck parlance, open up a can of whoop ass.

I try to calm my schipperkes but they'll have none of it. With the film crew looking on, I get down on all fours and coax the problem canine out from under the house. He is very furry and red. His tongue has purple splotches, which tells me there's some chow chow in the mix. His lower teeth are catty-whomped. His fur is matted and plastered with sticker burrs. His ears ooze an oily black substance. I pick up the little guy. He's built solid, a canine engine block, but I can feel his ribs. He licks my hand and bats his feverish big brown eyes at me. I fall in love. I say, "You look like Ernest Borgnine!" and the film crew agrees.

He is dehydrated, anemic, and riddled with multiple infections. I take him to a new vet who has set up shop on the outskirts of Crawfordville. She thinks he was on his own, traveling the countryside for a good, long time. I hold him against my chest, petting the length of him, and name him Ulysses, a wanderer in search of stories.

"That's a perfect name!" the vet says.

We clean him up, she gives him his first course of antibiotics and vitamins and an IV drip to rehydrate him. When we leave, the dog is already looking like he's poised to take on the world. Again.

But evidence of maltreatment persists. Ulysses freaks out— eyes too wide, a howl that is more of a moan, an attempt to hide under whatever is near (couch, chair, house)—every time he sees a man in white rubber crabbing boots. There are a lot of men along this coastline who wear white rubber crabbing boots, which in these parts are known as Panacea Nikes. I know in my soul, with a certitude made concrete by righteous anger, someone wearing said boots habitually kicked the dog. I know it's why the dog's teeth are catty-whomped. I know that one day the dog simply had enough and took to the road. What I don't know is why he picked me.

Atticus entertains me. Scout soothes me. Ulysses will prove to be my protector. He watches over me with fierce grace. He rarely leaves my side and stands guard all night, every night.

One afternoon, Ulysses and I are in the chickee. The beach is how I like it: empty. Ulysses sniffs the air, reading it the way a human reads the newspaper. I'm deep into my fifth reading of *Song of Solomon*. Milkman is in a Rexall drugstore buying perfume and powder for Magdalene called Lena when Ulysses erupts. I look up from my book and am instinctively, immediately frightened.

At the base of the dune line stands a man. Blue jeans. T-shirt. Unkempt. There is no light in the man's eyes, no glint of the stardust that signals us as being human, humane. Ulysses roars, bounding out of the chickee, charging the man, chasing him over the dunes, transforming into my own little Hound from Hell and sounding more like a lion than a dog. I follow behind, tripping once, twice in the sand. Sticker burrs sting my kneecaps and my shin is bleeding from where skin met stone. Still roaring, Ulysses stops at the road as the man scrambles into a white van and tears away. The man doesn't say, "Hey, call your dog off" or "I only wanted to walk down the beach" or anything else a normal person might say. He flees, just as if he were a coward who knew he was up to no good and had been thwarted. I watch the van head east, which I hope means he's heading off the sandbar.

Ulysses prances over, head high, tail wagging. I pet him and tell him what a good boy he is, but I am shaken. I think the dog just saved me. And then I have an outlandish thought, but it's one that will stick with me, a theory born of a heart that longs for a different past: Perhaps Ulysses is my father reincarnated. It's not as good as resurrection, but I'll take it. I mention my theory to no one because I don't fancy being institutionalized. But I pamper Ulysses every day. Extra pets. Extra treats. Extra love.

I found the calendar. I have lived on the sandbar, alone, for over a decade and in that time I have felt my body not age, but rather respond to the push and pull of the seasons. In springtime, I feel as if I'm eighteen and in love for the first time. In the harsh northern winds of winter, I wrap up in blankets and cook old people food—chicken soup, beef stew, corn chowder. In the summer, I fish and stargaze and spend hours in or by the sea, both by day and night. And in autumn, with the temperatures cooling, I begin putting some of my garden to bed and as I do I feel myself slipping into a desire for a long rest, but I can't succumb because there are butterflies and birds to feed for autumn is also a period of great migration.

But this fall, even though the sun's angle is slanting toward autumnal, the sandbar is seared in heat. I sit at my computer, my unfinished book on the screen, but I'm not writing. I'm staring at the blue water, imagining that not only will temperature never drop again but that it is going to get hotter and hotter and hotter until every living thing spontaneously combusts. Welcome to global warming. I'm daydreaming my own private Armageddon replete with baby squirrels turning to ash when I hear the familiar sound of the mail lady's car.

"Finally," I say, irrationally thrilled to have a valid reason for interrupting my lackadaisical writing session. I can normally count on the mail arriving four days a week; five is optimistic and six is an iffy proposition.

Barefoot, I enter the scorching light of midday. My skin feels on fire even though I've been under the sun's influence for only a few seconds. I pause at the mailbox and flip through envelopes. Junk, junk, bill, junk, Department of The Army. Huh? I tear it open but the sun is too bright.

Once back inside the shack, I have to wait a few minutes for my eyes—which are extraordinarily sensitive to sunlight—to adjust. Why on earth is the army writing me? As the letter slowly comes into focus, I get the suspicious impression the Department of The Army—the Jacksonville District Corps of Engineers to be exact—sent me a letter pounded out on a typewriter.

And I also succumb to a knee-jerk reaction of total panic. My mother hated the Army Corp of Engineers. One of my earliest memories is of her pulling me onto her lap (perhaps I remember this because the closeness involved in me being held by her was so unusual) and telling me about the horrors the Corp inflicted on all humankind, beginning with the ill-fated Cross Florida Barge Canal. "Those bastards destroy everything they touch," she said, patting my sunburned knee.

I think it's understandable, given her dislike of the Corp represented one of the few tender moments between us, a letter from them would send me into a tizzy. Did they want to recruit me? Arrest me? Censure my mother posthumously?

"Dear Property Owner," the letter begins, and I find its officiousness juxtaposed against the word "dear" mildly amusing.

Your property lies within the boundaries of the former Camp Gordon Johnston Military Reservation. This site was originally established as an Army amphibious training center and later redesignated as an Army Service Forces training center site, and comprises approximately 156,350 acres located along the Gulf of Mexico, encircling the town of Carrabelle and most of Franklin County, Florida.

Thank you for the history lesson, but why bother?

Various types of ammunitions were utilized during World War II for training purposes. A search of historical records (Archive Search Report performed by the U.S. Army Corps of Engineers) revealed that potentially dangerous ordnance and explosives (OE) may remain within the limits of the former training center.

Yes, the old-timers love regaling fresh ears with tales of their languid summertime hunts for ordnance, many of them claiming they picked the sandbar clean of all such OE years ago.

Current environmental laws require that the Army determine the extent of the OE contamination at these old Army sites and remove remaining OE. First, an informed decision must be made with regard to which areas would require further action. In order to make this determination a sweep of the area with a specially designed metal detector will be required. The metal detector will identify spots where ordnance may exist beneath the ground surface. A trained specialist will dig, with a hand shovel, to a depth no greater than 4-feet to determine the nature of the metal. The metal may be a nail, container or otherwise harmless item or it may be the shell of an intact piece of old ordnance, which is still dangerous.

Four feet deep? I look out at my yard. Every inch of it has been disturbed by a human hand—Anne's hands, my hands, the hands of septic tank installers, the hands of nursery workers who planted fruit trees and shrubs, the hands of the men who refurbished my oyster shell driveway. Any ordnance on my property were discovered and removed fifty-some years ago by exploring carefree, barefoot, shirtless boys.

Based upon the results of our investigations, areas of the former Camp Gordon Johnston Military Reservation which are most likely to contain ordnance will be identified and removal of ordnance found within those areas will be scheduled.

Enclosed you will find two copies of the Right-of-Entry for Environmental Assessment and Response, which grants the Government permission to enter upon the specified property, for a period of 24 months, to perform the work described above. You should sign and date both copies ....

I should sign and date nothing. I rummage through my giant refrigerator, find a can of soda water, crack it open, and gaze out at my beautifully xeriscaped front yard: fruit trees amid sea oats and salt tolerant wild flowers specifically chosen to offer sustenance to butterflies and hummingbirds. They will tear it all out ... fuckheads ... Mother was right about them. I read through the Right-of-Entry document. It essentially gives the Corps the right to stomp through my property for twenty-four months and store all manner of equipment anywhere they please. *All excavations will be backfilled and leveled.*

Over my dead body. I nearly lost the shack in the divorce and now here is one more entity trying to wreck my property. I wonder if I'm cursed and why I keep having to fight to save the shack and its environs. Am I being paranoid? Maybe. But the fact that there is essentially no amount of unturned ground on my property, that the military left over half a century ago, and that they sold plots of land they knew were riddled with live ordnance is perplexing on multiple levels. *Numerous ordnance items have been discovered by individual property owners since facility closure ... OE/UXO that may be encountered includes: 2.36" rockets (high explosive [HE] and practice), 105-155mm HE artillery rounds, 4.2" HE mortars, 4.2" smoke and white phosphorous mortars, 81mm mortars (HE and practice), 37mm HE projectiles, practice antipersonnel mines, and practice antitank mines.*

Jesus, sounds as though the dearly departed Princess Diana should have focused her landmine clearing efforts on Alligator Point.

I reach for the phone and call Wayne Coloney. He assures me there is no live ordnance on his property or mine. He says they can't come on our properties unless we sign the Right-of-Entry document. There is nothing to worry about, he tells me.

In the coming weeks, I will ask people in line at the IGA and at the fish market what they plan to do. As far as I can tell, no one will allow the Corps to dig up their yards. I call the information number included in the letter. I fear officials of any kind, a leftover from my mother dragging me into government offices, asking where our government checks were, and being treated like we were scum on the bottom of the bureaucrat's penny loafers. So my voice shakes as I speak to the Chief of Management and Disposal. She reiterates what Wayne told me: No one will come onto my property without my permission. But she also adds I must sign the form to insure "the safety."

"No," I hear myself saying, "absolutely not."

As the sun sets, the sandbar glows in a hazy, golden fog. I wander out to the backyard, spray on bug repellent, and begin deadheading my roses. The clippers are mildly rusted and snap hard on the necks of the spent blooms. The blooms plop onto the dirt with no grace whatsoever. As I gather them up and haul them to my clippings pile, I imagine that with every step I take, ordnance explode beneath me and I am blown to smithereens in tiny increments, as though my destruction is to be meted out in tandem with the slow, measured, slightly halting cadence of a tired gardener.

A few weeks later, it's nearing noon and I'm still in my pajamas, staring at the computer screen, trying to figure out what word comes next in a novel with innumerable moving parts. I'm just about to type the note *I don't know what this book wants to be* when the dogs go ballistic. I push back my chair and look out the window. What are those three handsome young men doing in my front yard? Wearing brutally starched identical shorts? Placing little white flags amid the sea oats so lovingly planted and cared for? I look a mess, but I have no time to shower, wash my hair, brush my teeth, sweep on mascara. I'm gleaming but stinking in my albino body.

I step onto my front porch—I don't even have on a bra and my hair looks like I'm Don King's daughter—and yell, "Hey! Hey! You guys! What are you doing?"

The one with short blond hair and a clipboard looks my way, seems surprised I'm speaking to him. Then he says something I can't hear to his compatriots.

"Hey! You! I'm talking to you."

"Oh. Hello, ma'am," Sergeant Clipboard says. "We're with the United States Army. We're here to clear OE from your yard."

What? They can't do this. I run through a quick mental check. No, I definitely did not give permission—written or otherwise—for the army to do so much as remove a teaspoon of dirt from my land. Sergeant Clipboard starts to refocus his attention on the setting out of white flags.

In a split second, I become the person I always promised I never would: my mother. "Like hell you will."

"Ma'am." He shoots me a military issue grin. "OE. That stands for ordnance and explosives."

"I'm very aware what it stands for. But you do not have permission to be on my property."

"Ma'am, if we don't do this you could get blown up. Lose a leg. Lose an arm. Maybe worse."

He's got to be joking. I've already lost everything I'm going to lose in this lifetime. "You will not touch one plant, one weed, one tree. I did not sign on any dotted line in the known world. Get out now. Or would you like me to release my dogs?" I am amazed and wholly ashamed at my forcefulness.

The three soldiers look at each other as if the unhinged woman on the porch was someone who really would sic her dogs on them.

"We're sorry, ma'am. There must be some mistake."

"You bet there is."

"We'll be moving on now."

"Good."

They pack up and head down the road, and I—appalled by my behavior—call after them, "Thank you for your service!"

The visitation from the Army has me jangled. If I'd been on a trip, for instance, I would have come home to a destroyed landscape. And once something is destroyed, it's gone. Father? Gone. Mother? Gone. All our possessions in that tiny Tampa demon-haunted cottage? Gone. Marriage? Gone. It would take years to bring the yard back to where Anne had it when I bought the place and even longer to regrow it into what it is now.

I tell myself, No harm, no foul; they won't be back.

But can I be sure? Is anything a given in this life?

Two days after my encounter with the army, in the shadow-dispersing light of a new day, I pause at a shelf that runs the length of my living room wall and try to regain my bearings. The shelf is cluttered with shells, bones, sea glass, matchbook Madonnas, and tiny books filled with incantations. I pick up a smooth-edged piece of cobalt sea glass, lift it to my eye, and gaze through it. The world disappears.

I set it down and wander into the kitchen where I'm startled to find a wren flitting among my dishes. How did it get in? Isn't a bird in the house a predictor of madness? Or is it tragedy? Does the wren want to make a nest amid my bone china? Will tiny baby birds open their mouths, mistaking the overhead light for the sun? Will I feed the baby birds with a medicine dropper I will purchase from the vet? Or will the mother bird force me from my home? I open the French doors. The smell of the bay—salt and desire—rolls in and the bird flies out.

"Don't go," I say, but already it is out of sight.

I brew my tea, feed the dogs, and head out for my morning walk. From my position in the high dunes, I see the beach is empty. Despite the occasional longing for greater human contact, I have found immense joy in solitude. And, in truth, it's nice to be able to go into the world and work with people who are committed to making the planet a safer, better place, and then come home and retreat back into the busy, vital cocoon of the sandbar. I feel my life has become that rare moment in the surf song in which there is no *whoosh*, no crash, no echoing roll. Only silence. In that momentary pause, bones heal, past traumas recede. I'm discovering solitude magnifies life. The sky seems vaster, the sea more insistent. I edge ever closer to *The Tropic of Capricorn*: "I wanted to be alone for a thousand years in order to reflect on what I had seen and heard …."

The rest of that sentence—"and in order to forget"—isn't a part of me. My time at Alligator Point has made me want to remember even more abundantly, more honestly, with a bigger, wiser heart.

I pause beside a beach juniper, a low growing evergreen unfazed by drought, flood, hurricanes, salt air, or heat waves. When crushed, the needles exude a scent that is both medicinal and woody. The bright green berries ripen into a dusky midnight purple. The birds love them, although they are not fit for human consumption—diarrhea—or as a cure for psoriasis—increased skin cancer risk—but some part of it is useful, otherwise there would be no gin. I wonder how difficult making a single batch of juniper gin would be? Perhaps Anne, with her pindo palm jelly and wax myrtle candle making, is proficient in bootleg gin brewing and just hasn't told me.

While not industrious or devious enough to distill illegal gin, I have harvested its branches and burned them as incense. Many ancient cultures, including those indigenous to the Americas, used juniper to purify temples, everyday objects, and people. Some cultures believed it heightened clairvoyance while others thought it protected them against evil spells.

I reach out, gather a handful of branches, run the spiny, faintly oily needles through my fingers, and all the seconds, minutes, hours, days, years, pain, glory, failures, triumphs, dreams unattained, dreams realized—a rosary beaded with anguish and hope—rush through me. When I open my palm I have a strange sensation my story will be written there in Sanskrit, an offering to the ages, but there is only skin and a wobbly lifeline; no history, no static signposts announcing this or that is exactly what happened and I am exactly the person I think I am and there is only one Truth inside each passage of my life. I study both hands and what I see is this: so many truths, so many passages.

I look beyond the dunes to the Gulf. It trembles—blue and relentless—on the lip of the world and I wonder anew, is this all a mirage? A hologram made from fate and luck? A form of sanctity born from isolation? A holy moment?

An oystercatcher switchblades the water with its long, orange beak. A beach mouse scurries past and disappears into a thicket of dune grass. That blacksnake is busy hunting. I can't see it, but in my solitude I've developed a sense about critters, so I know it's nearby, perhaps stretched out like an onyx necklace just beyond the next dune.

At this juncture in my island life—I am not beholden to a single person in the world … no partner, no children, no parents—I could recreate myself, leave writing behind and become a filmmaker or a shrink or a crafter of glass trinkets (for you, Grandmother). The strengthening sun induces temporary blindness. My eyes tear up—they are stippled with sand—and in a fleeting state of sensory deprivation, I realize once more time is not a fixed notion on the sandbar. The future commingles with the present, easing the past, prompting me to wonder, *What day is it? How old am I? When did I move here? How many years has that osprey been circling high and low, riding a thermal wind?* These questions thrill me.

Wiping my eyes with the hem of my shirt, not caring if the sea gulls catch sight of my boobs, I turn away from the wind and wait for the world to sputter into focus. When it does, I kick off my sneakers and head toward the water, past the chickee, which when I moved out here stood a couple of feet above the sand. Now the dunes threaten to consume it. Perhaps the movement of dunes is a more accurate marker of time than memory. And then there is this marker: The thatch roof was ripped away by a tropical storm that rolled through about a year ago and now it's crowned with tin. Oddly enough, once the thatch was gone and the tin was in place, teenagers began carving inane messages into its wood bench and spray-painting graffiti onto the beams. Julie, whoever you are, the world doesn't care if you love Stan.

A line of ducks stretches the sky into a giant V. They are the first ducks of the season, come south to winter. The shore is riddled with moon seashells, a species I only see in large numbers in autumn and winter. The last turtle nest of the season hatched a couple of days ago, and I'm sorry I missed seeing the newborns' epic, frenetic march to the sea. A battalion of giant gulls is gathered on the shoreline. They are all looking out to the horizon as if they are waiting for someone. I call them Yankee gulls because this particular species, like the ducks and snowbirds, live on the Point only during the colder months.

Here it is, the end of September, and temperatures are still hovering in the low to mid-nineties. But the creatures are following the calendar—that dictionary of time—chasing, perhaps, the shorter days and the sun's autumnal angle. They are positioning themselves, I decide, for whatever comes next.

I join the Yankee gulls (they don't seem to mind) and gaze out at the Gulf. A dolphin and her calf arc through the blue water. They are so close to the shore, I hear them chuffing, which is how they clear their blowholes, allowing them to take in life-sustaining oxygen.

I wear memories the way some women wear jewels: with daring and abandon.

Not long after first arriving on these shores, I went for a walk with my University of Kansas writing professor who was visiting from the Midwest, the novelist Carolyn Doty. Carolyn was short and round, drank more red wine than God could make, and famously never suffered fools. It was an early, clear morning during the depths of summer. We walked westward, pacing the journey of a dolphin that was extremely close in-shore—maybe ten or twelve feet.

This was the first time I attempted to click-talk. The urge rushed through me the way early notions that eventually become novels do. But with novels, you have time for contemplation and revision. On the beach that day with Carolyn, I was in a *carpe diem* situation. As if I knew what I was doing, I said, "Hey, watch this."

I stepped calf-deep into the Gulf and, unabashed, belted out what I presumed was dolphin speak. I'd recently heard their squeaky communications on a National Geographic special so, in my sudden enthusiasm, I thought that made me a scientist savant.

"What the hell are you doing?" Carolyn demanded from shore, and from our long history together I knew her fists were planted on her hips and her hair was on end.

"Just watch," I said, certain I was onto something, and, undeterred, resumed my high-pitched clicking.

Dolphins are shaped like mammalian bullets and can move like it, as well. They can also stun prey with one blast of their sonic song, leaving mullet helpless. But I am not a mullet, I thought. With a determination born to those who fail and survive, I squeaked and clicked for a good four or five measures.

I hadn't a clue what I was saying, but the dolphin did. With torpedic speed, the animal changed course and rushed straight at me.

Carolyn screamed. Unable to move through the weight of water quickly enough, I prepared for impact, bending my knees, digging my feet deeper into the ocean floor. A terrible fear swept through me. Had I just called the dolphin a salty whore? A shark wannabe? A no count loser with an ugly mama?

This massive sea creature created its own wave, which slapped at my thighs, and then, defying physics, the dolphin stopped no more than a foot in front of me, rolled slightly to one side, and gazed at me.

I gazed back.

Despite its great mouth forever curved into what humans assume is a smile, I had no idea what the marine mammal was thinking. Had my mangled dolphin-speak elicited curiosity? Love? Outrage? Bemusement? Shock?

"Holy shit!" Carolyn said. I glanced over my shoulder. Her mouth hung open in that lovely oval which signals profound surprise. A wave unfurled, water rushed knee-high, and with the conversation over—I was too stunned to keep clicking—the dolphin moved on, in shore, watching us. And we kept pace. It was as if we—two humans and a dolphin—went for a stroll together.

Carolyn shook her head, touched my wrist where one feels for a pulse, and whispered, "We can never, ever tell anyone about this."

Carolyn died of a heart attack on March 10, 2003. I miss her, but am grateful for the time we had together and for the lessons about writing and life she so generously bestowed.

After a few glasses of red wine spiked with ice cubes, Carolyn would inevitably tell the story of meeting Ernest Hemingway. She was a young, fledgling writer waiting tables at a resort in Sun Valley. On June 1, 1961, he was seated in her section and she served him lunch. She recited what he ate, which I can't remember, but she said he drank a lot of wine. The next day, at approximately 7 a.m., Hemingway shot and killed himself. Carolyn would gaze into her thinning merlot and murmur, "I wonder if I served him his last meal."

On this autumn morning, years after Carolyn's death, I turn away from the dolphin and her calf and journey north, back across the dunes toward my wobbly sea shack, empty save for my dogs. I walk down the oyster shell driveway toward the bay.

The sun-bleached oyster shells crunch beneath my feet, and—tangled for a moment in the shimmer of celestial pigment, sea light, the flash of an egret wing, and memories of the living and dead—I decide that what I'm glimpsing each second of every day in this fleeting life is infinity, and that is where forgiveness resides.

What makes this area so conducive to the perpetuation of marine life and the animals that depend on it—osprey for mullet, for instance—also makes it special in another way: the sandbar has one of the greatest potential storm surges in the world. The continental shelf is high here, thus the shallow waters, and it's also concave. The tide, when pushed by a cyclone, piles vertically—it's got nowhere to go but up—and rushes ashore.

I did not know this until a few years after I bought the shack. It explains a lot of things, such as the road being washed out every hurricane season and the frequency and speed with which we experience tidal flooding (so frequent I don't really notice it). I walk the Point from end-to-end, day after day, wishing the powers that be would let the Gulf take whatever it wants.

Hurricanes, flooding, erosion—it all fascinates me. I feel in tandem with it all. This place teaches me a single lesson over and over: Loss is not a cold, lightless grave. It is life.

After a hot autumn, a frigid winter, and an astonishingly vibrant spring, I find myself at the height of summer sprinting though the Atlanta airport, trying to make a tight connection that will take me to Italy and then Greece. I will be teaching on an Aegean island—who can imagine such a thing!—and am determined to not miss the connecting flight. I feel heady, as if I am a woman full of potential. This ability to run through an airport and fly to Greece is something else the sandbar has given me: moxie.

A few days ago, a storm entered the Gulf and began churning northward. Amid packing and list-making and getting the dogs to their sitter, I called my friend Pete Ripley, an African American and Cuban Studies scholar at Florida State University, and asked if he'd come down to the coast and board up the shack if it looked like we were going to get hit. Even though Tallahassee is only an hour away, my request struck me as desperate but required. Pete didn't hesitate to say yes, and in fact, seemed to view it as an adventure.

Hurricane Dennis is wall-to-wall on CNN, but I'm moving so fast I can't get a comprehensive view of the storm's predicted path. I make it to the gate seconds before they close the cabin door. I quickly find my seat and call my sister, even while the flight attendant is instructing passengers to turn off our cell phones, and ask about the forecast.

"Don't worry," she says. "It's going well west of you. Probably Pensacola." Her voice and assured weather report inspires confidence. I hang up and am about to call Pete to tell him not to bother boarding up the shack when the flight attendant stands over me and snaps with schoolmarm style, "Ma'am, you MUST turn off your phone NOW."

I arrive in Athens sans luggage. Delta managed to lose my suitcase and doesn't have a clue where it might be. Fantasies of looking sharp and chic (I'd watched *Roman Holiday* twice prior to packing) vanish. I wore a comfortable muumuu of a jumper on the plane and that will be my uniform for the next several days. Pride is this trip's first casualty.

A large Greek ferry transports the conference participants to Andros, a lovely mountainous island that serves as the jumping off point for the Cyclades. Dolphins surf the giant ship's wake, which causes a stir of excitement among the conference-goers. My room at the Andros Holiday Hotel overlooks the calm, nearly cobalt waters of the Aegean Sea. I watch huge ships and ferries enter and exit the channel. We are approaching a full moon and I am fascinated. How hard will the moon pull on these mythic waters? Will I be able to walk across the face of the Aegean? Will birds flock to the exposed sea floor to feast like they do at Alligator Point?

Tasso, the man who manages the resort, laughs when I ask about tides and explains there is no such thing as an Aegean tide.

"No tide?"

"No tide!" he booms, clapping his hands for emphasis.

I think he might be lying, having fun with the naïve American. So when I'm not involved in conference responsibilities, I sit on my terrace and stare at an outcropping of rocks near the channel, waiting to see the water level rise and perhaps overtake the rocks. It never happens. The moon, gravitational pull, hydraulics hold no sway. Gleaming like an Aegean fireball, the moon's watery reflection is as steady as the non-existent lunar surge. At a *taverna* in town, I strike up a conversation with a local fisherman who insists the Aegean has tides but, after downing a shot of ouzo and slamming his shot glass on the table, says, "Tiny. Tiny tides. You need a microscope to see them."

I spend my late night hours on the phone with someone named Sue in Delta's lost luggage department. Thanks to the time difference, the issue of my missing luggage can only be addressed post-midnight. Sue and I get to know each other better than we should, meaning that rather than giving me specifics about the hunt for my luggage, she talks at length about her decades-long struggle to become a published writer. On day four, as she prattles (I get the distinct impression she's lonely), I try spot cleaning my jumper, which is crusted in melted butter and emits an odor reminiscent of small children who refuse to bathe.

A Greek folk dance conference is taking place simultaneously with the writing conference. At first we're enamored with the music and moves. But after three days, most of us are muttering that if we hear one more *Oompah!* we're going to scream. No longer finding the other charming, we fight over which conference gets to use which rooms. *Folk dancer* becomes synonymous with *arrogant fuck head*.

After wearing my muumuu jumper for four days straight, a man whose name I believe is Dionysus, drives me to the ferry in a battered pick-up truck and—amid the barely controlled chaos of exiting cars, industrial trucks, and families on holiday—finds and retrieves my long lost bag.

There is only one computer at the Andros Holiday Hotel. It belongs to the manager's son—a sullen young man who clearly doesn't get along with his father—and though we're told we can check our email, he glares so contemptuously each time we sit down at the Soviet made machine I fear he might whirl into an expletive-studded rage. Still, desirous of news from home, one afternoon I take my chances. I log onto my email account. Just *junk, junk, junk*, and then this from a part-time sandbar neighbor:

> "Trust all is well and you have found Adonis (or a reasonable facsimile). House is ok. Grass in back yard is up to the fence and the boat is in the middle of the yard—but all looks to be ok. Power is out and it looks like it will be for awhile. There is no water and that looks like it will take a while. I have attached some pictures to give you a sense of what happened. There was a very large storm surge. (St Marks was under 8 feet of water.) The direction it came from it

really pounded the shore around the KOA--it's not there now. The road is torn up from about 1/2 mile to the east of the KOA to past the firehouse. There is no way in except by foot or ATV. If you look at the pictures the long aqua things laying about are the water pipes. I got down there but it was sure a long hot walk. I rode my bike back but had to carry the bike over the rubble—what fun. Angelos isn't. The deck is gone and there is not a window left. They think it will take over a year maybe two to get back."

I am half a world away, the last word I received was the storm would hit west of the Point, yet the sandbar got "pounded" and the KOA, the road, and Angelo's—the only restaurant nearby (at the northern base of the Ochlockonee Bay bridge and a favorite eatery for both locals and tourists)—are obliterated? And what does "House ok" mean? Whose house? Okay as in only the front windows are blown out? Okay as in half of it is still standing? I think the "boat is in middle of the yard" refers to my old wooden boat built by a blind man who lives near Carrabelle. The boat is very, very heavy and was on solid ground near the bay, its anchor affixed. For the water to move it into the "middle of the yard" means the storm surge was immense, that it breached the bank and might well have reached the shack.

Stunned, worried, 5,700 miles from home, a week of conference left, and there is nothing I can do about any of it. I try not to think about the wildlife, about what that kind of storm surge does to turtle nests, seabird eggs, anything that crawls or flies. To keep my cool, I will the Aegean tide to rise.

It doesn't. I'm out of magic.

Flying home improves my luck not one iota. I get stuck at Gatwick for a week thanks to Delta's hell-bent insistence on overbooking high season flights. When I finally arrive stateside, I return to a devastated sandbar. Twenty-three homes are destroyed and many others severely damaged. The frequently washed out portion of the road—long a boondoggle made worse by the county, the state, and the Feds courtesy the Army Corps of Engineers—is no more. Rocks and concrete from the destroyed revetment riddle the former road, making passage difficult and dangerous. The pine forest looks as though God tousled it good and then took off before putting things back in order. We appear war torn. Roofs gone, walls collapsed, trees snapped, water pipes tossed like Q-tips, but the shack stands untouched in its magic bubble, unharmed, looking as though it has simply received a good, hard scrubbing. I consider what condition it might have been in had that flight attendant not admonished me to shut off my phone.

After putting the yard back in order, emptying the stinking fridge, and hiring someone to haul away my battered wooden boat, I inspect Katie's grave. The sea did not breach it but came within a couple of feet. As I stand amid happy, sniffing, peeing, exploring dogs, a long simmering guilt boils over. Every time I leave the Point for an extended teaching gig, I feel like I'm abandoning my dead dog. And the fact that the surge nearly swept her away solidifies my concern. But what can I do? I have to make a living, which means occasionally going out among people. But Katie doesn't know when I'm gone or when I'm present. Can I really allow irrational guilt to trump common sense?

A rufous-sided towhee, looking worse for the wear, lands amid the tangled, leafless tangerine branches and caws, sounding very much like a bleating sheep with sandpaper for vocal chords. Could this be another visitation? Is this the Summer Haven towhee? Of course not. Get a grip. I think back to *Song of*

Solomon and Pilate Dead who goes through the world wearing the font of her strength—her name—in a snuffbox earring, waiting for the day it will sing beyond her existence. I imagine myself adorned with a transparent globe dangling from my ear, the ashes of my dog residing within.

This is insane. But I'd always have her with me. *Don't do it.* At least the bones.

I find a handyman from Panacea who is willing to dig up Katie. Once I have her bones, I'll cremate them. In this way—earring or not—I will have her with me wherever I go: Tampa, St. Augustine, New York, Paris. No guilt. No potential destruction from storm surge. This is a Perfect Plan.

With the house in order and the plan in place, I travel to central Florida for a temporary teaching job. Exhausted from international travel and dealing with the entrails of a mean storm, when I get there I decide to do something I rarely do: pamper myself. I book an appointment for hair, nails, and whatever else I think I can afford. And though I don't like strangers touching me (years ago someone insisted on buying me a massage as a birthday gift; the experience left me fetal), the new me, the one who gives speeches and travels to foreign countries, can do this.

The salon smells of cinnamon and champagne. Owned by a Turkish man, all the stylists are Turks who are exceedingly handsome and highlight hair so beautifully it's easy to believe they share a sole purpose in life—to make women happy—and who, for no extra charge, administer foot massages (yes, I'm going for it) with warm, fragrant oils.

There I am, my hair fully loaded with aluminum sleeves, looking like a tin man from the neck up, my feet propped on an ottoman (an ottoman in a Turkish spa!), a mustachioed Turk pouring scented oil into his palm—he is about to put his hand on my flesh—when my cell phone rings. I check the screen. My gravedigger in Panacea. This is very exciting. A foot massage and Katie's bones!

"Hello."

"Miss Connie?"

"Yes."

"Well, I'm here."

"Yes?"

"And I've dug all over the place. I mean, I dug down deep." He pauses, I think for dramatic effect.

"Go on."

"And, well … she ain't here."

I bolt upright. The Turk loses control of the oil bottle. It hits the floor and rolls underneath a display of expensive hair products.

"What do you mean 'she ain't here.'?"

"I dug and dug. But, Miss Connie, there ain't no bones."

Impossible! This cannot be. Where is she? I burst into tears and, phone in-hand, my head fully foiled, run out of the salon and into a bright day bustling with women in Chanel suits and co-eds in bikinis.

The Turk stands in the doorway, obviously concerned, offering what I interpret to be entreaties—*Please, come back inside, crazy lady!*—but he is speaking Turkish so I can't be certain. The gravedigger promises me his search has been both careful and thorough. But still, I weep.

"How long ago did you bury her?"

"Six years, maybe." I am so distraught, numbers make as much sense to me as the hairdresser's words.

"Well, honey, I think nature done took its course."

"What does that mean?" I'm very close to a snot-riddled meltdown.

"Her bones all turned to dust by now, Miss Connie. Ashes to ashes. Dust to dust. You heard of that?"

By now three Turkish men stand in the doorway, talking rapidly, their hands moving as quickly as their mouths. Frankly, they look frightened.

Surely the gravedigger isn't lying. Why would someone lie about a dog's bones? I thank him, hang up, and amid the horrified stares of well-heeled ladies, I step back into the salon.

The men expect an explanation. But how does one tell people you are not related to by blood or blood pact that you hired someone to dig up a dog's bones so that you could haul them around with you? You can't reveal that sort of thing to just anyone. I slump into my salon chair. One of them takes my hand. Another pours me a glass of bubbly. The third says, "What is this problem? Why your tears?"

I take a sip, then a deep breath, and find a way not to lie. "Someone," I say, trying to sound poised, sane, "someone very dear to me is missing."

Two days later, on a Friday afternoon, after meeting with my students, I drive five hours back to Alligator Point. As on the day I buried Katie, it's twilight and a gentle rain falls. I stand at her grave. The earth has been disturbed, but did the man truly dig deep enough? Did he try hard enough? Did he take the bones for himself?

Stop. Just stop.

Ashes to ashes. Dust to dust.

Remember: Metaphor, not grief, is your strongest amino acid.

Hurricane Dennis was not an aberration. The storm was part of a natural cycle. The facts involved in its formation, path, and timing are not evil. Or manmade. Or designed to single out any individual for punishment or retribution. Humans do that, not nature.

And nature heals its own. Oyster beds rebound. Mullet jump and have babies and try to avoid hungry dolphins. Osprey dive and feed. The stars still shine as brightly as they did before the cyclone. And the bay will recover. Soon crabbers and shrimpers and oystermen will forget all about the hurricane.

Human inflicted trauma—hydrocarbons and global climate change and polluted water tables and toxin-laden air and soil depleted of nutrients due to industrial farming methods and haphazard oil drilling? That's another story altogether. That's the stuff apocalypses are made of.

So. I do what I can. I call my congressman. I write letters. I show up at rallies. I cobble together a bully pulpit, which I use judiciously. And, I walk for miles every day, trying to save every sea creature that appears stranded by a low tide, ferrying starfish and living sand dollars to the shallows. I cart injured birds to a local wildlife rescue compound. I feed feral cats, take them to the vet, get them fixed and inoculated. I continue to plant flowers and shrubs and trees that will support the lives of winged and terrestrial critters. I try with all my might to do no harm.

These small acts of kindness are all I have to give this world I love so dearly.

It's Saturday morning and I don't have to be back in central Florida until Tuesday. Actually, I'm doubting the wisdom of going back at all. I have lived in small towns or rural settings for twenty years. The traffic down there frightens me. The noise is nonstop. The cafeteria bustles with strangers. I call an old friend in Tampa, someone who knew me long before I ever married. I tell her I'm thinking of cutting short the teaching assignment. She tells me I'm crazy. That I have been alone for too long. That I must get back to the "real world." She intimates that me living amid nature is unnatural, which makes no sense. Tampa's hustle and bustle has infected her brain. I hang up, grab my fishing gear, and head to the water. I don't catch anything, but that's okay. I didn't really want to. I just needed to reenter the silence.

That night, under an autumnal full moon, I fall asleep on the couch. Dreamtime is a dense fog from which I am being pulled by an otherworldly screeching. Faint at first, it grows louder, more sustained, until finally I am fully awake, as are the dogs. I sit up, ascending the brain fog.

The dogs mill about, shooting me furtive glances. They don't bark nor do they venture outside. They're scared. To be on the safe side, I close the doggy door. The howls are high pitched and seem to come from all directions. I creep over to the kitchen window and gaze into the night.

Coyotes. Five of them. In my driveway. Yipping. Howling. Their heads raised star-ward, their faces illuminated by moonlight. The sound is so full, so symphonic, I can easily imagine they are a pack of ten or fifteen. Apparently unaware of my presence, they continue their eerie song, one picking up where another left off, sometimes all howling in unison. They are glorious. And dangerous. From now on, I will close the gates to the back deck so the dogs don't wander into the yard where they could become a midnight snack.

The first time I ever saw a coyote was in Kansas while driving through the Flint Hills. I was actually more amazed by the cows' sense of survival than the coyote's hunting skills. The cattle formed a circle, their heads facing the interior center. The coyote approached swiftly but when it reached the cattle, the bovines powerfully kicked their hind legs—a sort of deranged chorus line—effectively depriving the coyote of an easy meal.

I watch the wild canines for a while longer, until their howling subsides and they trot past the window and down to the bay where they disappear into marsh grass and shadow.

"Well, that's that," I say to my pack. "No more wandering around at night without a big stick."

The dogs and I shuffle off to bed. I feel invigorated. The coyotes' visit feels like a benediction. I sleep well. No nightmares. No dreams. Just the occasional serenade.

Sometimes I think Dennis did something other than wreak physical havoc on the Point. It's as if it unleashed magic and all of Mother Nature is under its spell. I'd seen the occasional coyote trotting through the woods on the north side of the bay. But a pack of them in my yard? That is new. The morning after the coyote visitation, I went for a beach walk at dawn and came upon a small herd of deer. They were standing at the water's edge, gazing toward the horizon, as if they were dream walking. A white squirrel has taken up residence in my yard. It is not an albino. Its eyes are dark blue and its white fur is edged in gray.

I tell an old-timer this when I stop at the fishmonger in Panacea for my weekly pound of shrimp. He says, "They's a whole bunch of them upriver. White deer, too. Never heard of one this far south, though."

The fishmonger's son is hosing down the concrete deck, securing the walk-in refrigerators. I'm the final customer of the day. I slip my shrimp into my cooler and head home, surrounded by the softness of twilight and gentle rainfall, hoping one day

I'll stumble across a white deer. And why white deer and white squirrels? What happened to their DNA in the curly, winding wilderness of the Ochlockonee ecosystem?

In this prismed light, the marshes and waterways between Panacea and Ochlockonee Bay appear golden, the world bewitched. It's as if God's hologram got turned on its side, tumbling all the animals out of the woods and into the open. A fox emerges from the forest. A raccoon stands at the grassy edge, looking around, blinking. A small herd of deer grazes, seemingly oblivious to my presence.

What in blazes is happening? In this upturned hologram, the animals appear to have lost all fear. In a half mile I see deer, fox, skunk, nutria, raccoon, possum, armadillo, and birds galore, including turkeys. I check. The forest is not on fire. The animals have simply gathered *en masse* by the road, grazing, minding their own business, as if this peaceful conclave of different species happens daily. Charmed by the lion-laid-down-with-the-lamb moment, I slow to a crawl and still the animals gather. They don't cross the road. No bounding. No frightened, widened eyes at my approach. Something rises out of the ditch that abuts the marsh. I check the rearview. There is no one behind me. I stop the car as my brain scrambles to make sense of what I'm seeing. Huge. Majestic. Not a bobcat. Primal intelligence lighting its eyes, the broad, muscled chest, the confidence of a supreme hunter. Could it be? Yes, yes. A Florida cougar!

Nearly a century ago they were plentiful in these woods. But now these highly endangered cats are thought to reside solely in wilderness areas of south Florida. The big cat gazes across the road to the bay and marsh that leads to the Gulf, paying me no mind. In this enchantment, perhaps I am invisible. I wish I had my camera. But I don't, so I will simply have to commit to memory the animal's stillness, its certainty, its yellow eyes taking in the world, the way its black tipped ears and tail twitch as though testing the air, the coat that is the same gold as the winter marsh, the flash of white that is its underbelly. It is so beautiful and I am so lucky.

A car speeds toward me from the west. I flash my lights: *slow down*. They do, but not enough for my liking so I flash them again. I watch as they hurtle past; a male and a female who appear to be in their late twenties or early thirties. They are chattering away, completely unaware of the Arcadia they have just entered.

The cougar lifts its face to the sky, as if it is enjoying the light rain, and then trains his eyes again on the marsh leading to the Gulf. I take one more mental snap shot and then slowly move on, pondering my options. Should I report the sighting? Phone the media? Florida Fish and Wildlife? Rightly or wrongly, I decide to keep it to myself. Whoever I contact will probably dismiss me as a crank. Or some gun-toting jackass will blaze into the forest and kill the glorious animal. No, I decide, as I zip across the Ochlockonee River, this enchantment will remain my secret.

Eventually, the central Florida teaching gig runs its course and I am able to be home again, full-time. This is a good thing. Being around so many people taught me something about myself. I am not scared of humans—at least not anymore—but as my fourth decade of life begins to unwind, I realize I simply prefer dogs and cats and lizards and birds and dolphins and turtles and coyotes to some of the people I know. My preference is not a reflection on others. It's just who I am. And that's okay.

As I sip tea on the back deck while the seabirds head out into the Gulf, I consider Katie's empty grave. She has been dead a long time. Atticus, at age eighteen, finally succumbed a year ago. I lost Lazarus in the divorce. And Ulysses and Scout are getting old. Maybe it's time for a new baby. I finish my tea, get dressed—make-up, hair, everything—and venture up to the Leon County dog pound where I spend the better part of the day trying to figure out which pup to bring into the family fold.

One of the dogs is named Bubba. He's some sort of bulldog mix. I take him into the walking area. He is into everything. Exuberance is his real name. He's adorable but a handful, and I find that I keep venturing back to a little gold and white dog named Tamara. She is docile and very sweet. She's in with seven other very large dogs. They leap up when people walk by and often fall on top of her when they land. I'm afraid she is going to get stomped to death.

I ask for more details and learn she was spade only the day before so her stitches are new. They tattooed her belly—a long green line—as a permanent indication she is not a breeder. For the fourth time, I ask to see her. She curls up in my arms as if she were born to love me. They say she is a boxer mix. I believe them. I adopt her. I take my seven-pound baby to the pet store and buy her a diminutive doggy bed. She stays in the bed all the way back to the Point. I don't realize until later she is still groggy from the anesthesia. I also don't realize until I get home and look at the paperwork she is not a boxer mix. She is a pit bull mix. Perhaps that was the real reason for the tat: to give horrible people who fight dogs a visual confirmation she cannot be bred.

Tamara is too tame of a name for this dog who, once the anesthesia wears off, is bounding through the house and yard with wild-ass abandon. I rename her after the protagonist in my latest novel, Murmur Lee. She will grow into a seventy-pound love monster. She hasn't a clue how strong she is. She has never bitten anyone. And even when she is seventy pounds, she finds a way to fit her beautiful, golden, ample rear end into her homecoming bed. I appreciate that about her. She's like a woman who is a size ten who still manages, with the help of pliers and friends, to slip into her size seven jeans.

The bad thing about having pets is, unless you're willing to board them (I'm not), traveling is quite a challenge. I'm set to return to Greece in four months and there is not a dog sitter in sight. I've asked all the full-timers I know on the sandbar and everyone is busy. That's what they say but, really, how busy can retired beach bums be? Maybe they're scared of Murmur Lee and are too prideful to admit it.

In the meantime, I have a two-day book gig in St. Petersburg. I cajole a friend in Tallahassee into a weekend beach vacation with my dogs. I fly down and am picked up by a man named Mac, a conference volunteer assigned to drive me around. On my final night, we go to dinner, during which I discover he is a retired Navy pilot who carried nuclear payloads. He is writing a book. He is funny, big-hearted. If metaphor is my strongest amino acid, eccentricity is his.

In reference to absolutely nothing I can put my finger on, he looks up from his sandwich and says, oracle-like, "Don't worry. You'll find someone else one day."

"I don't want someone else."

"You don't?"

"No. I don't ever want to remarry."

"Oh." He pauses, obviously trying to recalibrate. "Then what do you want?"

"A dog sitter."

"Really?"

"Really."

"Well," he says, appearing so pleased one might have thought I'd just placed a stack of gold bars between him and his steak, "I'm your man!"

A week later, I'm holed up in my bedroom, reading student manuscripts for a novel workshop I will host in one week on the sandbar. I can't hear the surf because a hot, blistering wind is howling out of the north. It's as if Caicus woke up from his river slumber and decided to smother us. There are white caps in the harbor but the wind has rendered the Gulf smooth and flat. Everything is grounded—birds to butterflies—and the non-stop howling is starting to wrinkle the lining of my brain.

I reread the same paragraph three times. In the backyard, the dogs burst into a frenzy of barking. I ignore them, wanting nothing more than to get through this manuscript. I figure they will quiet down soon enough. But they don't. Their yapping is sustained, bordering on hysterical. Perhaps Wayne and Anne are here. I peek out of my bedroom window and spy not a soul. Except for the wind and dogs, the Point is silent today. I try to keep reading but the dogs won't allow it. Like a mother who knows the difference between her baby's fatigued cry and danger cry, the dogs are definitely barking to alert me of the presence of someone or something. I set aside the manuscript and head outside.

Standing at the kitchen's French doors, I peer into the backyard. The dogs are at the rickety wooden side gate that leads to the bird feeders and my studio. I step onto the deck to get a better look at what has them in a tizzy. Outside the gate, its nose sticking between the slats, is the biggest dog I've ever seen. It's huge … bigger than the cougar. Bigger than the mastiff a college friend owned. Bigger than that Saint Bernard

I saw in a St. Patrick's Day parade. I can't figure out what kind of dog it is. Some super-duper brand of Leonberger? One of those ginormous mountain dogs? He really seems to like it here. But, no, I can't adopt another dog no matter how awesome he is. The house is too small and that dog is the size of a ... oh my God ... a bear! A very, very large bear. A bear that wants to eat my dogs for lunch. I am stunned, delighted, frightened. I knew there were bears at Bald Point and in the forest, but I'd never seen one. They weren't supposed to be at the Alligator Point end of the sandbar.

"Come on, guys, come on in!" I call but the dogs have a sole focus: Kill the bear. I whistle. I clap. I call again. I wave my arms. Nothing. The bear and the dogs are ignoring me. This could get very ugly. I start to panic. I'm afraid to go down there but afraid not to. And then I'm struck with a brilliant idea, the idiocy of which won't dawn on me until later. I go back into the house, grab the giant bag of dog food, haul it onto the back deck, hold it over my head as if I'm some hot shot weightlifter, and shake it. Scout and young Murmur Lee take the bait and come running.

Thankfully, the bear does not.

I shuttle the two dogs into the house, close the doggy door, and rush back outside to try to save Ulysses' life. He is now nose-to-nose with the bear. Thanks to the bear pushing on it, the gate is beginning to bow. It will give at any second. I grab the closest object at hand—a conch shell—and hurl it, knowing if this doesn't work, I'm going to have to go down there and wrestle the dog away from the bear. And then the bear is going to kill me and Ulysses. And who will feed the dogs who are inside the house? I might not be found for days, weeks, months. What's left of me will rot under the sun. The starving dogs will watch from the kitchen as buzzards pick me clean. I track the conch's journey. It spins end-over-end. Is it just me, or is it suspended in time, taking forever to arc through the air and find its target? I hold my breath. *Please. Please. Please.* Finally, it lands by Ulysses' front right paw. Bingo! A small cloud of sand mushrooms and the fearless little dog trots onto the deck, looking exceedingly pleased with himself.

We're all inside, but I do not feel safe. The bear is pacing the perimeter. Obviously, he wants inside the fence. And given that a hard wind can blow open my back doors, if he gets inside the yard, he gets inside the house.

I grab the phone and dial 911. Typically, the sheriff has an extremely slow response time to Alligator Point. We're an hour away from the county seat, where they tend to hive. So I am grateful and astonished when he arrives within five minutes of my call. I run onto the front porch. The wind has blown open the screened door and it stands agape, like a flag.

"He's in the back yard," I yell over the sound of the gale wind.

The sheriff tips his hat and then rounds the side of the house. I follow and knock into him when he abruptly stops. "Holy shit, ma'am! That sucker has to be 375 to 400 pounds. You'd better close your screen door or he's going to get up there."

My mind flashes on an image: the bear lounging in my bamboo chair, and a part of me actually wants that to happen. But my good sense prevails and I, fighting the wind, latch the door. The sheriff is back in his car, calling, I think, for back up. I move cautiously across the porch, hoping to get another good look at the bear and hoping they don't kill it when it lopes right past me, the bird feeder bag of onyx black thistle seed in his mouth. He looks bemused, relaxed, a hippy who forgot to shave, as he slowly walks across the road and settles under the pin oak, downing the seeds as if they're rare, delectable. At any moment I fully expect him to lick his claws clean.

I'm standing in the middle of the road, watching the bear, when a Florida Fish and Wildlife officer arrives. He and the sheriff talk privately. I'm terrified at what they might do and I regret calling the law. I could have handled this myself. If they try to shoot it, I will throw myself in front of the bear and then we'll all be dead.

"He's not bothering anyone," I yell, but the wind rips my words out of hearing range. "He's just eating. I take back my call."

As if granting my unheard wish, the Florida Fish and Wildlife officer gets in his vehicle and speeds away. I hope he doesn't come back. The sheriff pulls out of my drive, rolls down his window, and says, "Ma'am, you need to get yourself a can of bear spray and keep it on yourself at all times."

I imagine myself showering with a can duct-taped to my calf. "In a wind like this, if I sprayed the bear, it would just blow back in my face."

"That," he says with perfect law-and-order logic right before tearing down the road, "is a chance you'll have to take."

Thus begins my life with bears. They become regular residents of the Point. They're smart. They know the trashcans will be full come Monday morning, overflowing with the detritus of weekend revelers. The road on Monday mornings becomes an obstacle course because the bears fling both the cans and trash willy-nilly. The big bear will bend my steel bird feeder pole into an arc for easy reaching (I think he likes to lie down while snacking). My trashcan, secured with bungee cords, will soon be mottled with bear claw and teeth marks. A mom and her two cubs will regularly traverse my back yard down by the bay. A young male will sit in the mulberry outside my kitchen window and eat birdseed out of the bird feeder as if it's a Pez dispenser, leaving sizable holes where he bites into it. The county—ever hungry—keeps approving ill-advised development, primarily in the form of catering to St. Joe Paper, which recently got out of the logging business and into real estate, but the economy has failed so housing projects are in a state of suspended animation. The bears aren't out here because of habitat destruction. They are here because the eating is easy. And some of them like to swim.

The big bear will be tagged. They tag "nuisance" bears on their ears. His tag is the number 007, so he is known by the locals as Bond. He will relax under someone's stilt house and they will be scared. So like me, they will call the law. The Florida Fish and Wildlife officers will shoot Bond in the butt with a tranquilizer dart. Freaked, Bond will run. Straight into the Gulf of Mexico. About twenty-five feet from shore. The tranquilizer will take longer to work than anticipated. One of the officers, a wildlife biologist, will realize the tranquilized bear may very well drown. So he does something that will make me love him for all time even though we will never have a single conversation. The biologist will run into the Gulf after the bear. When the biologist is within just a few feet of him, Bond will rise up on his back legs—all six and a half feet—and will look the biologist in the eye, bewildered, and growl. And then he will fall straight back, out cold, disappearing below the surface before popping back up. The biologist will put his arm around the disoriented bear. The bear will try to climb onto the biologist in a drug-hazed attempt to get out of the water. The biologist, whose feet will suffer barnacle cuts and one bear claw scratch, will stay focused and steady, carrying/floating/guiding the bear to dry land. Someone will show up with a front-end loader and scoop up the bear. He will be weighed. He is, indeed, 375 pounds.

After processing and tagging, they will dump his hairy ass in the Osceola National Forest. A month later, he will make his way back to the coast, where he will be seen swimming in the Gulf off of Keaton Beach. There is a horrible law in Florida known as three-strikes-and-you're-out. This applies to humans as well as bears. The third time a bear gets the law called on him, he is euthanized. It will appear as if Bond's time is up. But the Florida Fish and Wildlife biologist, Adam Warwick, who—like I said—I will love forever, steps in. He will call bear sanctuaries, begging them to take Bond. None of them will because of his size. Finally, as the clock runs out for Bond, the Hardee County Animal Refuge—a place with such meager funds they don't have a website—will agree to take him. I will write an email to the woman who is in charge of the sanctuary.

"Hello. I live at Alligator Point, Florida and was the first person who received a 'visitation' by the bear who subsequently went on to become something of a celebrity. I understand that after he was relocated to the forest near Ocala, he journeyed 110 miles back to the coast and that's how he finds himself at your refuge. Newspaper reports up here were a tad confusing, so as someone who feels sort of personally involved with the bear, I'm wondering if you can tell me what situation he is in. Is he allowed to roam freely or is he in a small enclosure? How is he adjusting? Also, many of us were quite taken with the bear and his journey. I'd be more than happy to advertise on my web page where donations might be sent to aid in the care and upkeep of the bear."

She will reply with good news.

"Hello, Connie. First let me apologize for taking so long to get back in touch with you. I had been off a few days and then when I got back to work our Internet connection had gone down and we just got it back today. (Things move slow in this part of the country). Anyway, let me give you a little update on "Bond" our new black bear from Florida Fish and Wildlife. He is really settling in nicely. The first few weeks he was very unsure of whom we were and if we were going to cause him harm. But every day he trusts us more and more. Of course he is still a wild bear so only time will tell how comfortable he gets. The enclosure he is in at this point is fairly large, with plenty of area for him to climb, watch other wildlife and wonder around. He has not been allowed to go out into our largest outdoor enclosure as of yet because of his 'wild caught' status but over time as he becomes more comfortable he will be allowed to go out into it where he can explore and be in contact with our other bears. The area he is in now allows him to see and communicate with them so there is a lot of bear talk that goes on. Seeing as we do not have our own website (due to lack of funds) it would be a great help if you would like to put some information on your website. We are in the process of trying to raise money to build another night house area and any help would be great and appreciated. I hope this answers your questions and please feel free to email any time."

I will call her and we will have a lovely conversation, but when I ask her if he has a place to swim, I think she begins to doubt my sanity. One more jewel in my Crazy Lady of Alligator Point crown. But that won't deter me. I will post about Bond on my website and people will send money. And I will feel better about Bond's plight, but I will wish with every cell of my being he was still running free, swimming in Gulf waters, eating thistle seeds as the sun sets all around him.

Four weeks after the visitation from Bond, Mac will drive his RV north to the sandbar and park it in my backyard, to the side, so I will retain my bay view. He will live in his RV where he will write his book, watch golf, and gamble in online poker games. He will also spend hours under my house, cussing, as he essentially creates a parquet subfloor so that my main floor doesn't collapse. The house, like Mac, has its eccentricities, which seem to grow with age. Mac's presence provides me the ability to freely travel; this is a great gift. And even though I insist to him I am wholly happy, that I do not desire a relationship or a vast bevy of friends, I can tell he thinks I'm either lying or deluded. I decide he simply needs to be out here longer so that the beauty and magic of this place infects him, too.

It's the Fourth of July weekend and I have no plans. Friends in Tallahassee have invited me to their parties, but I decline. Drinking and driving are not habits I have fallen into. Mid-afternoon, Mac comes up to the house and seems startled by my lack of holiday ambition. In the few weeks Mac has been here, I've learned something about him. Though he's a non-practicing Catholic, he will never recover. The Church's teachings—though he claims to have abandoned them—prompt him to try to save the world, strangers and all. I know that's why he's here.

Hands on hips, he says, "You're never going to meet someone if you stay hidden. You've got to go out into the world."

I mute the movie I'm watching, *Dead Man Walking*. My choice in films might be one of the reasons Mac is concerned. But the movie does not depress me. Rather, I'm fascinated with Sister Prejean and her capacity for forgiveness. "I've told you. I don't want to meet anyone."

"Yes, you do."

"No, I don't." I unmute the sound. "I am very happy," I say, watching Susan Sarandon walk down the death row hallway. "I have enough people in my life. I live in a beautiful place. No one bothers me."

The camera rolls in close on Sean Penn. That nun is something else.

"I would rather die than ever marry again."

"This is what we're going to do." Clearly Mac doesn't speak English. "You're going to get a shower and get dressed. And then we're going to get in the car and stop at the first bar we come to. We're going to go in. We're going to have some drinks. And you're going to start meeting people."

I begin to protest but he grabs the remote, turns off the TV, and points to the bathroom. "Go!"

Hookwreck Henry's is a tiki bar and restaurant on Dickerson Bay in Panacea. If the wind isn't blowing, you get eaten alive by the tiny flying demons known locally as no-see-ums. Luckily, on this hot, sun-choked afternoon there is a bit of a sea breeze.

Mac and I stand on the deck that overlooks the water. The crowd is mixed—families with small children, FSU students, FSU professors, fishermen, women on the make and the men who want them. I feel foreign, as in foreign to the human race. I look at Mac. What am I supposed to do? He jerks his head toward the bar and we find a spot at the end.

I ask, "Do you want something to eat?"

He looks over my head and turns away.

"Do you want to move to a table?"

Same thing. Evidently, Mac, in his ever-loving wisdom, decides to pretend one, he's deaf, and two, he does not know me.

So I am at the bar, essentially alone. I love being alone on the Point. But at a bar? Not so much. I try one more time. "How about a menu?"

Mac turns his back to me. He is seriously righteous about this. So I wave the bartender over, order a bowl of steamed shrimp, and attempt to disappear.

I have lived on the sandbar for sixteen years, give or take some excursions, yet I don't know a soul here. I find that both comforting and frightening.

To make matters worse, the guy next to me strikes up a conversation. The icebreaker? Football. I know nothing about football. He must figure this out because he changes the subject by asking, "What do you do?"

"I'm a writer."

"Really! What kind of horses?"

I have no comeback. I am simply overwhelmed. I hear myself say, "Appaloosas," but I think I say it only in my brain. I definitely say aloud, "Mac, how are you doing?" in the hope he will save me. But Mac simply nods, avoids eye contact. I'm going to kill him.

The guy who thinks I ride horses for a living gives up. I notice a very tall, longhaired, pony-tailed man at the other end of the bar. Several people—men and women—surround him. When they speak to him, he bends down, I think to hear them better. That's how tall he is. He seems to be truly listening. He doesn't look like he's on the make or has any particular agenda. He just seems … nice. As if I've suddenly fallen into a Fred Astaire movie, I think to myself, *Gee, a guy like that would never fall for a girl like me.*

Eventually, the wine catches up to my bladder and I head off to the lady's room. As I thread my way back through the crowd I bump right into Mr. Longhair. He's in the middle of the walkway. I move left, he moves left. I move right, he moves right.

He says, "Look! We're dancing!"

We start laughing and a natural conversation springs up. He works at Florida State University, maintaining their student health center. He rides motorcycles, likes to fish, is thinking of buying a sailboat. He is completely unpretentious. I like that. And those blue eyes? Yes.

Then the inevitable question, just like the guy at the bar: "What do you do?"

"I'm a writer."

"Cool. Have you published anything?" It's not a smart-assed question. It's sincere, as if he really wants to know about me.

He writes down my name and website. "I love to read," he says. "When I grew up in Indiana, my bedroom was the porch and they insulated it with books. It was cold but I read a lot."

I might have fallen in love right then. I'm not sure. All I know is that he asks and I gladly oblige: I scrawl my phone number and email address on a beverage napkin and hand it to him. He does likewise. Despite my best efforts to broker no favor with any man, I'm a bit smitten. Look at those beautiful crinkles around his eyes.

"I leave in two days for Greece." He is really tall. I have to look almost straight up.

"Greece! Wow! What are you doing there?"

"Teaching. Writers. And I'm staying on after the conference to see some other islands, to tour around," I say, hoping I don't sound like a Ralph Lauren-wearing jetsetter. Should I tell him I'm using my Skymiles? His arms are super-long. Nope. No wedding band.

"Well," he says, those blue eyes sparkling, "we'll just have to get to know each other the old fashioned way. Through email."

I have never been so grateful in my life for WIFI. The Andros Holiday Hotel's Soviet computer is long gone. My laptop and its Internet connection works beautifully. My luggage is again missing in action. But Andros is beautiful, the writers talented, the food amazing, the Aegean tide-less and sparkling, and every day I receive emails from Bill Hinson, the tall, longhaired, long-armed, blue-eyed man from the tiki bar. Because of the time change, he might write me in the afternoon, his time, but I will read it at midnight, my time, elated to hear from him.

I tell him about the colorful wooden fishing boats in the harbor. He tells me he's a boat builder so I take photographs for him of the Greek handmade vessels. He begins reading *Remembering Blue*, my novel about a Florida Panhandle fishing family. I don't tell him that Blue's house is fashioned exactly after my shack. Hopefully, he will see the shack one day and will make the connection himself. But I do tell him about the people I'm meeting, the high mass I attended, the one hundred steps I climbed to get to the church. He suggests we can talk from time to time, adding, "I will leave my cell on for as long as the battery holds out. I would love to hear your voice. I opened up a Hotmail account so I can get e-mail over the weekend."

These are banal exchanges, but they turn me into a fourteen-year-old: soaring heart, giddy mind, irrational hope. I hate the very idea of falling in love. I roll solo. It's who I am. But this thing that's happening feels so good. And if he wants to be in touch by phone and over the weekend when he doesn't have access to his work email, is he falling, too? Why do I want this? I must be insane.

It's our fifth day on Andros. We have tackled novels, visited the rough side of town, and consumed our nightly shots of ouzo while sitting on a terrace overlooking the Siren silence of the Aegean, the sky aglow with the big, bright moon. Sated and with my mind drifting toward thoughts of my nascent love affair, I say goodnight, wander back to my room, and turn on the computer. Bingo, another email. I eagerly scan the screen. Bill describes the night sky and the fluency of the stars. He actually has a very sweet way with words. I feel warm from the inside out, as if I'm floating in a deep and languid sea. And then the current changes.

"I don't want to hurt you or be misleading in any way with you. I believe in honesty so that is why I am asking you to be just my friend for now."

I reread the two sentences ten times. At first I think the ouzo has jumbled their order or meaning. But no. He's definitely putting on the brakes. Amid the sound of my heart plummeting to the Aegean floor, I think, *Fine. This was a folly. I should have never allowed Mac to take me to that stupid tiki bar. I already know that marriage is a fate worse than hell.*

For the next few days, I totally immerse myself in my teaching, my students, and this beautiful, ancient place. I try to behave as if Bill Hinson was someone I met briefly, like an ant on a ledge, who has no impact on my life. Give me birds. Give me seascapes. Give me snakes and turtles and trees. Just don't give me a man.

Still, I do not sleep. After three nights spent staring at the Aegean, my bed untouched, Amalia, the conference director, sees something is amiss.

I explain my head, my heart, my mind's refusal to rest. We go to Tasso and explain the situation. He immediately calls the village doctor and speaks to him in Greek.

"What's he saying?"

"He's telling the doctor you're dying from a broken heart."

Tasso hangs up the phone and says, "Go now. He'll see you now." He scribbles an address on a scrap of paper and hands it to Amalia.

I'm dying of a broken heart. How romantic!

Amalia and I gather our things and complete the short walk to the outskirts of town. As we head down the busy wharf-front sidewalk, we are suddenly engulfed in onyx crows: old Greek women dressed head-to-toe in black, rosaries clutched tight, whispering incantations, spells, prayers. News of my broken heart, it appears, has traveled quickly. Amalia and I look at each other and giggle. The women ferry us past open-air tavernas and through dark, winding, cinnamon and cumin scented alleys, chanting with each step, delivering us to the doctor's office. There, suddenly silent, they leave us at the door, rose water and mystic intention thick in the hot air.

The doctor prescribes Ambien, so science solves the sleep issue. And as for romance? Bill Hinson will swear the old Greek women of Andros cast a spell on him, intimating hoodoo healed his fearful heart.

People do not need to be in love to be happy.

But it helps.

I watch from my living room as a blue CJ5 Jeep zips past the shack, jerks to a stop, reverses, and then plunders into my driveway. I have prepared a shrimp boil that includes sausage, green peppers, onions, carrots, corn, potatoes, and, of course, shrimp. The preparation of the meal calmed my nerves, but now that Bill is here, I'm a schoolgirl wreck.

His arms are longer than my torso, his hands nearly twice the size of mine, and his hair is much longer than my tresses. Also, his hair is super straight. Mine is not. We are all about contrast. He walks through the shack, looking fully amazed. He says, "Oh my God. You have little altars everywhere."

Bingo.

He looks out to the bay, then the Gulf, and says, "You know I tried to buy this place back in the early '90s. I thought it would be a great place to raise the kids. The ex wouldn't go for it, though. She insisted on Tallahassee."

I think, *Oh. So you've come home, too.* I smile and say, "Yes, it is a great place to raise kids. Heck, I think I'm growing up here."

Even though he stands in the living room, he seems to occupy the entire house. I'm delighted to have masculine energy in the shack. The yin and yang of it feels right. This moment feels right. As I step into the kitchen to check on the shrimp boil and offer him a drink, I spy a glimmer of change: There I am, in my mind's eyes, by the shore, still immersed in nature but not wholly alone.

Bill and I will spend many nights in the chickee drinking red wine, dancing, surf and stargazing. One night, we will stay in the chickee until dawn, telling each other our life stories, and my hardened heart will soften, allowing me to truly fall in love even as a soft rain pings against the tin roof.

We will roam the entire peninsula—Bald Point, Alligator Point, the forest—in his Jeep, bird watching, collecting discarded treasures from which we will build stairs, fences, and bookcases. He will go into the bathroom and see the fabric I hung to hide the sink's plumbing, and he'll say, "This is Blue's house!" That's how I will know he actually read *Remembering Blue*.

He will come home one day from his job at FSU and in the Jeep will be a most beautiful, handmade, wooden pot rack.

"How'd you know I've been wanting a pot rack?" I will ask, running my hand along its fine, lipped edge.

"You said so in your book. So I made you one."

I will learn Bill Hinson can fix anything: cars, boats, motorcycles, lawn mowers, fishing gear, plumbing, electrical, ceiling fans, air handlers, broken windows, bodies inert or live. And, he can build anything: houses, boats, fences, pot racks, couches, chairs, desks, tables, shelving, decks, birdhouses, surf boards, paddle boards, tongue-and-grooved treasure boxes.

When the apocalypse comes, Bill and I will survive.

We fish. We swim. We get way too close to bears. We celebrate when the martins and butterflies arrive. We worry when they leave and try not to think about those who will not survive the trip. Bill loves this place the way I do: with an abiding awe at nature abundant, nature insistent. What an unexpected surprise! I now have someone with whom to share paradise.

Life on the sandbar, of course, is not challenge-free. Nature is resplendent but like a beautiful snake, it must be respected. Play by the rules or get bit.

I take Bill to the western end of the sandbar because one cannot truly understand the splendor of this place without experiencing the areas that remain untouched by human interference. We float down the bay side in my two-person kayak. We have on our brand new crabbing boots. I've packed binoculars, wine, wine glasses, and an assortment of good food in a wicker picnic basket. The water is smooth. The sky, clear. At the end of the Point sharks swim in the channel and baby mullet congregate close to shore. There is a sailboat moored in the harbor and we imagine ourselves on that boat—dogs and all—sailing the Florida coast and winding our way through the lovely islands and inlets of the Caribbean. We talk about building a dock and a widow's walk and more porches and more gardens and more bat boxes and more blue birdhouses. We drink wine and nibble sandwiches and dream. And when the sun begins to dip into the western sky, Bill says, "We should probably get back."

It is not until we are out on the open water that the weather changes. A sudden chop shatters the calm and a cold wind that threatens to become a gale replaces the gentle, warm breeze. We have to get home and fast. Once I was in the wooden boat with my nephew and a sudden storm descended from the north. I opened the little motor to full throttle as lightening and cold rain licked the back of the boat and the front remained dry and hot. Through personal experience I know the bay is mercurial, shifting without warning, and, like the snake, to be respected.

Bill looks over his shoulder and says, "Wow! Will you look at that sunset!"

Before I can say, "We need to keep moving," he plows his oar into the water in an effort to spin us around so we can take in the sunset's full glory. But you can't do that in a double kayak. A double kayak requires a gentle touch. He discovers this the hard way. We don't glide. We don't spin. We don't suddenly face west. We flip over.

Bill yells, "Kick off your boots," and after popping back up to the surface, gasping, I do just that. There they go, bobbing in the swift current, out of reach. In fact, everything is roiling away—picnic basket, oars, binoculars, life vests (there is a reason to wear them rather than tossing them into the hull), sunglasses, sunscreen, hats. A quick flash of the sharks gathered in the channel lights my brain on fire. Bill tells me to swim to shore while he goes after the kayak. I look towards dry land. I see people in houses, drinking, eating, laughing. I wave and yell.

Help! Help! I am invisible. I tell Bill to forget about the kayak but he won't hear of it. He tells me again to swim ashore. I try, but the current is strong and I don't think I'm getting anywhere. Panic starts to gurgle. I am going to drown. But the kayak will be saved. My intuition tells me to face the sky. I do. For some reason, doing the backstroke is a better way to go. Maybe it will confuse the sharks. But fear weighs me down. I don't know how long I flail and founder and make excruciatingly small progress in my bid for forward motion when finally big, tall Bill is by my side, dragging along the kayak as if it were a drowned bear. He reaches for me and pulls me, too, until my legs touch the bottom.

We leave the kayak on the shore. Bill will bring the Jeep back to get it, he says. "We're not dragging it home."

Barefoot, soaked, and cold, we set out for the shack. I'm limping from the stray pebbles on the road and shivering. He puts his arm around me and I feel better. Still in recovery mode, I mutter, "You and your fucking sunsets."

For some reason this sends us into fits of laughter.

"Fucking sunsets!" Bill yells.

"Fucking sunsets!" I chortle.

We look like a couple of drowned rats, like the walking wounded, like beach bums on a bender.

"Fucking sunsets!"

Amid our laughter and my certainty that things out there could have gone much worse, I realize Bill might have tumped us over but he also set us straight.

Several weeks later, we ride Bill's motorcycle over to St. Marks where we have a farewell lunch with my novel-writing students. They have been on the sandbar for the past three days and are full of new ideas and schemes for their various projects.

On our return, as we take a curve on the forest road leading into the Point, the back tire blows out. Bill keeps us upright and guides the bike to the shoulder. We're a fairly long distance from the house. The bike must be trailered home. We check: Neither of us has cell service on this particular stretch of road so there is no phoning for help. We wait, hoping someone will simply wander by. Within about twenty minutes, someone drives up in a truck and stops. The guy lives on the main road, rides cycles, owns a trailer. What good luck! We get in his pick-up and he takes us to the shack where Bill retrieves some tools. I stay at home, relieved we were rescued, that the bike is okay, that we weren't hurt.

As they head back to the motorcycle, I feel the accumulated tensions of the past few days slip away. Mac has reconciled with his ex-girlfriend and they are living in a house west of me. The writers are all gone. Bill is dealing with the blowout. Ahhh, golden silence!

I decide to mosey down to the bay and just stand there, just be, let the quiet wash through me. I reach the footpath that leads to the water. About a third of the way down, I spy a gray wing. Another dead heron, but this one has not been picked clean and is, I think, fairly newly perished. It must have succumbed to something horrible during last night's storm, which was a doozy. Do old birds, like old people, simply die? Did this bird decide enough was enough after hours of being pelted by cold rain? Again, I offer up that silent, retrospective prayer: *Please, I hope the bird's demise was quick, that it did not suffer. Rest in peace, little bird, rest in peace.*

I'll wait for Bill. We will bury the bird together. For now, I'm going to stand at the water's edge and simply be silent. I start to step past the heron but don't get far. The array scattered before me, all along the shore lining my property and into the sea grass, stops me cold.

Sunglasses. Wicker picnic basket. Two oars. One white crabbing boot—mine. Chapstick—Bill's. Hats—his and mine. Binoculars. Life vests. Nearly every item we lost weeks ago in the kayak accident has washed ashore in front of the shack. In fact, I think the only things missing are three crabbing boots.

Is this magic? Religion? Science? I didn't pray for any of these items to be returned to me. I only prayed Bill and I would not drown. Do the currents run in a circular fashion, hugging my particular stretch of shoreline? Did the storm—after weeks of our lost belongings floating willy-nilly—deliver them back to me? Is this all an accident? Is coincidence the voice of God? Since flipping the kayak, Bill and I took it out twice to see if we could find anything we'd lost. We figured the life jackets or maybe the picnic basket would have ended up on the northern and eastern shores because that is where they were headed last time we saw them.

I don't know what to say or what to think. This moment, like so many moments out here, really does feel enchanted.

When Bill comes home, I take his hand. "You aren't going to believe this."

He is as incredulous as I. He says the currents must swing around and come in close to the shore right where we live. I want to say if that's the case, why doesn't everything end up in our backyard—plastic bags to wallets? But I stay quiet because I don't have an explanation.

We bury the heron by the shore. We retrieve our magic belongings. I decide I can't throw away the boot. It went through too much to come home. I set it on the back porch next to the birdseed bin. Repurposed, the boot turns out to be an ideal scooper.

From my earliest days, as I set out to survive a surreal and violent childhood, I learned to simultaneously disengage from whatever violence was taking place yet somehow remain fully observant. Fueled by primal instinct, I managed to ferry my mind to a cool and observant space. My mind retreated to white space but my bones recorded every detail and later, in the clarion light of solitude, by seizing my own narrative, by writing down the harrowing moments as well as the sweet, I turned the interchange between dark and light into something useable, something life-saving. Art.

This ability to be, in a single moment, emotionally charged and exquisitely detached is what allows me to know this about my relationship with Bill: I am on drugs. Yes, love is a drug, blinding me to faults and magnifying the good. The powerful hormonal compound called love is a necessary evil. Without it, I suspect humans would rarely mate. And me? I am overdosing.

I read student manuscripts and think they are all brilliant. I stub my toe and do not cuss. Waking and sleeping, breathing and snoring: even the most banal activities take on a shine. But because I'm no longer eighteen, and I have one marriage behind me, and despite how potent the drug, I am aware my blood levels will eventually even out, these truths are clear to me: One day the shine won't glare with the same intensity. We will have arguments. Tears will be shed and voices raised. I know this while I'm still love-drunk. And I'm okay with that future moment because when the shine fades a bit, when it takes on the subtle glow of a patina, I will see him more clearly, with more context and complexity. It will be a truer form of love.

Bill and I get married twice: once in the living room with a handful of inner circle family present, officiated by our friend

Mike Underwood who is an attorney in Tallahassee, and then two months later in the chickee, surrounded by friends and family and the Gulf of Mexico. Pete Ripley, the long-time friend who boarded the shack in the hours prior to Dennis hitting the Point, buys his pastor's license from a classified ad in the back of *Rolling Stone*. My flower girl, who is also my hairdresser, is a transsexual and one of the prettiest women I know. Three men—my brother-in-law and two part-time neighbors, including Wayne Coloney—give me away. Yes, it takes a village to get me hitched.

The writer Janis Owens brings a whole smoked pig. Our bank provides the use of their smoker for free. We smoke oysters and grouper and any other delectables the wedding crew sees fit to slow cook. My Godmother and former high school Spanish teacher, Olga Barnes, brings jugs of her amazing, secret recipe sangria and cooks a giant kettle of black beans and rice. The Cuban bread she brings from Tampa's La Segunda Central Bakery is delicious. Annie Ferran, my friend from my St. Augustine days, decorates the outdoors with lace and ribbons and lights. Bill's boss, Deni Bloomquist, who is also his best man, brings liters of homemade wine. We put the writer Paul Yoon in charge of videotaping the wedding. But he can't stop pointing the camera at his soon-to-be-wife, my friend and former student, the writer Laura van den Berg. As Paul gets deeper into the sangria, his camera work gets wobblier, and he says things like, "Oh! Look! Look at Laura's toes! Doesn't she have the prettiest toes?"

It's a beautiful wedding, a true Florida wedding. The December cold snap gives way to a glorious warm day and the Gulf laps gently, its surf song a constant reminder that this world is ever changing and precious.

My only sadness on this day is that my best friend, the poet Rane Arroyo, and his partner, Glenn Sheldon, aren't here. Rane and I met when we taught together in Kentucky. For five years, Rane has been my go-to confidant on all matters professional and romantic. I've never had a friend like him. He is golden. He also suffers from a hereditary liver disease and needs a transplant. The doctors won't allow him to travel beyond a specific distance, and Florida is definitely too far given his health and the fact that, at any moment, Cleveland Clinic might finally have a long awaited liver for him. But he called me early this morning, wishing me the happiest of days.

"I wish you were here. I love you so much."

"I love you, too. You better look fabulous. I want photos."

And then we giggled, because that's what we do. When Rane and I aren't plotting, we're giggling.

Though Rane can't be here in person, he is in spirit and poetry. As Bill and I face each other before our community, in the shade of the chickee adorned with rosemary from my garden, my friend Zilpha Underwood reads a poem Rane wrote for our wedding. Even though she's reading, it's Rane's voice I hear:

Wedding Poem for Friends

Love teases us and then escapes us, often enough.
But there are times when it stays still and waits
for you to be there, be real, to feel the ambition

of a kiss. It needs you to talk about thunderstorms,
how lightning shines despite its danger, how two
multiplies into friends, family, the math of being,

how gentleness should be a Pulitzer Prize category.
Love changes the world because it is gentle and
patient despite all the push and rush to make meaning.

It's that slow walk and talk, it's that amazement
one feels when Love pulls out his pockets or throws
her purse out and there are no secrets to be found.

It's expectation with a strategic plan. Love is food
and most of us are hungry for what matters. On this
day, when two take vows, now is everything and I wish

you now, now, now. Love tempts us to trust and
that's the best gift, two becoming the future despite
the odds of being beautiful and handsome, two in love.

And now, now, now, here I am, at my own wedding. On
the beach. At the water's edge. Birds soaring and diving. Fish
jumping. Dolphins arcing through the air and sea. I wear a
hand-woven matrimonial shawl I bought in Lefkes, Greece, an
ancient artisan village on the island of Paros. When I handed
the weaver her money, I didn't know if Bill Hinson would ever
see the shawl, if his fearful heart would realign itself. But I was
certain that thanks to the Greek women's incantations, the odds
were in my favor.

I run my finger along the shawl's Aegean blue edge. For the
first time in my life, this wonderful thought wafts through my
mind: What an amazing life I'm having!

In *Before Women had Wings*, I named the two sisters after birds.
Nicknamed Bird, the protagonist's given name is Avocet. Her
older sister is Phoebe, which in avian terms is a black-billed,
sparrow-sized flycatcher. I'm not sure why I named the little girl,
who has an awful lot in common with me, Avocet. I think it's

because I love the sound of the word. The soft "a" coupled with the soft "c" sounds like a word with wings.

It isn't, however, a common sense choice. The avocet's breeding range stretches from the American northwest into Canada. Their summer range includes the Gulf coast states but it stops at Florida's western border and doesn't pick up again until the coastal areas south of Tampa. They are year-round residents of Texas. So I named my main character for a bird neither she nor I would probably ever see. That has resonance, the makings of more amino acids: metaphor.

When Avocet Jackson asks the only kind adult in her life about the existence of the bird, Miss Zora, not wanting to upset the fragile little girl, finesses the subject. "But creatures that have wings," she tells Bird, "can end up almost anywhere."

Bill and I are roaming the flats adjacent to Bald Point. The moon is full, the tide is low, so we are walking on the nutrient rich belly of the bay. A migratory flock of perhaps a hundred birds surrounds us. We keep our distance in order to not disturb them. They are supping mightily in the shallows. I watch them, some old notion, some scrap of knowledge, tickling the corners of my brain. The birds sweep their beaks through the water in a rhythmic arc, feasting on tiny marine invertebrates. I lift my camera and tighten my focus. Their bills are upturned. They have sienna-orange heads, graceful long necks, and white bodies. Black bands highlight white patches on their wings. Tall. Slender.

Oh my God.

Avocets!

"Avocets, Bill! Avocets!" The birds blur behind my tears, but I keep snapping photos, hoping for the best, knowing this might be a once-in-a-lifetime occurrence. Is it luck or providence, this juncture of hope, reality, chance, fiction turned nonfiction?

Bill has read the book. He knows what this means. Bird, the wounded little girl who was me, is seeing her namesake, a glorious gathering, a dream come true: another bone mended.

And another.

I have a single aural memory of my father: the sound of him dying. Growls. Moans. Monstrous inhalations and exhalations. The sound of his false teeth hitting the porcelain tub as he vomited into it. What I do not possess are any memories of his voice. And though I have searched my entire life for one of the rare recordings of him and his band, that gift has escaped me. Not even hours spent combing the Internet has turned up one thing.

Then, a breakthrough. A friend of my father's, a man I'd never met although his wife had conducted a radio interview with me in the 1990s, sends my speaker agent an email in which he writes, "I'm using your good office as Connie May Fowler's agent to let her know that I am in possession of an original 78RPM recording made by her late father Henry May many years ago."

I call Tom Rahner, the man in possession of the record, and he turns out to be one of the nicest, most generous, human beings I have ever met. We arrange for me to come to St. Augustine to retrieve the record, but I can't make the trip for several weeks so he offers to send the recording of "The Moon Reminds Me of Your Smile," a song my father wrote and performed, as an email attachment. I'm not a particularly tech savvy or confident person and doubted my ability to open the file. Plus, I am shaken to my core in the best way possible. I don't trust myself to listen to the song alone. I need support. I decide to sit tight until Bill comes home.

The roar of the motorcycle announces his return. I hurry over to the computer, pull up a chair, and wait. As soon as he walks through the door, I pounce.

"Are you ready?" I ask, not giving him a chance to even take off his leather jacket.

Bill places his hand on my shoulder. "Let's do it."

"It probably won't work." I tell myself I'm okay with that. I've lived without his voice this long. What's the rest of my life?

"It's going to be fine," Bill says.

I position the cursor over the attachment, hesitate, and click.

My father's voice—a voice I haven't heard in over forty years—fills our sea shack.

My dreams are all broken. You took them with you.

Oh, Daddy. Oh, Daddy!

Maybe my mother was a metaphorist herself. Maybe she wasn't really talking about the surf song that day so long ago in the Rambler as we headed south to Tampa. Maybe she was speaking code because the actual words pinned to the actual truth were too painful, too raw, too absolute. Maybe what she meant was neither she or her children would ever hear her beloved's voice again.

But I did.

In my nearly two-decades out here, I've become an adept reader of tracks. Bear tracks thrill me beyond reason, especially their depth, width, and that signature sweep: the curvature of their claws. I know if it's a lone bear, a big or young bear, or a mom with cubs. The tracks that confuse me the most are deer tracks because I still can't reconcile them being seaside animals. But the forest here meets the sea. So why shouldn't they enjoy the view, too?

This is what I'm telling myself as I look at a flurry of deer tracks near the dune line. They'd been pawing the ground, but for what? Small, loose bones lay scattered on the sand, the same color as the sand but without the glittery shine. I pick them up. I hold them close to my chest because I can see them better in shadow than in light. They are pristine, no chips, no nibbles, simply bones free of the ligaments that once bound them. *I close my eyes in order to see.* In fact, I close my eyes in an attempt to be a bone reader. I feel their heft and shape. They are too substantial to be bird bones but not substantial enough to belong to, say, a deer or a coyote. And why are they out here, lying in the sun, almost as if they were placed in my path by a careful hand?

How does one learn to be a bone reader?

Five days in a row I revisit what I've started calling the bone yard. Everyday there are new bones. The science of it escapes me, but somehow they are working their way to the surface. Because erosion, accumulation, and storm surge all scour and rebuild the beach, these bones could belong to a sea creature. That's my hunch. And on day ten, when the bones of a foreleg and shoulder girdle and shards of a carapace lie atop the bone yard, my hunch is proven correct. These are the bones of a large, old sea turtle.

The bones will continue to surface for over a year. More magic. More bones to care for. More evidence of death, endurance, the migratory miracle of life.

The notion that the old sea turtle made it back to these shores to lay her final clutch of eggs and then succumbed to nature's need for life to begat death, death to begat life, deeply moves me. I mean, maybe something horrible happened offshore and she died out there, her remains tossed out of the Gulf's gullet. But I don't think so. The bones are too far away from the surf line.

I turn the bones over and over in my hands, trying to imagine what she saw and did in her lifetime. Was she a free spirit? A vagabond? A take-no-prisoners explorer of the high seas? Do sea turtles have those choices in their lives?

Lifting a bone to the sky, I study it: curves, flat planes, an interior labyrinth of holes like good bread. *Eat this in remembrance of me.* The sea turtle came home to die. To that extent, she controlled her destiny. And I, too, will control mine.

As I gather the bones, a certainty overtakes me: I will perish here amid the constancy of life and death. Once my sentient self departs this good earth, my ashes will hitch a ride on the wind, eventually disappearing into the white sands, the bones, the cerulean waters. One day the impulse people called "Connie" will regenerate into a railroad vine's opulent white, big-lobed blossom; or the bemused glint in the ever-searching eye of a piping plover; or the vast, brief pulse of a shooting star held aloft in a salty breeze on a deep, black, new moon night.

Oh, yes, that would be heaven: to be the heat—the celestial engine—that drives a dying star across the sky's infinite hip, one last tour of the fading gasp that is the Big Bang.

Reading bones, taking care of a new husband, tending the dogs and gardens, writing, teaching, hosting writing conferences here and in Cedar Key: These are not my only activities.

It's fall, 2009, and our state legislature, greased by Big Oil money, is poised to jettison long-standing laws prohibiting oil exploration in Florida waters. They want to place the rigs three miles from shore. They claim the rigs will be "virtually invisible." I write an open letter to Governor Crist. I sign petitions and call my representatives. Environmental writer Susan Cerulean, along with authors Janisse Ray and A. James Wohlpart, ask Florida writers and those who have experienced oil spills in other locations to contribute essays for an anthology, *UnspOILed*, that will be used to raise awareness about the threat offshore drilling poses to our environment, our livelihoods, our health. We, in a collective case of massive naiveté, believe our book might move the legislature to vote "No" on oil exploration.

My fondness for facts and figures slips into my essay: "Big Oil also would have us believe that offshore drilling is an accident-free endeavor. But according to the International Tanker Owners Pollution Federation, between 1997 and 2007, there have been 242 spills from tankers, combined carriers, and barges (acts of war not included). On July 27, 2009, an underwater pipeline owned by Shell Pipeline cracked off the coast of Louisiana, releasing approximately 63,000 gallons of crude oil into the Gulf of Mexico. If you conduct a Google search for 'oil spill Gulf of Mexico' you get approximately 166,000 hits."

That number seems huge to me. It points to the ongoing potential catastrophe we flirt with each time we drill for oil in the Gulf. Surely, I think, the politicians will come to their senses. They must. The stakes are too great for them not to.

I end the essay with a shivering nod to an unthinkable possibility: "May we never be so lost we say, 'Oilrig? You mean that virtually invisible monstrosity right out there? Where paradise once lay?'"

Like me, I suspect most of us who contribute to the anthology pen our essays with a mixture of outrage, panic, and hopefulness. We're all Don Quixote, chasing down the threat of oilrigs, insisting the pen is more powerful than the pipeline.

Rituals. We all have them. Necessary, repetitive motions turn the ordinary into the sacred. Maybe we always drink coffee out of a blue cup. Maybe we always check to see if the newspaper is on the front stoop prior to taking our first sip. Maybe Facebook every day at 2 p.m.—*like, like, like*—is where we pay penance for sins we do not speak of. Maybe we go to mass on Sunday mornings and offer the stained glass Virgin Mary a sly wink even as we genuflect and take communion and utter to the stranger next to us, "Peace be unto you." Maybe we dance under a solstice moon wearing nothing but silver bangles. Maybe, our skirts heavy with fresh blood, we bury the placenta of our first born beneath a weeping willow tree.

Or maybe we direct our hearts and minds to that depression in the sand and mark off the days on our wall calendars (thirty, forty, fifty days) and make forays into the night, looking for cast away eggshells and, best of all, tiny turtles scaling mountainous ridges of forgotten footprints.

Rituals provide entry into that which we cannot fathom.

Every summer, every early fall, since moving to the Point, this has been my ritual:

I stand on my moonlit, sandbar beach with friends and strangers, and we find ourselves part of the sea turtle's journey as temporary travelers on that watery silk road newly jammed with of hundreds of hatchlings.

Resembling moonlit traffic cops, we shoo away birds that understand "easy pickings." We scoop wayward babies out of crab holes and ferry them to the water.

We watch, amazed, as the surf rolls over the turtles. At first contact with the sea, the tiny animals metamorphose into beings that behave as though they possess invisible wings. They struggled and lumbered through the sand. But now, enveloped within the sweet waters of the Gulf, they fly through an atmosphere with an oxygen quotient nearly opposite of what they were born into, seemingly alert to life's purpose: sure and wondrous even in the face of death's inevitability.

We will not see the male turtles again, for they wander far and wide, rarely returning home, just like many a man I've known. But the female hatchlings are already essential and ongoing participants in the affairs of this place, for they will revisit these sands with ritual compulsion for the rest of their days. They will know intimately the sea and the land. They will be reptilian poets, understanding the geography of the wanderer. They will not be strangers.

Indeed, generationally speaking, they—even at the moment of their birth—will have more of a claim to this sandbar than I.

Amid the scurrying and ferrying and stumbling and wiping away of stray tears, those of us bearing witness to the turtles' maiden voyages are awestruck. We surprise ourselves with our sudden sense of purpose and sanctity. Without forethought or malice, we offer up humble, confused prayers—ephemeral as smoke—to whatever god or goddess or universe we believe in, fervent homilies based on religions we keep secreted in the unreachable hollows of our hearts. We pray the way you're supposed to—in unorganized, spontaneous bouts of irrational sincerity—silent and not, simple and true, with the intent that these small creatures—no larger than a communion wafer— will be blessed with safe passage, that they will complete their destiny, one that is both a shape and a song.

May their circle be unbroken.

We are one decade into the new century and spring is glorious on the sandbar. All manner of new life—winged, finned, footless, and four-footed—is emerging on land and in the sea. The estuaries and marshes are alive with activity as birds mate, lay eggs, tend to their young. The water churns with promise: baby fish, newborn dolphin, tiny sharks. Life below and above the surface is abundant. It's as if my known world is throwing a party.

The frog that lived in my shower all winter has moved to my garden. The banana spider (AKA "Banatula") is spinning a splendid, huge orb just outside my living room window. In the early morning it shimmers with dew diamonds. Cedar waxwings were here for one delightful day, ascending and descending in balletic perfection from the pines towering above my studio. Purple martin scouts arrived three days ago; their families will soon follow. I dig in the dirt on the kitchen-side of the shack and discover a cache of pearly white, oval eggs the size of my little fingernail. So, it seems, the lizards are doing their part to keep up with the promise of spring. A rat snake has taken up residence on the back deck. The dogs keep their distance. Wrens fly in the house, swooping, darting, as they hurry to find the perfect nesting site. A pair of mating osprey obsessively brings sticks to the platform at the top of the osprey pole where they are engineering a very messy, large, but functional nest.

Nearly everything out there in the deep blue sea is heading my way.

Embattled, overfished blue fin tuna are spawning. We're only one of two marine nurseries on the planet that host the blue fin. They favor the Gulf's northern slope, which is a critical habitat for them. Indeed, as the Gulf goes, so goes the blue fin tuna population.

Gag grouper, other species of grouper, snapper, and spiny lobster are also spawning. And all their babies, over the course of the next few months, will migrate to the estuaries and marshlands of the northern Gulf where they will find safety and nourishment. They will grow. Life abundant will happen. Again.

Brown shrimp are at their reproductive best April through May and September through November. Their eggs float through the Gulf, eventually turning into larvae. Plankton is the larvae's manna. As they grow stronger, nourished by plankton, they, too, travel into the northern Gulf along with their seafaring cousins. There, amid the nutrient rich estuaries and marshes, they will begin to resemble shrimp.

Bottlenose dolphins, full-timers in the Gulf, are giving birth right now: March, April, May.

Oysters, the beleaguered lifeblood of my zip code, are spawning in the waterscapes of my front and back yards.

Some sea life remains in deep water as they trek northward, but those requiring oxygen, such as sea turtles and the twenty-eight species of dolphins and whales that make the Gulf home for at least part of the year (twenty species are full-time residents), necessarily spend much of their time near the water's surface.

To celebrate the Gulf's bounty—it's vibrant cycle of life, life, life—nearly every coastal village and hamlet hosts seafood festivals. There seems to be one close by every weekend. Oh what I would give to be crowned Panacea's Blue Crab Queen! But I'll settle for a T-shirt and the knowledge that nature's delicate balance appears steady, prolific, bountiful.

In the midst of all this new life I, too, have given birth of a sort. *How Clarissa Burden Learned to Fly*, my seventh book, is winging its way into the world. This inevitably means I have to follow it out there to places far from the sandbar. I hate leaving the Point in the spring. And I also still feel very much like a newlywed, which makes sense given Bill and I have been hitched only a few months. So I bop back and forth, spending as little amount of time on the road as I can, always hurrying home so I can measure how much progress the jasmine has made (a lot), if baby mullet are jumping yet (yes), if the baby osprey are flying yet (no), if we have any crabs in our traps (sometimes yes, sometimes no), if Bill's blue eyes still make me shiver (yes).

Bill doesn't waste any time. As soon as I hit the road for my book tour, he takes it upon himself to paint the interior of the shack, put up new shelving, and renovate the kitchen, including the addition of recessed, built-in shelves. I call him from a central Florida hotel room that smells like wet swimsuits and stale beer.

"I miss you," he says in a southern drawl that confounds me since he is a Midwesterner.

"I miss you, too."

"I love you."

"I love you, too."

"You sure do have a lot of things."

"What do you mean?" I thought I lived the life of a frugal hermit.

"Your altars. I'm having to disassemble them so I can paint."

"Oooooh." I imagine my poor husband collecting all the bits of bones and shells and dried flowers and spell books and feathers and more, gathering them into assigned portions of the kitchen table so he doesn't lose anything, so the altars can be reassembled just the way he found them.

"Pile it all up and I'll deal with it when I get home," I say, sensing his unease at the responsibility he feels for the ephemera of my life. But I also know the painting, the building, the renovating: It's his way of nesting, of making the shack *ours*, not just mine, of him working his way into the mysterious nooks and crannies of married life and paradise.

The newlywed in me has decided to cook a five-star worthy dinner every night, using homegrown ingredients whenever possible and creating every morsel from scratch. Though it looks like I'm cooking (and I am), I'm also casting spells. I whirl through the kitchen, seeking spices and solutions. Heart, home, love. Heart, home, love. Heart, home, love.

I've just finished kneading my dough for tonight's dinner bread: Cuban bread complete with a palm frond down the vertical length of the loaf. My whole body—crown of my head to tips of my toes—is dusted in a thin layer of fine flour. I think about working my way up to *pain de campagne,* a daunting recipe in Julia Child's *Baking with Julia.* It requires "capturing and nurturing airborne wild yeast" which floats in the air only after many days of tossing yeast about as part of the bread baking ritual. I've never had the nerve or need to "coax wild yeast and bacteria and harness their energy." That sounds like a job for a physicist. I sneeze. Flour, if not yeast, flies through the air, resembling dust motes. I catch my reflection in the mirror that hangs on the wall closest to the living room. I appear painted, ready for battle. I study the birdfeeders hanging from the rafters of the deck. A bevy of hummingbirds sup. My back aches. My hands hurt. Why didn't I just pick up a loaf of French bread when I was in town? Who am I trying to impress with all this homemaking mania? He'll be home soon and I've got to get this place cleaned up ... o*h my God.*

I tiptoe over to the door, snowing flour as I go, trying to make less sound than the wind. Perched at the same feeder are a rose-breasted grosbeak and a blue grosbeak. The blue grosbeak could easily be mistaken for an indigo bunting, but the grosbeak is larger and has broad, cinnamon wing bars. I don't think there is any other bird one could mistake for the rose-breasted. Its deep crimson shield glimmers against its white belly and black head.

These, like the avocets, are two birds I thought I'd never see—individually or together—unless I move to Mexico where they winter or the Great North where they breed in the summer. Once again, I experience the thrill of living on the edge of the world, a cusp where water and forest meet, a dynamic wonder-ground.

I do not take lightly the responsibilities of living at a migratory crossroads. Seed in the feeders. Parsley for the swallowtail caterpillars. Milkweed for the monarchs. Bee balm and hibiscus and honeysuckle for the hummingbirds. Clean gourds for the purple martins. Bat houses for the bats. Seashells placed in the birdbaths so butterflies can drink without risk of drowning.

It is April 20, 2010, and all seems right with the world.

The following day, April 21, as the sun descends into the Gulf's blue horizon, washing the cumulus-slurried sky in ribbons of purple, gold, aqua, and radiant hues as yet unnamed, Bill and I are enjoying what we call "bull bat hour"—cocktails amid the bats newly emerged from their slumber, mammals on the wing feasting on mosquitoes and no-see-ums.

Out here on the sandbar, twilight shimmers. Dragonflies stir the air with the metallic thrum of transparent wings; they hover and flit, dive and ascend, resembling tiny bursts of tumbling stained glass, occasionally resting on a stem, a limb, a blossom, my hair. Purple martins pierce the jasmine laden breeze, competing with the bats—the former eating supper and the latter breakfast. Seabirds return to their roosts. Overhead, terns chatter so raucously my dogs bark at them. As the birds glide out of sight and earshot, the dogs exchange satisfied glances. I believe they think their barking drives away the noisy aviators. My favorite pair of great blue heron plaintively squawks, their voices calling each other home to their nocturnal rest in the sentinel oak at the edge of the harbor.

If one is lucky enough to be on the water at bull bat time in a calm wind, you will hear the creak of the pelicans' wings as they skim the water on their way to the western end of the Point where they gather in a great feathered conclave, on a beach populated only by ghost crabs and what the surf brings in—star fish, sand dollars, sea urchins—until daybreak when they take to the sky again.

But it is the bats I watch. Their scientific name, *chiroptera*, means hand-wing, surely one of the more appropriate and poetic designations ever made by science. Evolution has gifted these animals to the point that it is only a minor exaggeration to say, physically, bats are exquisite wings attached to tiny faces.

I have had many close encounters with bats, the first being when I was perhaps eleven or twelve. It was a blistering August evening and I was watching "Sanford and Son" with my mother when I happened to look down and see a saucer-sized bat resting atop my sweaty bare foot. I said, "Oh, oh!" instead of "Holy shit!" because my mother was the only person allowed to cuss in our house.

Fear spiking, I was trapped in a quandary: stay hidden and still while hoping for the best (translation: maybe the bat would just fly away) or run into the world—visible, shouting, flailing (translation: risk the ridicule of my mother and all humanity).

Inaction versus action and its attendant but unknowable results is a puzzle that confounds me to this day.

Mother, steeped in her own time zone, laughed as Redd Foxx grabbed his chest and delivered his classic quip, "Elizabeth, I'm coming to join you!" With her cigarette bobbing between clenched teeth, she glanced at the bat—the whites of her eyes flashing with Bette Davis flair—and muttered out of the left side of her mouth because the right side was in charge of the cigarette, "Son of a bitch! Goddamn it. Don't move."

She marched into the kitchen—I remained immobile, fearing any movement would inspire the winged Fury into a feeding frenzy—and then returned with her pine-handled broom, which she held aloft with fierce conviction, her pose reminding me of the Joan of Arc prayer card I kept hidden in my top dresser drawer beneath a nest of fading underwear.

I was terrified Mother was going to beat the bat to death and, in the process, reduce my foot to pulp (she swung a mean broom), but instead she simply proceeded, her cigarette fashionably akimbo, to chase the bat out of our roach-infested rental, screaming "Out, out, you bastard!"

Fearing my foot might be infected, I dabbed it with what was left of my Coca Cola (the boys down the street had told me Coke could take rust off a radiator, so surely it would fizz bat germs from flesh). I looked up. Mother was back, her hair on end from the struggle with bat and broom and screen door.

"How do you think it got in here?"

"How the hell do I know?" She tilted the broom against the doorframe, flopped onto the couch, lit another cigarette using the ember-end of the old one, and that was that: my first bat encounter.

But it would not be my last. Indeed, walking at twilight remains hazardous. Bats simply don't see me. When foolish enough to take an evening stroll, I bob and weave in an attempt to avoid head-on collisions, looking as if I'm performing a spastic imitation of Mohammed Ali's graceful ring dance.

My theory (untested and probably without a shred of scientific merit) is that the bats' echolocation bounces right through me, rendering invisible my corporeal self, this being a result of low blood pressure (mine, not theirs; I'm not even sure if bats possess blood pressure).

And, yes, surely there are other explanations: the bats are drunk, having feasted on fermented fruit; a rabies epidemic, they just like to fuck with me. I don't know. I'm sticking with the low blood pressure-echolocation theory because it makes a good story.

But the plot thickens. On a sultry summer night in 1996, I walked to my downtown Nashville hotel after a book event. I felt pretty full of myself. I'd given a good reading and signed lots of books. The storeowner was delighted. Even the sales rep who'd made a surprise visit seemed appropriately satisfied. So I might have had a bit of a swagger. I might have even caught my reflection in a skyscraper's plate glass window and not recognized myself. In short, I was happy.

As I approached the civic center, which was a mere two blocks from my digs, chaos splintered the placid evening. People driving home after a production of "Carmen" honked and cut each other off and made obscene hand gestures and behaved, generally, the way folks normally do in a traffic jam: as if their very lives depended on them being the ones to lead the elephant parade.

The cast and crew milled about on the sidewalk, waiting for busses to take them to their next tour stop. Their hump-backed equipment, scattered hither and yon, resembled brooding prehistoric snails. I noticed most in the gathering were male which, probably due to anthropological reasons, made me both fearful and excited. When this realization tumbled to the front of my brain—poof!—Confident Connie was gone, and in her place stumbled a gal haunted by her past, riddled with self-conscious angst.

No longer buoyant, I threaded my way through a Gordian knot of noisy masculine chatter—all of it in Spanish or Italian, I wasn't sure which, maybe both—bodies and shadows in motion, cased musical instruments, suitcases, props. I felt unmoored, as if the night had suddenly been infused with a bad case of buckle your seatbelts; it's going to be a bumpy ride.

Out of the corner of my eye, I glimpsed a dark shadow glide through the air and then felt it unfurl in a soft embrace against my neck. It fluttered, gentle and feminine, in the light Southern summer breeze. An image of Isadora Duncan (whom I desperately wanted to be once I got over the shock I would never, ever look like Sophia Loren no matter how many hours I laid in the backyard dirt while slathered in iodine-laced baby oil) wafted through my consciousness: Isadora dancing through life, a fabulous long scarf floating in her wake. One of the men— they were yelling and wildly gesturing—must have tossed into the Tennessee Williams night a crepe paper streamer.

In addition to hoping the paper was yellow or pink so it would complement my pale linen suit, I did what my mother taught me to do when men acted the fool: I ignored them.

But it didn't work. Their catcalling escalated. Still, I marched on. *Don't you dare look at them, you little heathen.*

The crepe paper caressed my skin in a rhythmic beat normally reserved for something with a pulse. Since when, I wondered—my fear nebulous, unfocused—did crepe paper possess cadence? I grabbed at my neck, took hold of something soft and warm—the men screamed—gazed at my hand, and delivered (at least in my emotional mind I did) a shriek that scarred the night.

In my very own hand—a hand that only moments prior felt very ordinary—I held a small bat. Or rather, it held me. The creature clung to the fatty rise of my palm, pinching my skin with something tapered and sharp. Fang or claw? I did not know. I flicked my wrist as hard as I could. The bat's talons—or were they teeth?—dug deeper. Its wings fluttered in black vampire perfection against my chunky, yellow Bakelite bangle. The goddamned bat, as my mother would have said, wasn't letting go.

The teeming mass of male humanity shouted what I assumed was advice. I did not speak their language because, though I made As in high school Spanish, I retained very little knowledge except that one should never develop a crush on the new guy, at least not while he's still new and untested.

Clueless as to the meaning of the men's swift phrasings, the rapidity of their words in all likelihood fueled by fear, I continued to vehemently shake my arm. I could not bring myself to pick off The Creature of The Night, which was unfortunate because no matter how hard I shook, flung, or gyrated, this demon seed of Dracula remained attached to me like a black diamond wrist corsage.

There, amid the heat and wavering light and cacophony of male counsel, I brought the bat closer and inspected, faintly fascinated, and praying I wasn't bleeding. Its little face resembled that of a wee dog with giant ears.

The bat looked at me as though I was a mere curiosity and it held all the power. The good news: It had not fanged me. The bad news: I realized bats possessed tiny, powerful thumbs crowned with flesh-ripping claws.

I am superstitious. Of this, I am unashamed. After all, I was raised by a woman who believed she spoke to demons. How could I not believe in signs, ghosts, spells, Barnabas Collins, and the possibility that all bats are secret goatsuckers? I didn't need a refresher course in the occult to know a clinging winged rat was not a good omen.

Panicked to the point of nearly losing control of my mind and bodily functions, I flicked my hand so violently I distended my wrist. The bangle flew off, ricocheting into the tangle of men and equipment. Pain radiated up my arm and fissured in the maze of my elbow and shoulder. The bat, possibly suffering from thumb distension or shriek-induced deafness, did, however, release me, promptly disappearing—a shy apparition—into the chaos of moon-filtered chiaroscuro and city bustle.

Before I could begin to track down my Bakelite or worry myself into a frenzy over how many agonizing rabies shots I would have to endure, a young man jumped in front of me, danced an agitated jig, and said in a thick accent, his eyes wide with what I interpreted as both fear and wonder, "No worry, ma'am, no worry. Bat good luck!"

What the hell was wrong with this guy?

"It was a fucking bat!" I said, rubbing my wrist, the sensation of the creature's claws and wings haunting my neck and hand. I triple-checked: no broken skin, which I was pretty sure meant (a) I didn't have rabies and (b) I remained an outsider among the ranks of the vampiric dead.

"I know, I know!" His feet slowed as did his speech, and he repeated himself, allowing the syllables to hang in the air longer than necessary, each vowel oozing into a viscous slur. "Noooo wor reee. Baaaat goooood luck."

Fourteen years and many trials later, I stand on my back porch, testing fate again, wondering what sort of luck I would have had *without* that bat encounter. Bill hands me a glass of wine as I watch the evening's first wave of *chiroptera* flicker though the gathering twilight—black silhouettes shattering a prism sky. I take stock. Was life a series of mistakes and trials interrupted by small moments of joy? That would suck. Was it a mixture of luck and fate, good karma and bad, depending on a cosmic roll of the dice? Did cataclysmic things happen to decent people just because? Did the Old Testament God occasionally wake from his eternal slumber and screw with people simply for shits and giggles?

A bat swoops within a foot of me. I don't flinch.

"That was close," Bill says, bringing his Jim Beam on ice closer to his chest, as if he suspects bats have a proclivity for brown liquor.

"Do you think Job deserved those boils and plagues?" I ask, slapping at a no-see-um.

"Absolutely not," Bill says, keeping his gaze pegged to the sky that is now quite crowded with winged creatures. I think Bill is about to expound on what he thinks of God's treatment of Job and it probably isn't complimentary of the Lord Almighty, as a faded relation of mine oft refers to Him, but our attention is snagged by a thread of conversation emanating from the house. We had, like poor earth stewards, left on the TV.

A CNN talking head reports that overnight in the Gulf, gas, oil, and concrete from something called the *Deepwater Horizon* oilrig exploded up the wellbore to the deck, where it caught on fire. Eleven platform workers are missing. Rescue and recovery operations are underway. A Coast Guard petty officer insists there is no sign of a leak.

"A rig exploded and there isn't a leak? How can that be?" I ask Bill. I gaze out at Alligator Bay, worry mushrooming through every corpuscle in my body. I can't survive the destruction of this pristine estuary, this amazing ecosystem where if you are a fish, a marine mammal, a land mammal, an insect, a bird, a mullet, you've found one of the greatest places on the planet to birth babies. Or, if you are a grown woman with a painful past, you find solitude and grace, states of being that if you're lucky lead you down the path toward forgiveness and new love.

"They're lying again," Bill says, a matter-of-fact nonchalance lacing his words.

One of the herons glides to its roost in the big tree. It lands amid gnarled branches and squawks—a warning, an avian sigh, an issuance of old pain, a call to its mate (*I'm home. Where are you?*): Which one I don't know. But I fear Bill is right.

I rest my head against his shoulder, watch the winged world feed, my memory flashing on a horrific ingrained image: oiled birds dying horrendous deaths in the wake of the Exxon Valdez disaster, and I find myself praying to whatever is out there. *Please, dear God, no.*

Then I voice a hope that makes no sense, at least not to my husband. I slip my hand into his and say, "The sky is full of good luck tonight."

Before reaching the final line, however, he had already understood that he would never leave that room, for it was foreseen that the city of mirrors (or mirages) would be wiped out by the wind and exiled from the memory of men at the precise moment when Aureliano Babilonia would finish deciphering the parchments, and that everything written on them was unrepeatable since time immemorial and forever more, because races condemned to one hundred years of solitude did not have a second opportunity on earth.— Gabriel García Márquez, *One Hundred Years of Solitude*

LOST

April 21, 2010, Day 2

Potential environmental threat is 700,000 gallons of diesel on board the Deepwater Horizon and estimated potential of 8,000 barrels per day of crude oil, if the well were to completely blowout—Coast Guard log.

I lived in the shack for over a decade before finding the words *Alligator Point* on a contemporary terrestrial map. The land was there, of course, but we were of such little importance, no one bothered to pencil us in.

When I finally spied our reptilian moniker thanks to Google Earth's omnipotent efficiency, the disappointment I felt was so great that for an entire afternoon I made plans to move to some other uncharted corner of the world.

But where could I flee? A quick Internet search, fueled by the phrase *isolated islands*, led me to one of the most difficult to reach, but climatologically fabulous, places in the world. The Marquesas. I could walk around in almost nothing, just like at the Point, but it would be more interesting because of the islands' history of cannibalism and the fact that I could spend an inordinate amount of time trying to disturb Gauguin's ghost.

But there were practical considerations. How would Bill and I, with four dogs, actually get there? Would we have to leave my sole maternal inheritance—Mother's hand mixer—behind? Would I have any need for shoes and, if not, what would become of my addiction? Did people in the Marquesas Facebook?

I close my eyes in order to see.

Pithy statement. But maybe Gauguin lied. Maybe he closed his eyes to occasionally take a respite from the Marquesas' extravagant, unyielding beauty in the form of flower, forest, beast, human. After all, for a painter, the opened eye is a necessary state of being. The closed eye does something else with joy. It plays the fife; it listens to a symphony. What is the point of seeing if not to celebrate the sparrow, the color red, the newborn child, the laughing man, the woman's hip curved like a cello?

Since moving to the sandbar nearly two decades ago, I've learned the importance of the open eye. A closed eye might miss something. That trail of fire ants building sand castles across my drive. Or the flock of snow geese that one chilly spring morning happened to fly over my shack—*my* shack out of all the shacks in the world—just as I stepped into the front yard in search of the new season's air. Or the lizards that formed a graceful lime green double helix: a gentle composition of swirled tails and entwined bodies pulsing as they went about the business of creating new life on the shack's western facing wall. I have fought an estranged spouse, survived incompetent carpenters, battled vermin, shouted at soldiers, and stared down innumerable hurricanes to remain here. Despite a rash of new vacation homes, a small condominium complex that loses some of its plastic siding in every run-of-the-mill storm we have (I believe our county commissioners have never seen a development plan they don't like or a tree they want to save), and ever growing numbers of ignorant-to-beauty visitors, I trick myself into believing Bill and I are alone in this deceptive microcosm of river, sea, sand, and sky.

As I cut a piece of paper into a three by five-inch rectangle in order to create a new map of my beloved world, a prayer, a mantra, an intention wafts through my brain: There is no environmental threat. No leaking oil. No leaking oil. No leaking oil.

No.

It will never come to that.

April 22, 2010, Day 3, Earth Day

I'm in Atlanta for a reading at Charis Books, but my mind is on the Gulf. I scan the news every chance I get. No one seems to have a firm idea of what is happening. Conflicting statements from BP, the Coast Guard, and the White House, though, all have a similar theme: Don't worry, be happy.

I roll my hotel room chair close to the TV and study the map CNN has flashed on the screen, pinpointing the Macondo well. Who had the bright idea, I wonder, to name a deep-water well after Gabriel Garcia Marquez's ill-fated village in *A Hundred Years of Solitude*? A village that was perhaps merely a mirage? A mythical land wiped off the face of the earth, condemned in its solitude? Who is in charge of naming oil wells, and how well read is this person?

In my personal hundred years of solitude out here on the Point, I have found abundance. I know birds from their calls. I've seen stars most people will never glimpse. I've witnessed animals behave with intelligence and kindness and wit. And I have found a partner with whom to share it, a man who doesn't want to control it. Or destroy it. He simply, like me, wants to be part of it.

If the map is right, the accident site doesn't appear to be that far offshore. A CNN reporter says the well is forty-one miles south of Louisiana. The Gulf is approximately 600,000 square miles. It ebbs and flows through 16,000 miles of American coastline. The Gulf of Mexico basin contains 643 quadrillion gallons of water. How much oil does it take to ruin 643 quadrillion gallons of water?

The Coast Guard reports the rig has sunk and a one-by-five-mile oil sheen floats on the water's surface. Rear Admiral Mary Landry: "This is a rainbow sheen with a dark center." How descriptive of her. She says there is not much to worry about because the sheen "probably is residual from the fire and the activity that was going on on this rig before it sank below the surface."

Eleven platform workers are still missing. But that's not too concerning either for the Coast Guard. They seem to be daydreaming out loud. Perhaps the workers made it onto a lifeboat and we don't know it yet. Perhaps they're out there bobbing around. The water is calm and warm. What can go wrong? They can last for days in calm, warm water. Chances are, the Coast Guard insists, the missing workers will be found. Furthermore, this is not an act of terrorism.

Well, talking Coast Guard head, perhaps your definition of terrorism needs to be expanded. Big oil, with their lies and destruction and greed, might be the most dangerous terror group out there.

I push back the chair and wander over to the window where I gaze at Atlanta's high-rise-tortured sky. I close my eyes and imagine home. It's still untouched. The animals will remain unpoisoned. The oil will stay in the well. BP will fix this. There will be no devastation.

CNN announces BP is moving equipment into the area that will "minimize the environmental impact of any spilled oil."

Any spilled oil. Don't cry over spilled milk. A little yeast in the air makes bread rise. I'll take just a splash of rum in my coke. A little dab will do you. One teaspoon of vanilla is all you need. One drop too much and everything is ruined. A drop in the bucket. A drop in the ocean. Iota. Scintilla. Fragment. Trace. Tittle. A dandy little oil spill. Don't worry your pretty little head about it. BP and the Coast Guard are taking care of everything.

"Up to 336,000 gallons could spill into the Gulf, based on the amount of oil the rig pulled out daily, (Coast Guard Senior Chief Petty Officer Mike) *O'Berry told CNN. And up to 700,000 gallons of diesel fuel could also leak, Coast Guard Petty Officer Ashley Butler said."*—CNN.

I rearrange my schedule and catch a flight home after the reading. I need to be back in the shack with my family. I need to dip my toes in clear water. I need to breathe the sea air. I need to see the birds and the dolphins and the mullet and decide for myself if everything is okay, if I still live in paradise.

I read the *New York Times* on the flight home. Even though officials insist there is no sign of a leak, the EPA authorizes the use of 100,000 gallons of dispersant just in case. As the plane's tires touchdown on the Tallahassee runway, I find myself wondering, what is dispersant? Can fish swim through it? Will we, the Gulf's coastal inhabitants, be sprayed with it?

April 23, 2010, Day 4

A few minutes past 5 a.m., Bill fires up his motorcycle and leaves for work. I listen to the loud pipes, tracking where he is until I lose the sound. It fades somewhere near where the KOA once stood.

I try to go back to sleep, but my worry over this thing in the Gulf keeps me awake. I reach for my robe while Scout attempts to lick my armpits. The newest addition to our family, Pablo Neruda, a Jack Russell mix we rescued after an alert was posted on Facebook, leaps through the air and plants a wet doggy slobber directly on my lips. With talent like that, he should be on You Tube. I head for the bathroom and the Listerine.

Murmur Lee stamps her heavy feet as she watches me pee. She believes, I think, there is a gorilla in the backyard and I am preventing her from her prize.

Ulysses follows at my heels as I thread my way through the house to the back porch. I pause before opening the gate and pet him. He buries his head in my hands and sighs. I look out at the calm, blue bay. Has the oil come ashore? Are they telling the truth yet?

Before fixing tea or filling dog bowls, I flip on the TV. Coast Guard Rear Admiral Mary Landry is telling CBS's Harry Smith, "At this time, there is no crude emanating from that wellhead at the ocean surface, er, at the ocean floor … There is not oil emanating from the riser either."

"That is impossible," I say to Ulysses, who has just re-entered the house via the flung open French doors. I bend down and rub his ears. "Absolutely impossible."

I walk into the kitchen, confused as to whether the rear admiral is outright lying or simply misinformed. What is a riser? If it emanates from the wellhead, wouldn't oil be gushing forth? What do I not understand? I reach for my teapot, look out the window at the day's first flight: a long line of pelicans heading for the Gulf. *I close my eyes to see.* How do politicians see? How do corporations see? By sleight of hand: *See no evil, hear no evil, speak no evil while we throw down shit so bad you can't imagine it.* An image of oiled birds, inspired by the Prince William Sound disaster, mushrooms again. *No, dear God, not here.*

The teapot slips from my fingers, rolls on the floor, clatters to a stop by the kitchen table. Ulysses, eyes wide, runs. I do not follow him. Rather, I look again out the kitchen window. The pelicans are nowhere in sight. What is happening out there in the blue, blue sea, where turtles dream of the shore and dolphins the sky?

I slump on the floor. The dogs, including the returning Ulysses, quickly gather around me. I reach for the teapot. The round hip of its blue enamel is oddly cold. I hug it to my chest, unable to shake the sensation that time has buckled—a cosmic earthquake—and amid a flailing earth, we have been hurled into a dimension where nightmares rule the day.

Ulysses licks my hand, nudges my arm, yet still I feel that old poison rise. It's in my mouth, the very taste of it.

I'm cleaning the floors, clearing out drawers, dusting altars, trying desperately to convince myself I have control over something in my life because I sure don't have any control over the oil. And amid all my cleaning, yes, I watch the news. Incessantly. I think I am looking for redemption, for that kernel of good news that will make the nightmare go away.

No such luck.

Despite yesterday's optimism, the Coast Guard cancels the search for the eleven missing rig workers. Coast Guard Rear Admiral Mary Landry states, "We've reached the point where reasonable expectation of survivors has passed."

I wander out to the front porch and watch the patch of blue. The surf song today is frenetic, uneven. Those men are out there somewhere in the big blue. And here I go again, a dogma-free person, praying.

I hope they did not suffer. I hope that when the rig exploded they simply vanished—whoosh!—no lingering in pain or horror or sadness. Just release. At least that.

Rest in peace, little bird, rest in peace.

A murder of crows rises out of the pine canopy and darkens the eastern sky. It's only Day Four, yet, according to the Gospel of BP, we have already passed the point of reasonable expectation.

I mute the TV when I hear the distant roar of Bill's motorcycle. Sounds like he just hit the straightaway. I check the time. It is nearly five p.m. He has been gone twelve hours and I'm still in my pajamas. I have not bathed or brushed my teeth. My hair is on end.

A small mountain of tissue surrounds me because whenever some expert starts talking about *worst-case scenario*, I panic. And for some reason, with me panic almost always gives rise to tears. Despite this, I'm glued, trapped in a twenty-four-hour news cycle that after an hour or so isn't news anymore. It's regurgitation, supposition, posturing. BP officials behave as if they have everything under control but when their PR folks look into the camera and utter meaningless phrases of assurance, I think I see the dead light of fear darkening their eyes. And why, oh why, do I have to watch TV for news about something happening in my front yard?

The motorcycle draws near. I zip to the bathroom and quickly wash my face, brush my teeth, smooth my hair. I rush into the bedroom, throw on a bra and a clean T-shirt. Bill cannot know how undone I am. I've got this, I tell myself as I slip on cinnamon-colored lip-gloss. He's in the driveway. I glance in the mirror. My pajama bottoms are disgusting. Bag Lady Connie. Fast, I shimmy out of them and pull on a black, cotton skirt I sewed by my own hand. I hear him gaining the back steps. I check. I look okay. Not unhinged. Maybe.

The dogs are, as always, boisterous in their greetings. Murmur Lee whines and prances, a Nylabone firmly gripped in her jaws, an offering to her triumphant human dad who, through unnamed acts of courage, made it home again. Bill sets down his gloves and helmet and pets them all—Ulysses, Scout, and Murmur Lee—but not Pablo Neruda who barks, runs up to get petted, runs out of reach before he can; abuse has made him a little schizoid around men, even Bill.

"So," he says, still petting the brood, "what's going on?"

I look at him sharply. Does he know I've blown the entire day? Does he know, thanks to growing up with a mother who always expected her child to fix whatever calamity was at hand, I possess a compulsive, fucked up need to stop the oil all by myself? Does he know last night I dreamed of super heroes— fit men and women in spandex body suits and silk capes who parted the waters and capped the well? Captain Concrete was particularly effective.

Bill stands, the full length of him, and I wonder how he fights the urge to hunch over, to not feel as if his head might hit the ceiling. He leans in and kisses my cheek. He smells of salt air and exhaust. I have all my feelers out. I don't think he has any idea about my true condition.

I jerk my head toward the TV. "No one knows anything."

"They haven't stopped it?"

"No. And they say the men are dead."

"All eleven?"

"Yes."

He looks from me to the Gulf, worry etching ever deeper. I know what he's thinking, because it's what I'm thinking. How bad will this get? How much oil is out there? How long before it gets here? What about the animals? What about us?

If the well were to completely blowout, there could be a potential release of 64,000 to 110,000 barrels a day.—BP

April 24, 2010, Day 5

Just in case. Just in case. Just in case.

I sit before my computer and search for news. BP is stockpiling dispersant—something called Corexit—because, you know, just in case.

Today, the government authorized in situ burning, just in case.

BP makes plans to open a command center in Houma, Louisiana, just in case.

And I begin to worry about everything we might be breathing as they carry out their "just in case" measures.

I click over to the Associated Press website and read:

"The U.S. Coast Guard discovered Saturday that oil is leaking from the damaged well underneath a massive rig that exploded this week off Louisiana's shore, while bad weather halted efforts to clean up the mess that threatens the area's fragile marine ecosystem.

"For days, the coast guard has said no oil appeared to be escaping from the wellhead on the ocean floor. Rear Admiral Mary Landry said the leak was a new discovery but could have begun when the offshore platform sank on Thursday, two days after the initial explosion.

"'We thought what we were dealing with as of yesterday was a surface residual [oil] from the mobile offshore drilling unit," Landry said. 'In addition to that is oil emanating from the well. It is a big change from yesterday .... This is a very serious spill, absolutely.'"

Now I know the reason for my obsessive tears: Just in case is here.

April 25, 2010, Day 6

The disaster isn't even a week old and I'm already incredulous at the inadequate response from BP, the Coast Guard, the federal government. NOAA? Where is NOAA?

BP's plan for Day Six is to throw a Hail Mary pass. They are sending robots 5,000 feet below the sea's surface. The robots will attempt to activate the blowout-preventer, the gizmo that was supposed to do exactly what its name says, which is exactly what it did not do: prevent a blowout.

I'm completing an online interview with a blogger—*Why didn't Clarissa Burden leave her husband sooner? Because there would have been no novel* is what I want to write—when my computer lights up with news alerts: The robots' attempt fails. The oil unfurls into the Gulf unrestrained. Pandora's Box roiling with poison. Pandora's Box with no lid. Pandora's Box spewing into the Gulf the bowels of Hell. I stand in the center of my living room and scream. But the only sound I hear is silence.

What an odd feeling: meeting the responsibilities of your life as though nothing has changed, yet you know out there, in the Gulf, something horrific is happening, something you have no control over, something that potentially will blow to smithereens your entire known world.

I make quick one- and two-day trips through the south to promote *How Clarissa Burden Learned to Fly*, but I'm not 100 percent on the road. The unfolding disaster dominates my thoughts. When I'm home, I walk the beach, looking for signs of the BP apocalypse: an oiled bird, a dead dolphin, crude-soaked sands. I watch the news in sterile hotel rooms, sifting through conflicting statements, waiting for someone—BP, the government, Super Woman, Spider Man—to stop the gusher.

In my more benevolent moments, I draw a sketch in my mind in which all the players resemble Keystone cops. They aren't evil; they're simply inept.

In my less forgiving moments, there is no sketch at all. Only rage.

In my naïve moments, I remember what I believed when I first met my new husband. *When the apocalypse comes, Bill and I will survive.*

April 28, 2010, Day 9

Red-headed woodpeckers, rose-breasted grosbeaks, blue grosbeaks, titmice, house sparrows, American crows, blue jays, mourning doves, ring neck doves, ground doves, thrashers, black capped chickadees: It's a good day at the feeder.—My Facebook post.

As my morning tea grows cold, I log off of Facebook, save my manuscript file (I started a new novel but it's going Nowhere), and bring up *The New York Times*. Accompanying a story headlined "Size of Spill in Gulf Larger Than Thought" is an aerial photograph of the Gulf. Its surface is covered in veins of orange and deep black. My heart seizes.

I venture out to the front porch. I scan the Gulf, what I can view from my perch, anyway. I see only blue. The oil is not on my doorstep, not yet, but my doorstep isn't what matters. There is never a good time for an oil spill but springtime in the Gulf of Mexico has to be the worst. It's tantamount to a category five hurricane hitting Miami Beach on a three-day holiday weekend during a full-moon high tide, a train derailing off a mountain with all its cars filled with children, a fire consuming a music hall during a sold-out concert, a barefoot child going missing in a blizzard, a pregnant woman falling, falling, falling, falling down an endless staircase that leads only to more falling.

Returning to the computer, I dive back into the *Times* article. "In a hastily called news conference, Rear Adm. Mary E. Landry of the Coast Guard said a scientist from the National Oceanic and Atmospheric Administration *(there's NOAA … finally)* had concluded that oil is leaking at the rate of 5,000 barrels a day, not 1,000 as had been estimated. While emphasizing that the estimates are rough given that the leak is at 5,000 feet below the surface, Admiral Landry said the new estimate came from observations made in flights over the slick, studying the trajectory of the spill and other variables."

And, "Wind patterns may push the spill into the coast of Louisiana as soon as Friday night, officials said, prompting consideration of more urgent measures to protect coastal wildlife. Among them were using cannons to scare off birds and employing local shrimpers' boats as makeshift oil skimmers in the shallows."

And, "Part of the oil slick was only 16 miles offshore and closing in on the Mississippi River Delta, the marshlands at the southeastern tip of Louisiana where the river empties into the ocean. Already 100,000 feet of protective booms have been laid down to protect the shoreline, with 500,000 feet more standing by, said Charlie Henry, an oil spill expert for the National Oceanic and Atmospheric Administration, at an earlier news conference on Wednesday."

My Facebook post about birds at the feeder will be my last upbeat report for months. Slay the oil. Save the birds. Save the sea turtles. Save the dolphin. Save the fish. Save the people. Damn BP all to hell.

April 29, 2010, Day 10

My email inbox becomes a virtual clearinghouse for disaster-related information. More often than not, what gets sent from neighbor to neighbor, scientist to neighbor, fisherman to neighbor, never jibes with anything BP says.

With each passing day, it is apparent that the ever-growing, ever-expanding oil slick coming from the remains of the Deepwater Horizon is headed this way.

As the slick now approaches a massive 2,000 square miles and as crews work feverishly to contain the mess, several news reports show that offshore currents are now turning the spill towards Florida's western and southern shores.

That is the message from a mass e-mail sent by former Tallahassee Mayor Scott Maddox. The email's subject line is a nod to *Macbeth,* one of Shakespeare's greatest tragedies: "Something wicked this way comes."

I have no idea what to do. Screaming—silent or otherwise—does no good. Crying does no good. So far, writing politicians has done no good. I push back from the computer and go into the backyard. Swallowtail butterflies are consuming the parsley: a moment of light on a bleak day.

The notion of light dispelling darkness propels me into a memory of my mother's feet, her golden-shod feet. She, unlike me, did not have a shoe addiction. At home, she was always barefoot. If she had to go out, she wore basic, unadorned, work-a-day, sensible shoes. But somewhere along the way, she found a pair of gold *lamé* stretchy flats and fell in love. She bought several pairs and from that day forward, when she went into the world, her feet gleamed in her golden shoes.

When she died, my sister, half-brother, and I decided she had to be buried in her gold *lamés,* but we discovered that in the long months and years during which alcoholism spiraled her into a knot of angry and unrealized dreams, she had managed to lose or throw them away. So we went to the mall and searched shoe store after shoe store. In an effort to not look stark raving mad, we shied away from revealing the fact that we were buying shoes for a dead woman. Inevitably, a clerk would say something to the effect of, "Do her feet tend to swell?" This would send us into paroxysms of laughter and out of the store. We finally found the shoes at a strip mall discount place. We bought them and immediately delivered them to the funeral home.

This is what's stupid about our search and insistence she be buried in her favorite shoes. None of the funeral attendees could see her feet. She hated shoes but we, in an attempt to be good children, decided that for all eternity she would wear the only shoes she felt any affection for. And because her feet were not visible in the casket, we have no way of knowing if the funeral home folks even put them on her feet.

But we were well intended.

As I pinch the newly emerged buds off my basil bush, I consider if BP is well intended. They didn't want the oil spill. But they caused it. And the government didn't want the spill, but by approving oil drilling at depths we don't understand and at depths that need safety measures not yet invented, they, too, caused the spill.

I watch Scout bite the sprawling rosemary bush that is covered in white moths. He suddenly looks cross-eyed. He opens his mouth and a moth flies out. I watch the moth float unsteadily toward the bay, away from the dog. And I'm struck by what for me is a new truth: Intentions aren't nearly as important as end results.

If they didn't mean for an open vein of oil to bleed endlessly into the Gulf, they should never have let it happen.

Bill and I make love in the pre-dawn darkness. Pablo scurries to the foot of the bed in order to avoid being kneed or elbowed. Scout jumps to the floor and onto the couch. Murmur Lee simply tries to take up more room.

Later, while Bill is getting dressed to go to work, he says to Pablo, "I'll sure be glad when Mommy and Daddy can make love without there being 100 dogs on the bed."

He says this frequently. And normally I laugh. I envision he and I and 100 dogs, the only thing visible beneath a pile of pups: our toes. But this morning, I am unduly angered by what is, for all intents and purposes, an innocuous, harmless line. I want to snap something mean and ridiculous such as … *well if this bed isn't good enough for you* … but I stop myself, sensing I am irrational and knowing that, of late, everything angers me. It's as if the oil has sucked away my sense of humor and replaced it with dread so great it is an immovable object.

A mockingbird sings outside our window. It's perched in the Confederate rose, amid white and pink blooms.

"I wish he would shut up," I say, and I wonder if Bill knows I don't really mean the bird.

Bill and I still roam the sandbar, but instead of looking for treasures we now look for tar balls, oil sheen, dead animals.

Having a task helps. One, it gets me away from CNN's annular disaster coverage. And two, it tricks me into believing there are positive approaches to the cataclysm unfolding all around me. So I become Connie May Fowler, Recorder of My World.

Every day, twice a day and more if need be, I photograph everything I can: sand, water, dune line, creatures. Document my home in its pre-oiled state—that's my instinct, a mission I take on without conscious forethought.

After a late afternoon session documenting migrating butterflies, including what food sources they are availing themselves to, I check my email. A friend has forwarded instructions from a biologist who works with the U.S. Fish and Wildlife service. These instructions are not without forethought. They are not instinctual. They are designed to counteract complacency born of greed: "If you are on the beach please take pictures to document what the beach looks like now—so if something happens we can show before and after."

April 30, 2010, Day 11

I read over the latest pages of my novel-in-progress and all confidence in my abilities as a wordsmith slip away. I can't seem to link two sentences in a row that have any verve, any discernable logic. Where the hell did my talent go?

When something isn't working, the best thing to do is try to get some distance from it. So I slather up in sunscreen and head for the garden that is, in all honesty, in need of a caring hand: pruning, transplanting, watering, weeding (except for the dollar weeds; Anne Coloney was right: I had to learn to love them because there is no stopping them).

First, I tackle the roses in the backyard. Five years ago, I moved the oyster pit to beyond the fence, close to the bay, and planted roses in the ashes and sand. Here, on the north side of the shack, the roses are protected from the direct onslaught of hurricane gales and salt-laden air. They flourish.

I snip the nearly black spent blossoms of the American Beauty rose bush, which is fairly covered in beautiful red blooms. I remember the oyster roast I held for my sister, her husband, and Sean the last time they visited. The roses weren't here then and I hadn't yet moved the pit. I check a leaf: mealy bug free. Excellent. I'm happy, in a rueful sort of way, that I introduced my nephew to the glories of the Apalachicola oyster before they were all gone. There is no way the oyster beds will survive an oil spill. Just no way. I move on from the American Beauty to the Voodoo, a specimen with big, bright orange blooms. I position my clippers at the base of a burgeoning rose hip but stop. Something isn't right. I tilt my head to the wind and sniff. Yes, it's unmistakable. I smell oil. I do not know if this means the spill has moved in or if the prevailing winds are carrying the scent of oil being burned off the surface of the Gulf. I don't know anything. Zero. Zip. Nada. I sniff again.

"Fuck." I toss down my clippers on the wooden bench facing the garden and hurry into the house. Temporarily blinded by the move from light to dark, I trip over Ulysses and bang my knee into the kitchen counter. I let out a string of expletives that would have made my mother proud and then bend down to pet and comfort the startled dog.

When I can see again, I send an email to a friend who is a member of the Alligator Point Turtle Patrol, wanting to know if he has smelled anything. Or am I simply losing my freaking mind?

He responds, "Didn't smell anything today but I went out late a couple of nights ago and got a distinct smell of oil—couldn't believe that it could be coming from over three hundred miles away so I walked all around trying to place where it was coming from—never found anything to explain it and it went away."

His email points to a larger issue. I am not alone in feeling as if I'm coming unhinged. We all feel that way. The phrase "waiting for the other shoe to drop" has taken on urgent meaning. It's as if BP, the government, and the oil are all separate parts of the same Boogey Man, an omniscient and all-powerful monster adept at smoke and mirrors, hazing and gas-lighting, lies and half-lies, ineptitude and ass-covering, as a disaster of epic proportions swirls through the Gulf.

As I read my friend's email, another one arrives from a friend who is a shrimper's wife in Carrabelle. Clearly alarmed, she tells me to check out Sarasota's Save Our Seabirds web page. "We need to get out the word," she writes. "No telling how bad this will get."

I click over to the Sarasota site. The seabird advocacy group is preparing for an avian Armageddon. "The response unit is currently in need of electrical extension cords, heating pads, Dawn detergent, plastic clipboards, pliers, and linens."

Automatically, my mind imagines why these various items are needed. Seabird triage. Birds coated in oil, blinding them, suffocating them, poisoning them, killing some quickly and others slowly. I close my eyes and will the images away. *I close my eyes in order to see.* Eventually, I will toughen up simply by virtue of these sorts of lists becoming commonplace. Indeed, the emergency list will be amended, fine-tuned, expanded, by rescue groups all along Florida's 5,095 miles of Gulf tidal shoreline.

Even in the house, I smell oil. I forget all about the garden. I turn on CNN and stay glued. When Bill calls and innocently asks what I'm doing, I fib. "Working on the novel." After a pause, I say, "I smell oil. I really do."

Bill sighs and mutters something about us being totally screwed.

I hang up and open a new computer file. "Oil Spill." I begin jotting down the day's highlights. This will become a ritual for me, just like the daily photography excursions and beach walks, which are no longer about joy or relaxation or communing with nature. These rituals are seated in despair and a wild groping for control as the Gulf becomes a killing field. I write:

On this day, Governor Crist issues Executive Order Number 10-99, declaring Florida is in a state of emergency.

On this day, oil washes ashore in Venice, Louisiana.

On this day, I smell oil.

On this day, my eyes begin to burn.

On this day, President Obama orders a stop to all expansion of offshore drilling.

On this day, I post to Facebook, "Let this not be our generation's Silent Spring."

Thanks to the many hurricanes and tropical storms that wallop the northern Gulf coast, residents here know how to prepare for a disaster. And though helpless to staunch the oil flow, we go into overdrive trying to mitigate its damage. While our inboxes fill with rumors, facts, and expressions of desperation, Facebook quickly becomes a war room. Groups pop up simultaneously.

Some of them solely exist to disseminate oil disaster related news. Others focus on organizing and mobilizing. Our triage list grows: sheets, Pepto-Bismol, new toothbrushes, heavy duty rubber gloves, kennels (small to extra-large), towels, adhesive bandages, shovels, and rakes.

If I think about the list too long, I cry. *Stay busy, don't dwell on the details. Action, not rumination.* I email Bill. "Hey, honey. Can you find any of these supplies at work?"

Bill puts out the word at FSU's health clinic. Within the week, he has to drive the car to Tallahassee in order to collect the deluge of donated items. In the meantime, I scrounge the Dollar Store in Panacea and my shed. We have multiples of every item on the list. We deliver them to a veterinarian east of Panacea who is heading up a citizens' response team.

Perhaps out of a growing sense of helplessness or perhaps because I have become quite vocal on Facebook, in ever greater numbers emails from government officials are routinely, quietly, forwarded to me. After we get home from delivering the triage supplies, I check my inbox and find a forwarded message from the Florida Fish and Wildlife Conservation Commission: "Staff in the FWC and the U.S. Fish and Wildlife Service has been working together to develop Florida's response to the potential impacts to our nesting beaches, nesting females, nests, and hatchlings due to the Deepwater Horizon oil spill event. We will be forwarding a summary of nesting beach protocols for this season to ensure that all Marine Turtle Permit Holders and the marine turtles you strive to protect are considered if oil occurs on your beach and cleanup is initiated. There are very strict state and federal requirements for who can do what once oil hits the shorelines or occurs in near shore waters. We will be working very closely with you on these issues and contacting each of you directly to discuss the protocols and how we can best protect sea turtles during this difficult time."

Yes. Difficult. A difficult time. A time of tribulation.

I close out my email and type into the browser *time of tribulation.* Wikipedia's definition is the first hit: " ... the Tribulation is a relatively short period of time where everyone will experience worldwide hardships, disasters, famine, war, pain, and suffering, which will wipe out more than 75% of all life on the earth before the Second Coming takes place."

"Well, ain't that dandy?" I whisper. I don't know about a first coming, a second coming, or even a third coming of anyone, whether it's God or his son or his mama or one of my many dead relatives. But I sure as hell know a tribulation when I see it.

May 1, 2010, Day 12

I ask my Facebook followers to join a new disaster recovery group named "Help Prepare Florida for Oil Spill in Panhandle." To underscore the gravity of the situation and to help people understand some of the ways in which the oil causes death, I copy a post from the group's page:

"This is the nesting season and the neo tropical migration season in the gulf. Black skimmers, sandpipers, laughing gulls, oystercatchers, all kinds of herons are nesting and raising their hatchlings. Once the birds come into contact with the oil, they will no longer be waterproof and they cannot fly. When the parents go out to get food for their young, they are unable to fly back to their nest and the young will starve. Also, if the parents have oil on their feathers, they will bring the oil back to their young in the nest. The oil spill affects everything in the water. Sea turtles will come into contact with oil when they come up to breathe. The biggest impact will probably be shellfish and birds. Anything that uses water to get its food is in danger of not surviving."

I add an entreaty, knowing that in Louisiana and Alabama, the living hell described in the post is already in full swing: "Please, locate local groups who are preparing to aid in the cleanup and rescue. I've posted several such organizations on my FB page. We don't know if we will be affected but we must prepare now. Please watch the bird cleaning video I posted. Also, volunteers will need BLUE Dawn, towels/linens, heating pads, extension cords, and more (full list also posted on my page). Our hearts are breaking. But we can't dissolve into despair. We have to act now. If you live on the coast, please clean up all man made debris today and tomorrow. This will facilitate cleanup operations if they become necessary. Please repost this."

Panic fuels our good intentions. People offer use of their boats, their businesses, their expertise in far-flung fields. One person posts on the group site, "I don't know much about wild life, but I do have some time I can spare."

We have become weeping children trying to save our burning house.

May 2, 2010, Day 13

The morning finds me at the beach, staring southwestward, attempting to read our future via the scent of the wind. When the breeze blows out of the south or west, the smell of the oil is strong. My eyes burn with greater frequency and as of yesterday, my breathing is not 100 percent. I feel asthmatic. Yet, despite the rise of physical ailments, I'm still filled with a sense of reverence by the beauty of this place. Sunrise, this sunrise, is glorious, all gold and orange with whorls of purple. I watch as various species of seabirds take to the sky, flying south and southwest over the Gulf.

"No," I whisper. "No. Don't go out there."

I wander home, sit in front of the computer, and click open the Audubon Society's website. In addition to filling out their volunteer form, I sign up for intensive training classes— HAZMAT to injured animal transportation. How will I, a too-sensitive person when it comes to animal suffering, pull this off?

"Nerve pills."

I grab my phone, look up my doctor's number, but I don't dial. For some reason, I feel I have to go through this tragedy anesthesia-free.

May 3, 2010, Day 14

BP curtails our volunteer efforts. The veterinarian who is organizing our rescue response, the one to whom Bill and I delivered triage supplies, sends an email that, in essence, instructs us to stand down. "As of this writing (1:00 p.m. on Monday) it appears that BP has turned wildlife issues over to an organization that specializes in these matters. I have contacted them and offered support and told them that I have access to an army of eager volunteers. I have a feeling that they will assume total control of the situation, if indeed it develops, and will provide their own people to assist. That is good for the wildlife—if anything can possibly be good at this point—but that leaves my able comrades all dressed up and no place to go."

On the surface, it sounds like BP is trying to be helpful. But something about it sticks in my craw. I forward the email to Bill and voice my concerns: "Very interesting. BP is saying they have taken over the rescue/cleanup effort, farming it out to 'an organization that specializes in these matters.' I want people involved who know what they are doing but that also includes local involvement. I'm not liking the sound of this."

The evening news reports that at least twenty-five dead sea turtles have washed ashore in Mississippi. The report is accompanied by images of turtles suffocating in an oil sea. I feel as if my skin is being removed, ripped off my muscles, so that it can flap in a diseased wind. I'm freaking not cut out for this. I don't think there is a nerve pill on the planet strong enough to see me through whatever comes next.

Tomorrow I leave for a writer's conference in Miami, and despite BP telling us to butt out, our band of volunteers plan a beach cleanup for May 8. I'm not scheduled to return until the ninth so I call my publicist and ask her to change my travel itinerary. Within the hour, my flight is amended. I'll be back home on Saturday by 9:30 a.m., helping with the cleanup. Our goal: keep the beaches debris-free so that oiled and distressed animals aren't further booby-trapped by human trash.

In Miami, I land on a different planet. It's as if folks haven't even heard of the oil spill. They chatter, laugh, drink espresso, walk the beach hand-in-hand. It's astonishing. I'm an extra in a disaster movie that won't end and, all along, an alternate, happy universe exists just a few hundred miles away. I wish I could step fully into this disaster-free dimension and hobnob at their cocktail parties, but I can't. When I start to talk about the spill—I'm incapable of *not* speaking about it—people's faces go blank and their eyes glaze over. *Fuck you*, I think. *Wait until that shit gets picked up in the current and ends up in front of your condo.*

May 6, 2010, Day 17

I love my Miami students. They are bright, inquisitive, talented. Returning to a hopeful world composed of words and ideas is good medicine, but the calamity in the Gulf stalks me.

After my workshop, I zip back to my hotel room and turn on CNN. I'm caught in a seemingly endless string of commercials when my phone rings.

It's Glenn Sheldon, Rane's partner. That's weird. Glenn almost never calls. He must be phoning to tell me Rane is finally headed to Cleveland Clinic for a new liver. What wonderful news! Rane will have a new lease on life. A huge worry erased.

Glenn sounds like a ghost. He whispers the news. Rane took a terrible fall. He's in the hospital. He's not expected to recover.

I ask him to repeat what he just said. I listen closely but words and their meanings don't align. I ask for details. I seek clarification. I ask innumerable questions. In reality, what I'm doing is buying time so I can figure out how to wake up from this nightmare.

Tonight I sleep with the cell phone next to my ear. When it rings, I check the time: 4:06 a.m.

"Glenn," I say.

"He's gone," Glenn says.

For the next several months, Rane's death and the oil disaster become part of the same monster: The world as I knew it and loved it is gone.

My dreams are all broken. You took them with you. —Henry Jefferson May

May 8, 2010, Day 19

When I get off the plane, Bill and I head straight to the beach cleanup. There are a handful of volunteers and we are oddly cheery, buoyed by the community effort, eased by the relief being proactive brings. There is actually very little trash on the beach, which leads me to think weekend visitors are being mindful of what they are being told: Take your trash home lest you make this fuckery even more difficult.

I find a silver dollar in the sand as though it were placed there just for me. I do not pocket it. I wade into the water and toss the coin as far as I can, whispering to Rane, hoping he can hear me.

After the cleanup, Bill and I wander home but any sense of a job well done evaporates under the weight of bad news. BP's latest attempt to staunch the gusher—the placement of a containment dome—fails. Evidently, methane is freezing at the top of the dome, which renders such a method useless.

I watch CNN and curse. *Thank you, Mother, for teaching me the joys of a foul mouth.* It's as if everything about this disaster is a surprise to BP. How is a company granted the right to drill 5,000 feet below the surface of the water when they have no idea how to deal with a worst case scenario? And that's what this is: worst case. BP's behavior—its apparent disregard for safety, its lack of transparency, and its continual low-ball estimates of leaked barrels per day—is beginning to feel abusive.

My instinct is to Gather the Facts. Armed with facts, maybe I can stop the gusher. This is the same instinct, I think, that led me to scrawl stories on grocery bags when I was a little girl: *Figure it out.* So I spend the rest of the day researching BP's safety record, which, it turns out, is abysmal.

The oil giant has been fined by OSHA 760 times. Its cousin Exxon, on the other hand, has been fined once.

In 2005, BP's refinery in Texas City exploded, killing fifteen workers and injuring 170. The U.S. Chemical Safety and Hazard Investigation Board concluded that BP's cost-cutting, particularly as it applied to safety measures, maintenance, and staff training were contributing factors to the explosion.

A year later, a BP pipeline in Prudhoe Bay, Alaska, sprung a leak, resulting in the worst ever spill on Alaska's north slope: approximately 267,000 gallons. Prosecutors cited BP's lax maintenance and safety measures and their knowing neglect, including the fact that the pipeline was corroded (the company knew calcium was building up in the pipeline, which would in all likelihood cause a rupture). According to a September 7, 2006 article in *USA Today*, BP, per their own report, admitted their corrosion-fighting program was based on budgetary concerns and not the worsening situation with the pipeline. BP pled guilty and under The Clean Water Act was fined $25 million dollars, which might sound like a lot but not when you consider BP's 2005 profits.

In their annual review to stockholders, BP's Group Chief Executive, Lord Browne of Madingley, wrote glowingly of the year BP had: "In terms of financial performance, 2005 was an exceptional year for BP, with profits of $19.3 billion, representing a return on average capital employed of 20%. High oil prices, which averaged $54.48 during 2005 against $38.27 in 2004 (dated Brent), contributed to the result but the underlying performance of the company is strong. These results reflect not just a positive operating environment but were the consequence of the long-run strategic position of the company and improvements in each part of our business."

Fifteen people died and Lord Brown crows about profits and improvements. Fines levied by OSHA and the courts, evidently, are simply the cost of doing business for BP and in no way prompts them to improve safety, maintenance, or training. In all these cases, and more, clear signs of imminent operational failure were identified and ignored.

I reread the stockholder report five times, trying to divine the magnetic tug of a moral compass, but all I come up with is devastation: The Gulf was a tragedy waiting to happen thanks to BP's corporate culture that rewards cost-cutting while quietly muttering "oops" when the inevitable happens: human fatalities, dead animals, a ravaged environment.

I glance into the backyard. Bill is burning brush, wholly unaware of my burgeoning hypothesis-induced mania. Alone, free to engage in whatever behavior I sense might ease me, I push away from the computer, stand, and do ten jumping jacks. The house shakes. A framed batik image of a dolphin crashes to the floor. The dogs scatter. I don't care. My breath is labored and something strange is going on in my mouth—a thickness, a stickiness—but I do ten more jumping jacks anyway. My form sucks but my intent is pure: work it out, work it out, work it out. With each upward sweep of my arms, I wonder how on earth this company is allowed to keep operating and why they are given *carte blanche* to drill at depths we don't yet understand.

Texas City. Prudhoe Bay. Something referred to as the Torrey Canyon spill in England back in 1967 that affected the UK, Spain, and France. The Gulf of Mexico. And these particular environmental and industrial disasters represent only a handful of what's on BP's rap sheet.

Jumping, looking profoundly deranged, I imagine myself becoming a BP stockholder so I can attend a board meeting … just one. In my imagination, I cut my hair short. I even straighten it. I wear a gorgeous midnight blue suit. I look very, very corporate. I walk up to the microphone and say, "Fellow stockholders, BP is a criminal entity that puts profits over the earth and all humankind. Divest now!"

Their corporate goons manhandle me as they drag me away from the mic. But I look good. And everyone is cheering. Cameras are flashing in this Hollywood fantasy.

But that's okay. A bit of diversion from real life is what I need right now. I see myself yell into BP CEO Tony Hayward's shocked, pinched face, "BP is an environmental terror organization!" An inordinate amount of satisfaction sweeps through me as I imagine the coppers putting him in handcuffs while the now divested stockholders jeer at him.

May 13, 2010, Day 24

But Hayward is not in jail. Evidently, he's simply rich and oblivious. Displaying an astonishing lack of concern, he tells the British newspaper *The Guardian*, "The Gulf of Mexico is a very big ocean. The amount of volume of oil and dispersant we are putting into it is tiny in relation to the total water volume."

I reread the statement aloud, to see if it sounds better than it reads. Nope. It's just as outrageous; maybe more so because when I speak it, I hear his upper crust accent, not my coastal drawl. Ulysses, as if to ease my anxiety, nudges my leg. I pet him. I tell him what a good boy he is. Again, the urge to do jumping jacks slurries through my veins. I ponder the likelihood that privilege combined with wealth combined with greed is actually the formula for what we call evil. Right there and then, ten more Jacks. More shit falls off the wall. Maybe I should try push-ups.

When Bill gets home, we have cocktails on the back deck. He says he thinks he smells oil or smoke.

"They're burning the entire Gulf," I say, knowing it's an exaggeration but a good one. "And don't sit down until I wipe off the chair."

"What's wrong with the chair?"

I swipe the cloth across it and show him: black yucky stuff, like fine soot. "It's coating everything. I'm worried about the computer, the printer. It might even be messing up our cars."

"Jesus. You need to file a claim. They need to pay it. And then we need to get the hell out of here."

I look at him as though he has said, "I am going to kill Ulysses." He sips his Jim Beam. I know he doesn't mean it. One exaggeration meets the next.

"You won't believe what Tony Hayward said today." My words come out thick. The weird sensation I felt in my mouth a few days ago has worsened. Gluey-ropey masses keep forming. It's as if my mouth is harboring mutant mucous. It's disgusting.

"What's that asshole doing?" Bill asks as I turn my back and clean out my mouth. The stuff sticks to my fingers. I wipe it off on the soot cloth and then tell him about Hayward's latest gaffe.

He nearly spits bourbon out of his nose. "That's just great. That's like me saying, 'Here, honey, drink this glass of water. I only put a tiny dab of shit in it.'"

Sometimes I find Bill's plainspoken musings shocking. But here in the cool twilight, I can't argue with his logic.

May 14, 2010, Day 25

We're not quite one month into the disaster and already I feel my way of moving through the world has been irrevocably changed.

Time no longer unfolds as something fluid, winged, magical.

Now, time is unbendable, static.

Now, time is measured by soundbites, top-of-the-hour news reports, 4 p.m. press conferences.

Now, time is a steady drum. Beat. Beat. Beat. *One more beat, just one more, please, goddamn it, dear God ....*

Now, time is a dirge.

No longer do I blithely spend hours, days, weeks without knowing or caring what day it is.

No longer does the confluence of memory and reality delight me because a new reality is taking over and this new reality sucks.

No longer is my life tied to the moon, the sun, the tides, the stars, the migrations.

No longer do I live according to nature's rhythms.

Now, BP's ticking clock dictates my life, my every breath.

One barrel, two barrels, three barrels, four.

Twenty-five days of oil gushing means we have endured nearly 600 hours of trauma. And in that time, I have been humbled by the grace with which my neighbors are dealing with the destruction of their livelihoods.

The community approaches the challenges with long-suffering practicality, making decisions based on what we've read and seen about other oil spills. Despite BP telling us to butt out of any rescue efforts, some of us take HAZMAT classes, we continue to collect supplies that will be needed for impacted wildlife, and churches hold vigils.

But as the ordeal wears on, the weight of a slow-dawning realization crushes us: This isn't a garden-variety oil spill. While terms such as blowout-preventer, containment dome, containment boom, top kill, junk shot, and dispersant become part of our daily parlance, it is obvious BP—one of the richest corporations on the planet and a "supermajor" leader in the petroleum industry—doesn't have a clue how to fix the horror it has wrought.

I've added a new obsession to my disaster watch. I penitently study projections of where the oil will creep next. Experts project tidal currents will bring oil to Florida shores in June.

Day-by-day, the government closes more of the Gulf to fishing and BP creates the Vessels of Opportunity Program, an Orwellian name for a project that seeks to employ the very people they put out of work: fishermen.

Franklin County Emergency Management sends out a press release stating, "BP is looking to contract with vessels for hire (shrimp boats, oyster boats, etc.) to deploy boom in the Gulf of Mexico."

Over a dinner of pasta tossed with chicken, black olives, sundried tomatoes, and herbs from my garden—we don't eat seafood any longer—I say to Bill, "It's terrible work. Making people who rely on the Gulf for their livelihoods clean up BP's mess. And you know, being out there among all that oil is going to make them sick."

"What can they do? If they don't take the work, their families starve."

No, I want to say. It's dishonorable, Machiavellian. How soul-killing it must be: forced to work for a company that killed off your present happiness *and* murdered your future.

May 15, 2010, Day 26

Today's new horror also happens to be the lead news story: Marine researchers have discovered underwater oil plumes, some up to ten miles long. Researchers say the plumes are composed of millions of dispersant-induced droplets of oil. Some are caught in sea currents that will carry them to the shore. Plumes plucked not from birds but the bowels of the earth.

This is just the start.

A few days later, University of South Florida marine scientists aboard the research vessel Weatherbird II will discover a plume over six miles wide and twenty-two miles long. Just below the sea's surface, it extends approximately 3,300 feet down and—as if we need this news to get worse—the researchers will contend the plume is heading toward an underground canyon essential to the Gulf's food chain. The canyon contains sea currents rich in various types of larvae that other sea animals depend on, especially during this time of migration and birth.

I drink hot tea but it coagulates with the mucous ropes. I wipe out my mouth and then wipe the sooty dust off the computer screen. I toss the Kleenex and paper towel into the trash. I get on the floor and attempt ten push-ups, reciting my most oft repeated refrain, "We are fucked, one. We are fucked, two. We are fucked, three ...."

May 17, 2010, Day 28

CBS reports BP is acquiescing to Massachusetts Democrat Rep. Edward Markey's demand that they release video of a live feed of the gusher. They quote Markey as saying, "This may be BP's footage, but it's America's ocean. Now anyone will be able to see the real-time effects the BP spill is having on our ocean."

I'm amazed that BP has a camera down there. And I'm thrilled that Markey is giving them hell: "BP thinks it's their ocean."

The CBS news article goes on to say Markey, "... blasted the Coast Guard for what he described as letting BP call the shots ... Coast Guard officials were on a boat with BP contractors who stopped CBS News cameras from viewing an oily beach, and the Coast Guard—which is in charge of the investigation—admits it's had access to the live video since Day One but wouldn't let Congress or the public see it ...."

Markey said there was "no excuse for withholding live video for 23 days."

"Damn straight," I say. But then a wobbly light bulb goes off in my brain. When the rig exploded, for four days BP and the Coast Guard stuck to their guns: No oil is emanating from the well. On Day Five, they reversed course, with Coast Guard Rear Admiral Mary Landry saying, "It is a big change from yesterday. … This is a very serious spill, absolutely."

But if Rep. Markey is correct in saying the Coast Guard now admits it had access to the live feed from "Day One," I can easily deduce—at least suspect—the Coast Guard lied to the American public for four days. Did they only go public when they realized BP's bag of fix-it tricks was empty? If so, knowing there was no end in sight, they had no choice but to fess up. I grab a piece of paper and map out what they said and when they said it. Day Two: … *if the well were to completely blowout,* but thanks to the live feed, they must have known it already had. Day Three: The Coast Guard insists the eleven workers will be found. Day Four: *We've reached the point where reasonable expectation of survivors has passed.* Day Five: Suddenly we have a serious spill.

Has their release of information been an orchestrated attempt to dribble out the truth in order to try to soft-pedal the severity of the situation, to keep the media at bay, to keep stockholders holding on?

I grab my phone and head over to the beach. As I crest the dunes—the air smells poisonous yet the sky teems with seabirds—I think about Rep. Markey's "no excuse" comment. I pick up a sandblasted plastic bag bubbling on a mound of wildflowers and decide actually there is an excuse: BP is determined to control the narrative. If they control the narrative, they control public thought. And to achieve that, I decide, no amount of obfuscation or lying is beneath them. I hold my phone aloft and take a panoramic shot: dunes, sky, shoreline, water.

At least this won't go away. No, not this. Not ever.

Every day the water looks heavier, more viscous. Indeed, we are having fewer and fewer days of clarity of both mind and sea. I've wondered if this trend is in my imagination but, no, there is no denying the water is dark and leaden.

When I get back from my beach patrol, I wash out my burning eyes under running water at the kitchen sink.

I sift through my pantry, gathering ingredients for supper: an eggplant and zucchini timbale. I turn on National Public Radio. I pause all dinner preparations when the topic turns to the disaster. The news breaks my spine: Up to 70,000 barrels of oil a day is gushing into the Gulf. This amount is tantamount to suffering through the Exxon Valdez disaster every four days. I wash the eggplant and slice it into rounds. With each vertical slide of the knife, I mutter, "Every four days. Every four days. Every four days."

It is when my knife is poised above the second eggplant, after I've just uttered "four" for the third time, that I realize how desperately I want to crawl out of my brain, just leave it on the kitchen counter and stumble away. Who in their right mind would want to be a sentient being during The Tribulation?

May 18, 2010, Day 29

Bill hovers over me as I reheat last night's timbales and toss a salad. We make small talk and I try to avoid saying anything about the disaster because that's pretty much been our sole topic of conversation for nearly a month.

I glance up from my little pyramid of homegrown yellow pear tomatoes. Bill is silent, gazing at the Gulf. He is a study in sadness. We used to dance nearly every night. Sometimes he'd head into work, having had only two or three hours of sleep. Love and dance somehow lessened our need for slumber. But we haven't behaved that way since the news broke on April 21.

I tell him I posted on Facebook information about our Cedar Key writing conferences. He loves Cedar Key and is so friendly, affable, some of the locals dubbed him The Mayor when we were there for a conference earlier in the year. The prospect of spending a few days wandering the seaside fishing village should cheer him up. I show him the post and he reads it aloud. "Even amid the tragedy in the Gulf, we still have to make a living, still have to try to follow our bliss. I hope you will join me in Cedar Key for a three-day workshop-intensive writing conference. We will write and learn and write some more. Two chances: July and September."

He breathes out hard and glances Gulf-ward. "You think anybody will come? With this happening?"

"I think so. July is already almost full."

I slip my hand into his and kiss his cheek before returning to the salad—a spritz of olive oil, two dashes of red wine vinegar. I cannot entertain the possibility the oil disaster will affect our conferences. I pull the warm timbales from the oven and whisper, "Please, dear God, don't let BP fuck that up, too."

After dinner, Bill flips on the TV. I check my email. A friend has forwarded a press release put out earlier in the day by Florida Senator Bill Nelson. I read the release's first paragraph and chant, "No, no, no!"

"What?" Bill asks, hitting the mute button.

I read to him just the high points: "A new oil-spill tracking forecast, prepared by four experts relying on five computer models, says part of the slick from the Deepwater Horizon may reach the Florida Keys in five-to-six days and Miami just five days after that."

"We are so fucked." It's Bill's mantra, too.

I don't respond. Fighting the desire to leap up and do a round of mind- and body-numbing jumping jacks, I keep searching the Internet, looking for some glimmer of good news. I don't find it.

Two hours later, the head of the Alligator Point Turtle Patrol, Bill Wargo, sends an email detailing possible and recommended responses should oiled turtles come ashore here at the sandbar. The email includes pdf's of official documents we'll need in order to follow protocol and the law. NOAA's Chain of Custody Record form includes phrases such as "Date and Time of Seizure," "Evidence/Property Seized By," and "Defendant/Company Name and Remarks."

A government form titled "Sea Turtle Stranding and Salvage Network—Stranding Report" requires detailed information such as turtle species and condition (from "alive" to "fresh dead" to "moderately decomposed" to "severely decomposed" to "dried carcass" to "skeleton—bones only").

The "Sea Turtle Identification Key" includes turtle diagrams and descriptions with artful renderings of the faces of leatherback, green, hawksbill, loggerhead, Kemp's ridley, and olive ridley turtles.

An "Oil Spill Event Instructions for Completing a Sea Turtle Stranding and Salvage Network (STSSN) Report Form" instructs in all caps, "ALL TURTLE STRANDINGS WITHIN THE DESIGNATED OIL SPILL RESPONSE AREA NEED TO BE SALVAGED FOR FUTURE NECROPSY / ANALYSIS."

A document titled "Deepwater Horizon Oil Spill Response 2010, Sea Turtle Nesting Beach Survey and Turtle/Nest Protection Protocols" goes into even greater detail, stating, "Nests deposited on beaches that have oil evident on the surface but the sand in the area with the nest is mostly clean sand (80 to 99% clean) should be left in place and not relocated unless in accordance with existing sea turtle permitting guidelines. Surface sands should be visually inspected for the presence of oil. If a nest is covered with oil, please call the number identified below for the State in which the nest is located; these organizations will in turn contact the local Incident Command System Hazmat cleanup crew to request the sand above the nest be removed and replaced with clean sand and take the appropriate steps for chain-of-custody documentation."

If the worst happens—nests hatch out as the oil laps the shoreline—the document offers this solution: "Due to the uncertainty as to which beaches will become oiled and concern that emergent hatchlings may depart from the nesting beach and encounter oil in the water, nests may need to be screened with restraining cages to enable collection of hatchlings at emergence should alternative release sites be necessary, depending on the location and extent of the oil spill."

Perhaps in order to drive home the severity of the situation, Bill Wargo also attached a photograph with a file name that perfectly sums up the situation: Sea Turtle in BP Oil Spill. The turtle appears to be trying to swim out of the oil; its head is the only part of its body not submerged in the deadly sea. In less than a second, the image sears itself into my memory. I don't want this memory. I must find a way to erase it.

I shut down my email, pour myself a monster glass of red wine, clean more glue ropes out of my mouth, and start wading through the latest news articles. I don't get far. *The Daily Telegraph* reports Tony Hayward stated the impact of the disaster on the Gulf will be "very, very modest."

"You motherfucker." I seethe. This isn't teatime and the crumpets are stale. This isn't a case of the Queen inadvertently flashing a side boob. The impact is already immodest. It was immodest the moment the well exploded and killed eleven people. It was immodest even before the explosion, during the years and months BP and its subcontractors cut corners. There is nothing modest about greed. Nothing modest about lies. Nothing modest about the Gulf suffering an Exxon-Valdez-sized spill every four days.

I'm starting to remind myself of the character on "Treme" played by John Goodman, the one so depressed by the aftermath of Hurricane Katrina he committed suicide, just threw himself off a ferry boat, drowning his body and his troubles.

Of course, I won't do that. Or would I? *No, no, you won't.* But the magnitude of the disaster and the shell game response by BP and the government has planted a seed of hopelessness deep in my belly. I feel it grow with every labored breath.

I once knew a very bright five-year-old. We were very close and I love him to this day. However, when something ordinary would go wrong—a broken drinking glass, a torn shirt—purely out of curiosity, I'd ask what happened. The sweet child would always claim not to have a clue, as if glasses spontaneously fracture. And though I understood—thanks to the child development book I checked out of the library—that this is how five-year-olds deal with what they think might be a crisis, I worried about what would happen out there in the real world if the little boy grew up to believe the fix for every problem was to simply pretend there was no problem. How could I know that multi-national corporations such as BP ran their affairs precisely so? And if BP did take full responsibility, if they spent as much money on cleanup and restoration as they do on commercials touting how wonderful they are and how much they care, would my anger ease? Would my despair flag? Maybe, by a quarter inch or so. But the Gulf isn't a broken glass; it's one of the most important, complex ecosystems on the planet. And here it is, Day Twenty-nine, and the only clear piece of knowledge we have is that BP does not care about the environment. That's not their job. Their job is to make money, money, money and the destruction of the Gulf is little more than collateral damage.

I drink my wine, close my eyes, and what I see faintly fascinates me: I am in a long skirt and flowing lace top. I am entering the sea, deeper and deeper and deeper. I am submerged. I am adrift in oil.

I am collateral damage.

May 19, 2010, Day 30

Nineteen percent of the Gulf is deemed a no-fishing zone by the U.S. government.

Tar balls are washing ashore as far east as Alabama.

Oil washes onto mainland Louisiana. This, of course, means the barrier islands—and the birds that nest there—are suffocating beneath an oil blanket.

Satellite photos are released that show the oil extending into strong ocean currents, which is potentially devastating news.

I stand in my backyard, watering roses, the tangerine, the pear, the sprawling rosemary, my abundant herb garden, my veggies. The eggplants are doing particularly well this spring. As I garden, the wind picks up and a chemical, metallic-laced scent washes over the sandbar. It sets my teeth on edge as it wafts and disappears, wafts and disappears, and wafts again.

As I pull the hose across the yard, through the sand and over railroad ties, more mucous glue clogs my mouth. I try spitting it out to no avail.

I am, I believe, suffering from a reaction to Corexit. The poison is drifting over land. Just like with chemicals sprayed from a crop duster. Spray drift is a real phenomenon. There is no way aerosol particles aren't picked up by the wind. It's science 101.

May 20, 2010, Day 31

I need to get away.

I need to stop obsessing.

I need to create something, grow something, immerse myself in a different vista.

Instead, I descend into my new normal: see Bill off, feed the dogs, patrol the beach, watch CNN, search the Internet, and freak.

Today the *Washington Post* reports the government is concerned about BP's unprecedented use of Corexit. Are they actually beginning to listen to scientists and not BP officials? Is this a bead of hope, something I can carry with me, stuff in my pocket like a long overdue good luck charm? "The Environmental Protection Agency informed BP officials late Wednesday that the company has 24 hours to choose a less toxic form of chemical dispersants to break up its oil spill in the Gulf of Mexico, according to government sources familiar with the decision, and must apply the new form of dispersants within 72 hours of submitting the list of alternatives."

The article goes on to state, "The move is significant because it suggests federal officials are now concerned that the unprecedented use of chemical dispersants could pose a significant threat to the Gulf of Mexico's marine life."

I phone a friend who is an environmental attorney and I read to her the article. "They won't do it," she says.

"What do you mean?"

"BP won't stop using Corexit."

"But why not? The government has ordered them to."

"BP is in charge of the cleanup. They can do what they want. And for some reason, what they want is Corexit."

"Then what do we do?" I ask, picking at my fingernail bed because physical pain sometimes edges away the psychic pain.

"Someone who matters has to follow the money. But look, BP is the fourth largest corporation in the world. They own everyone who matters."

I pull the phone from my ear and look at it as though the phone, and not her assessment, is offensive. I actually want to hurl it across the room, the way disgruntled people in movies do. But I also know it wouldn't help, and it's not the phone's fault or my friend's fault, and maybe, just maybe, the idea that BP owns everyone who matters is an idea I ought to closely consider.

After we finish our conversation, alone except for my dogs and whatever amount of Corexit is being blown in by the sea breeze, I again clean out my mouth that is nearly bubbling with glue ropes. I sniff it. I detect no odor. But, still, it's worrisome. If I go to my doctor and say, "The Corexit is making me sick," she won't believe me. We have entered, after all, uncharted territory.

I sign into Facebook, and type, "Despair, despair, despair."

May 21, 2010, Day 32

BP complies with Rep. Markey's request and releases to the public the underwater live feed of the spewing oil. It boils forth, roiling through the water in shades reminiscent of death: gray, black, putrid brown inflamed with swirling ribbons of deep orange. It actually appears angry, evil, as if it truly is Pandora's Box full of Hell.

I watch, transfixed, terrified, helplessly praying for a miracle. Maybe I need to go talk to a priest. Or a nun ... one of those terrific feminist nuns who are in trouble with the Vatican. Someone with a direct connection to Jesus who is, let's face it, the ultimate super hero. But do the world's major religions consider themselves spiritual earth stewards? Or do they concern themselves exclusively with human-on-human sin? Does BP own them and what would that even mean? Want a new convent, orphanage, cathedral, mega-church? Well, here, choke on our money.

Have the world's primary religions intentionally sent nature into exile? Is this how we landed here—a dying Gulf, global climate change, a poisoned food chain, cancers galore—because Big Petroleum owns us?

This live feed, I know, is exactly what my obsessive compulsive self needs. I'm an oil-disaster-aholic. Twenty-four hours a day, I can watch the oil spew. I keep the spew-cam open on my computer's desktop, accessing it with the click of one key. Every time I walk by, I check. Yep, still spewing. The motherfucker is more reliable than Old Faithful.

We have not had a single bit of good news since the well exploded a month ago. Everyday there are new, higher estimates as to the amount of oil flowing into the Gulf. I watch arguments break out on Facebook between Americans damning BP and their English friends for whom BP is a point of national pride. Trolls who are adept at twisting people's words and intentions pillory disaster-focused Facebook groups. They call people liars and morons as they spread disinformation across the Web. Some groups actually close and reopen using new names in an attempt to evade and outsmart the trolls. As I sit in front of the glow of my computer screen, trying with each keystroke to find a glimmer of hope, a rational and competent solution, the word "extinction" pops into my mind repeatedly, randomly, as if my subconscious is trying to prepare me for what lies ahead.

May 22, 2010, Day 33

I rise early, right along with Bill, and as soon as he leaves the shack, I head to the beach. I stand at the water's edge but am careful not to let it roll up on me. Rumors are rampant regarding people swimming in the new toxic stew that is the Gulf and getting sick: lesions, ulcers, respiratory damage, and more.

It seems to me the dispersant has simply spread the oil over a larger area. And the water quality continues to decline; it is definitely darker, thicker, than it was a few days ago. I watch a pod of dolphin chase bait fish into the shallows. Pre-April 20, the sight would have delighted me. I would have felt connected to something greater than myself, a divine plan spun by a divine world. But today, I see the animals and am filled with worry ... worry that grows right alongside my hopelessness.

In an attempt to cope, I trudge back to the shack, sit before my computer, and begin composing something—an op-ed, an essay ... anything that will keep me off of Facebook and away from the news. Maybe if I write it all down, a pattern will emerge, common sense will take over.

"I live on the edge of the world: a peninsular sandbar in the northern Gulf of Mexico in Franklin County, Florida. For generations we have, directly and indirectly, depended on the sea's bounty for our living. Red tides, hurricanes, and pollution flowing downriver from population centers to our north have persistently presented challenges to our maritime way of life. But no prior natural or human-driven disaster has prepared us for what we're currently experiencing as a result of the Deepwater Horizon oil spill.

"This is a world of rivers, estuaries, bays, oyster reefs, and wide-open seas. The complex cocktail of nutrients flowing from freshwater rivers into saltwater shallows helps create a biodiversity studied by scientists worldwide. Our bays provide nurseries for all manner of sea life. The Gulf's heartbeat—its wildlife—begins here. And then, of course, there are those world famous oysters. Apalachicola Bay oysters comprise ninety percent of the state's supply and ten percent of the nation's.

"I'm a native Floridian who has lived on these shores for nearly twenty years. Five years ago this July, Hurricane Dennis destroyed thirty-five homes in my neighborhood and wiped out much of the oyster processing facilities in nearby Eastpoint. We took it in stride, rebuilt, and carried on without much help from the government or anyone else.

"But what's happening in the Gulf feels different. Amid the occasional debate over whether we're imagining the stench of oil, smoke, and chemicals, there's a sense of finality in the air. New phrases are slipping into our everyday lexicon: HAZMAT training, oiled seabirds, sea turtle rescue, oil-spill tracking forecasts, deep water oil plumes, dead zones.

"We watch hyphenated lines of pelicans cruise overhead and are stricken with the sickening fear of what the future might hold for them and us.

"So we organize into small flotillas of volunteers, only to be told by BP to butt out. We call the BP volunteer hotline, navigate the system, and leave messages that are never returned. The Audubon Society scurries to organize folks to be 'bird stewards' who will 'help ensure beachgoers and individuals preparing for the spill do not enter nesting areas ….' The closest bird steward program they offer is 200 miles to our south. That old familiar feeling of abandonment in the face of disaster looms.

"Earlier this month, BP notified a grassroots organization started by a local veterinarian that it had opened an office in the adjacent county for the purposes of offering HAZMAT training. Their automated system to register for the classes didn't work. Not until one of the group's organizers, after private efforts failed, publicly chastised BP, did the company address the problem.

"On Monday, Gov. Charlie Crist, who has received high praise for his prompt attention to the spill, appointed oil-industry lobbyist Jim Smith to head the state's BP response legal team. Smith and his son lobbied for BP via Florida Energy Associates, a group that has for years pushed for offshore drilling in Florida's Gulf waters.

"The theater of ecology—how politicians and corporations respond to this disaster with hubris bordering on arrogance—is becoming a major issue. President Obama lambastes the CEOs of BP, Halliburton, and Transocean for finger pointing, but in the meantime quietly approves twenty-seven new offshore drilling projects. What happened to the moratorium? The very company responsible for the spill trains our fishermen in boom placement. But the counties under the oil gun can't put those booms into place until BP gives the okay.

"Oil continues to hemorrhage unchecked into the Gulf with the closest thing to what we're told is a real solution three months out. We can't wait three months. I cannot find a single person—scientist, politician, or oysterman—in this county who believes our economy and environment can survive a four-month long oil spill. Politicians and oil executives continue to talk about offshore drilling as though it's a perfectly safe proposition and that the Deepwater Horizon event is an anomaly. But when does an anomaly become a catastrophe of such colossal magnitude that quaint or politically convenient notions of 'safe' no longer apply?

"Those of us out here on the edge sense that a new nightmarish reality has just begun: living without solutions or leadership amid a multi-generational ecological disaster. We write our legislators and president. We post information on social networking sites. We look out at that beautiful Gulf and grieve, fearing we and this place we love have become expendable."

I reread and polish amid a veil of tears. I zip it to the op-ed desk of *The New York Times*. They do not acknowledge receiving it. They do not publish it.

Even though Florida waters are still open, no one is buying Gulf seafood. When I made my weekly stop at my seafood monger, he shook his head and fought back tears. "The market in New York turned our trucks away. We've got the best seafood in the world and this oil has made it worthless."

The training session for fishermen who want to participate in BP's Vessels of Opportunity program takes place near the end of May. While some fishermen plainly state they don't want to work for BP, what is their alternative? I grudgingly admit Bill was right when he said fishermen have no choice if they want to keep their families fed, housed, clothed: work for the hand that bit them.

So many people sign up for the training session held in nearby Wakulla County, they have to move it to a larger venue. In the meantime, commercial fishermen receive this email:

> "The captain and crew ("Contractor Vessel Party") **must** participate together in the scheduled local orientation and training session to become eligible for the VoO program. It is recommended that the vessel owner also attend, but it is not required. During this session you and your team will learn the requirements to become eligible and active in the Vessels of Opportunity (VoO) program. These sessions will

include: Health, Safety, and Environmental Review. Contract Review—A contract will be issued to the Contractor Vessel Party during the session. You are not expected to sign the contract immediately and are encouraged to review with your attorney if desired and return the signed contract at a later time. Your Contractor Vessel Party will be mailed a copy of the contract from BP at a later date."

Three days after the training session, President Obama issues a six-month moratorium on drilling in 500 or more feet of water and scientists hit the airwaves to say they believe oil is leaking at a rate of 798,000 gallons of oil a day. They reiterate we are experiencing the worst oil spill in our country's history.

The amount of volume of oil and dispersant we are putting into it is tiny in relation to the total water volume.

Here, honey, drink this glass of water. I only put a tiny dab of shit in it.

I'm a mess. I look at myself in the bathroom mirror and barely recognize the gaunt-eyed woman staring back at me. I've got to change my ways or this disaster is going to kill me. Personal hygiene: paramount. I take a shower—my first in six days—put on Coltrane, and pull my *Baking with Julia* book down from the cookbook shelf. I turn to section titled "Mixed-Starter Bread." The instructions include a two-day bread-making plan. This bread is complex. It's not for sissies. You have to focus, watch the clock, be engaged. Make the first starter, let it rise for eight hours, make the second starter, let that rise for four hours, and chill everything for another eight hours. The second day of preparations begin at 7 a.m., according to the instructions, with the loaves finally being baked at noon. Kneading, rising, resting. Sounds like Catholic Mass. I can do this. But my heart, because it likes a challenge, wanders. I flip over to the recipe for *pain de campagne* ... *But if you persevere with this bread* ... heck, if I can persevere with this disaster, I can persevere with bread that depends on airborne yeast for its success.

But will the starter bread provide enough yeast to properly feed the *pain de campagne*, which in my head I start calling *pain de my ass?* I'll just make sure it does. I break out the flour, yeast, olive oil, tepid water. In only a matter of minutes my kitchen and I are covered in flour. Every time I pass the jar of yeast, I take a pinch and toss it in the air. I remind myself of a sumo wrestler, the way they toss sacred salt in the air to please the gods during their pre-match rituals. Maybe if I toss enough yeast, I'll wake up the right god, a crazy Old Testament god who will put an end to the gusher before there is nothing left to save.

Not until I knead the flour and notice droplets landing on the elastic dough ball, do I realize I'm crying.

May 23, 2010, Day 34

It's a beautiful Sunday in spring. From my spot on the front porch, I watch butterflies and hummingbirds engage in the three F's: feed, flit, and fly. The surf song unfurls slowly, again and again, a metaphor for the ebb and flow of life. If we didn't know any better, Bill and I could pretend we are living in a pre-spill world.

While the mixed-starter bread is on its final one-and-a-half-hour rise, Bill and I mend the rips in our porch screens using bedazzled hot glue. Fish swim across the Gulf-facing screen, adorned in jewel-toned pieces of broken glass. The glue dries to a transparent sheen and light passes through both the glue and the glass. Everything shimmers. Bill has created a mother, father, son, and oak tree depiction on the screen door that is inspired by the ghost family in *How Clarissa Burden Learned to Fly*. It reminds me of the Tree of Life. Surrounded by my hot-glue-and-glass artwork, I love this front porch more than ever. And I wonder why everyone doesn't bedazzle their screens, torn or not.

Eventually, Bill sets aside the glue gun and wanders inside. There is an unspoken tension, a constant ripple of how bad is this going to get mingling in the air right along with the yeast, the Corexit, the smoke. I pause for a moment as I consider the possibility that the yeast I've been tossing in the air is adhering to a fine mist of Corexit and that I might inadvertently be baking poisoned bread. Jesus. Life in a spray field.

I finish hot gluing a blue and green mosaic fish, glass shard by glass shard, onto the screen. It's beautiful: a happy fish resplendent in shimmering jewels. Maybe one day the entire screen will be a sea-themed mosaic. I unplug the glue gun, sit in my low-slung bamboo chair, and flip through my notebook. Staying busy is the key to survival. I'm juggling helping to plan a memorial for Rane that will take place at the Associated Writing Program's annual conference, the country's largest gathering of writers and academic programs; preparing for appearances to promote *Clarissa*, and fine-tuning the next writing conference in Cedar Key.

While I check my notes to see how many people have responded to a request to read from Rane's poems at the memorial, I hear Bill flip on the TV. A CNN talking head promos the upcoming segment—something about dispersant, so I set aside my notebook and join him in the shack.

"Should we watch this?" I mute the commercial.

"The commercial?"

"No. The story."

"Probably not. Just more bad news."

"Yep. Probably." Still, when the commercial break is over, I flip on the sound.

CNN reports what we already know ... unprecedented amounts of Corexit are being used ... many countries have banned it ... no end game insight. They run footage of a plane spraying Corexit over wide swaths of the Gulf.

"I feel like we're being crop dusted," Bill says, "like we're twenty-year case studies."

"My breathing and the gunky ropes in my mouth are getting worse."

"You need to see a doctor. A specialist maybe."

I get off the couch and go over to the computer. There it is: Old Horrible spewing at full tilt. I do a Google search for news about Corexit and stumble upon a *ProPublica* story written by Marian Wang. "As we've reported, Corexit was also used after the Exxon Valdez disaster and was later linked with human health problems including respiratory, nervous system, liver, kidney and blood disorders. One of the two Corexit products also contains a compound that, in high doses, is associated with headaches, vomiting and reproductive problems."

"Bill, they are trying to kill us," I say.

"We've got to get the fuck out of here."

I look at him sharply. This is the second time he has said something like this. He knows that's impossible. *At least this won't go away. No, not this. Not ever.* "We're not going anywhere."

But he's not looking at me. He's staring at the TV. Images of Louisiana's Chandeleur Islands flicker across the screen, the mangroves and birds coated in oil so thick it looks like mud.

Fearing the images will send me into a total mental and emotional meltdown, I turn back to the computer and click over to Wikipedia's Corexit entry: "Dispersants are mixtures of surfactants and solvents that are commonly used to break up floating oil slicks into small droplets, which are submerged underwater. This reduces shoreline accumulation but increases the amount of oil underwater. This also increases the surface area of the oil and, in theory, accelerates the destruction of oil by naturally occurring bacteria. Dispersants are themselves a form of pollution that can be toxic to marine life, and the increased activity of bacteria from their presence can deplete oxygen in nearby waters, causing further harm to marine life. There are important trade-offs that must be considered in their use, such as the relative level of toxicity of the dispersant versus the relative toxicity of the spilled oil, to ensure that dispersant use mitigates an oil spill rather than to make the problem worse."

There are rumors that when rainstorms blow in off the Gulf, they carry Corexit with them. If true, it's far more dangerous than spray drift. It's spray immersion. I ask Bill if he thinks it's possible.

"Who knows? Probably. Like you said, they're trying to kill us." Bill is acquiring the deadpan honesty of the defeated.

But that's just about everyone's response: Who knows because BP isn't telling us anything and it doesn't really matter since we don't trust a word they do say.

Later that afternoon, when the bread is in the oven, a storm barrels in off the Gulf. I run out to the backyard with a mixing bowl and collect the rainwater.

It's still lightly raining when I say, peering into the bowl, "Bill, come look at this. Am I crazy or are there tiny, oily droplets in the water?"

"Maybe it's residual from something that was in the bowl," Bill says. He looks at me, obviously concerned, but I don't know if he's worried because our paradise is becoming something that can kill us or because he fears I'm losing it. Maybe both.

Going crazy, I know, is easy. Gloria Steinem once riffed off of the John 8:32 Bible verse, quipping, "The truth will set you free, but first it will piss you off."

Amen, sister, amen.

These are some of the truths known to me. But they do not set me free. Truth: Thanks to a post-Exxon Valdez law that requires the responsible party take control of the cleanup, BP is in charge of their own crime scene. Truth: BP is free to destroy evidence because they have control of the corpse. Truth: The real reason they aren't allowing volunteer groups to aid with animal rescue is that they don't want the public to see the crime. Truth: BP, with the aid of the Coast Guard, is hassling journalists, scientists, and photographers, sometimes threatening them with arrest when they, for instance, try to report from oil-soaked beaches. Truth: Everyday more and more areas of the Gulf become part of the crime scene and are being closed off to fishing. Truth: A sheriff is posted at the BP claim office in Crawfordville because tempers are on the rise.

Later that evening, as the sun slurries the sky in purple and gold, we will sit at the picnic table on the back deck after I've wiped off the soot that has accumulated during the day. We will drink wine and eat cheese. We will pretend nothing is wrong, that the truth is not a bitch peddling despair and destruction.

We will eat the tears I spilled, the ones I baked into the bread.

The oil gusher and its attendant fuckery have reopened old wounds. How can this present madness hurl me into the past, back onto that pile of broken bones? I can't figure it out. And I can't stop it.

One memory in particular hurts like a blade to the gut. I am in the grocery store with my mother. I'm small—maybe six or seven years old—and I feel totally hollowed out. I miss my father. Of course I do. But if parental death for a child isn't bad enough, my mother tells me at random moments throughout the day, often between sips of bourbon and Coke, that I killed him, that I was such a bad daughter he preferred death to life with me. So on this day in this grocery store I am trying to be extra good. After all, I don't want my mother to leave me, too. We're in the canned goods aisle and I'm looking at the shapes and colors of beans ... round, oblong, kidney, red, yellow, black. A woman with a tiny baby in her cart reaches past me and grabs a can of beans that shares the name of one of my favorite candies: Boston baked. I gaze up and down the aisle. My mother—*whoosh!*—is nowhere in sight. I zip down the next aisle. No. I check the beauty aisle. No. Medicines. No. Bakery. No. Panic and fear hurtle through me. Mother is gone. She has left me. I am so bad she can't stand the sight of me. Sensing I will be forever alone, I wail.

I won't know the word until years later: derisive.

Her laughter reaches me before she does, silencing the wail, slowing me into tear-stained hiccups.

"Look at you, you big crybaby. Grow up!"

The same woman who grabbed the Boston baked beans strolls by. "I'm sorry if my daughter is bothering you. She's incorrigible."

Mother played this demented game of abandonment in grocery store aisles until I was old enough to not care.

Even as an adult, it played out in nightmares until this spit of land, this world with nature as its center, purged the fear. But on this night as I sleep, the old fears return. Mother enters stage right. I stare at the beans. I wear gold lamé flats. A menagerie of animals hides in my hair. I close my eyes. Yes, for sure, Mother is gone. I wander through the ages, calling, "Mommy! Mommy! Mommy, where are you?"

When finally she appears, her laughter rings with more evil than derision. I watch as her mouth grows bigger and bigger and bigger. Her head explodes but is replaced by my father's face. He laughs the same demonic laugh until he, too, explodes. And then there is Carolyn's face and Rane's face and my mother's face, my father's face. It's a carousel of abandonment. It swirls me out of the nightmare. I sit up, gasping for air. I look through the darkness. No exploding faces. Just my dogs and my husband who are deeply asleep, their breathing heavy and steady.

I pull Scout over to me. He curls against my ribcage. His presence, the trust such physical contact requires, soothes the nightmare jitters.

May 30, 2010, Day 41

"There's no one who wants this thing over more than I do. I'd like my life back."—Tony Hayward

May 31, 2010, Day 42

I'm standing in line at the Crawfordville Winn Dixie. In my cart is a five-pound bag of flour—I'm running through a lot of flour these days—a jar of active yeast, and a decongestant. My breathing problems are eased by a few degrees when I take the decongestant, but nothing affects the ropey, gluey masses. If I had to give a reading today, I wouldn't be able to do so.

An old man wearing crabbing boots, a gold cross necklace, denim shorts, and nothing else—his face creased from countless hours working in the sun, trolling through Gulf waters—stands behind me, holding a carton of milk and a package of Ding Dongs.

"How's the crabbing?" I ask.

"It ain't," he says. "You can't give 'em away."

"It's a crying shame," I say, but he shrugs off my comment and keeps talking.

"That fella from BP wanting his life back? What about MY life? That sonbitch shows up around here and he'll be shark chum."

"I don't know what we're going to do," I say.

"Starve," says the woman in front of me who has a toddler in tow.

Her Panacea Blue Crab Festival T-shirt and spandex exercise shorts are a wee too tight but that's how a lot of people roll around here. A tattoo of an anchor edges just below her shirtsleeve. Her little girl is blond, blue-eyed, and has a smattering of what appears to be grape jelly around her lower lip. I feel an immense wave of guilt wash over me. I'm sure she's a fisherman's wife. Her cart is full of baby formula so she must have another child at home. The crabber and this woman are suffering far more greatly from BP's negligence than I ever will.

"That chemical they're using?" the old man says. "It's way worse than the oil. You just wait and see. We're all gonna get sick."

"What's that stuff called?" the woman asks, her fingers sifting through the child's curls.

"Corexit," I say.

"Correct It? That's a joke," she says, rolling her eyes.

June 1, 2010, Day 43

As soon as Bill leaves, I set aside my steaming cup of hot tea and pull down from the shelf what has become my Bible:

Baking with Julia. I am discovering something mystical, something holy, about the act of baking bread. I'm not talking about the alchemy that occurs with flour and water and yeast and heat. I'm talking resolution, resurrection.

The Christian tradition tells us Jesus is the bread of life and I get it. I understand the metaphor. But I am not a person who in the best of times blindly adheres to articles of faith. I am a seeker. A woman wracked with questions. Now, in the midst of this apocalypse, I am something more: an active participant in a spontaneous religion, cooking up my own private dogma on the fly.

Bread baking is not merely an attempt for me to stay busy and avoid the bad news babble that is CNN. It's about trying to make this pain, these tears, mean something. I am not baking bread. I am casting spells, recreating the earth out of flour, water, yeast, heat, an earth un-scarred by gushing oil.

And the tears I shed and bake into the loaves? Maybe I'm channeling the Canaanite war goddess Anat whose tears were so powerful they brought her dead brother, the God of storms, the master of thunder, Ba'al Haddad, back to life.

As I flip open the book and study once more the complex instructions for *pain de campagne*, this psalm, memorized eons ago in Sunday school, wafts through my mind: *My tears have been my food day and night, while they say to me all the day long, "Where is your God?"*

While contemplating that question, which is surely a dangerous one, my email alert buzzes on my phone. I push away the cookbook, that wayward Bible, and click open the mail.

Bill told me this would happen but I had refused to believe him, relying instead on my faith in Emily Dickinson: *Hope is that thing with feathers / That perches in the soul.*

Penitent, I reread the email three times. My first Cedar Key writing conference participant is canceling due to "concerns about the oil spill."

"Don't panic," I whisper. I set down my phone and return to my Bible. But I have lost my place. I flip through the pages, leaving small rips as I go, chanting a new prayer. *Please, no one else drop out. No one else. No one else. No one else.*

My hope has no more feathers. I've been plucked. I can't make this truth fly away: The disaster has not only blown asunder my physical home, it is—beam by beam—destroying my financial house of cards.

My chant falls on deaf ears. By June 15, my cancellations reach one hundred percent. My conference business—my main source of income—is finished. The economy is in the dumpster, with publishing being hit astonishingly hard. Writers are being told by their agents they don't even want to shop their books until the industry recovers. Despite the economy's dire condition, I was managing to get by because the conference business was chugging along, allowing me to remain financially solvent until publishing regained its bearings. It seems as though everyone who lost a job wants to write a book and they are more than willing to drop a few dollars to learn how. But those same people don't want to risk exposure to the toxic nightmare that is the Gulf. I don't blame them.

When Bill comes home, after he's had a shower and a beer, I give him the bad news.

He's surprisingly calm, as if he expected it and had already come to terms with my financial ruin. He hugs me and repeats something he has been suggesting for weeks. "Baby. You need to file a claim."

I literally wring my hands as I say, "I don't think BP will approve it. They probably won't help out anyone other than fishermen."

"Try anyway," he says.

I cry as I print out a claim form. I cry as I read through the labyrinthine instructions—tax forms are less complicated. I cry as I gather all of the required financial documentation. I cry as I make photocopies of pieces of paper that prove what I earned and what I have lost. I cry because the company that has rendered me financially insolvent, emotionally fractured, and physically embattled is operating from a stance that suggests they believe I, along with everyone else caught in their hell-storm, am lying. I cry as I sign on the dotted line. I cry because a part of me doesn't want their fucking money. I cry because their money cannot give me back my peace of mind. I cry because they cannot fix this enormous wrong. I cry because out there, in that once beautiful blue sea, life is suffering, life is dying.

I cry.

But there is a silver lining, a tiny bird of hope, at least as it applies to my finances. In a few weeks, I leave for a new part-time teaching gig in Vermont. I approached Vermont College of Fine Arts (VCFA) back in February, before the disaster, when everything was good in my life. It's not a great payday, but it fills in some gaps. And I'll be gone only for ten days. Between the new job and what Bill brings home, we ought to avoid my worst nightmare: being homeless.

But, in truth, financial concerns aren't the only reasons I'm thrilled about the job. VCFA has a sterling reputation, being consistently ranked number one or two among the nation's low residency writing programs. And teaching at VCFA keeps me in the game, which I need. I learn so much from my students: books to read, music to listen to, movies to watch, new ways to think.

Despite the bright light cast by the possibilities of the new part-time job, June is shaping up to be monstrous. In addition to my conference tanking, conditions along the sandbar worsen. The first dead baby dolphin washes ashore, the first dead turtle washes ashore, and deep-sea fish enter the shallows.

A friend who is a recreational fisherman stops by one afternoon and expresses his delight that the big fish are in-shore. "I've never seen anything like it!"

"They aren't supposed to be in this close," I say, holding onto the porch rail, fearing my anger will hurl me into the sun.

"But they are and it's great!"

"No, no it's not," I snap. "They are trying to escape the oil. They are, essentially, running for their lives. There is nothing even remotely great about it."

On June 10, the government ups its estimate yet again, saying that more than a million gallons of oil are being spewed into the Gulf every twenty-four hours.

One million gallons. Per day.

The water quality at Alligator Point continues to decline. In addition to the mucous glue, I have developed a wheeze that comes and goes without logic. We are not allowed to clean up the carcasses of sea creatures that wash up on the shore. They are marked with bright orange paint and are left for days. I do not understand why they are left to rot under the hot, hot sun. Why even mark them?

I read a Huffington Post article written by Exxon Valdez survivor and marine toxicologist Riki Ott that sheds some light on the treatment of the dead sea life. She writes:

"With oil undisputedly hitting the beaches and the number of dead wildlife mounting, BP is switching tactics. In Orange Beach, people told me BP wouldn't let them collect carcasses. Instead, the company was raking up carcasses of oiled seabirds. 'The heads separate from the bodies,' one upset resident told me. 'There's no way those birds are going to be autopsied. BP is destroying evidence!'

"The body count of affected wildlife is crucial to prove the harm caused by the spill, and also serves as an invaluable tool to evaluate damages to public property—the dolphins, sea turtles, whales, sea birds, fish, and more, that are owned by the American public. Disappeared body counts means disappeared damages—and disappeared liability for BP. BP should not be collecting carcasses. The job should be given to NOAA, a federal agency, and volunteers, as was done during the Exxon Valdez oil spill in Alaska."

Nearly every day while walking the shore, I come across more dead sea turtles, baby dolphin, large and small fish. Because of the large number of dead baby dolphin washing ashore, marine scientists suspect the toxic chemical brew is causing miscarriages.

Everything about this disaster pushes all the buttons I have: abandonment, death, greed, cruelty, injustice, animal suffering. I don't sleep. Rather, I worry about the turtles trying to make it to the coastline. I worry about what will happen to the turtles after they lay their clutches of eggs and return to the poisoned water. I worry about the turtle eggs that will hatch and the hatchlings that will enter a sea composed of oil and dispersant. I worry because I know the truth: Those baby turtles that successfully make the Herculean journey across the gullied sand to the sea? They're all going to die.

June 25, 2010, Day 67

I am back in this odd church of my own making. It's 8 a.m. and already Julia Child's cranberry-walnut pumpkin dough sits in a Pyrex bowl—a modest chalice—on my kitchen counter: first rise out of two. I reread the *pain de campagne* recipe. *If you were the type of student who never minded when the teacher sent you back to the drawing board for the third time, this recipe is for you. Because this loaf is made by the centuries-old chef-levain method, which depends on capturing airborne wild yeast, it's an iffy project that comes with no guarantees. You might work on this bread for four days and get a loaf as flat as a pizza—or the bread of your dreams. Wild yeast is like that.*

Wild yeast? I have been prepping the air for months and I just noticed the most important part of the equation: wild. Have I not been tossing the right kind into the air? How did I miss that? *Pain de my ass* morphs into *Pain de Corexit.*

REM's "Losing My Religion" wafts through my head and I actually laugh because it dawns on me that my faith is like French bread: full of holes. I leave the kitchen and pull out my Yoga mat from its hiding place underneath my desk. I unfurl it in the empty triangle of light in front of the French doors and begin. My downward facing dog thrills my canine crew. They gleefully jump on me because they think Mama is playing and *oh what fun, she's nearly upside down!* Pablo Neruda manages to lick me right on the mouth again—that little guy is fast—and just as I'm considering putting the dogs in the bedroom, I hear the thunder of a semi-truck hurtling down the road. From my head-down position I see it fly by and at first its giant, rubber tubes folded and piled on its trailer like sleeping anacondas don't register. I stand in time to see a pick-up truck, following the semi, speed by. "Unified Recovery Group, Disaster Recovery Team" is emblazoned on its door. And then it hits me. "Boom. They are deploying boom."

At this moment, with dogs jumping on me and frolicking on the mat, my head feels exactly like that: boom! I grab my phone and keys, jump in the car, and head west. The semi-truck is maybe a half-mile down the road. The driver backs the semi up over the dunes, destroying them. I snap a series of photographs from the safety of my car. I do not think they've seen me. I want people to know the oil really is here. Our fishery really is shut down. Animals really are dying. People's livelihoods really are being stripped from them.

I hurry home and post the photos to Facebook. The images say more than I can, so I simply write, "A photo album of Alligator Point as we deal with the oil disaster."

My neighbor one county over, environmental activist and photographer Melissa Starbuck, responds with a sentiment that speaks volumes: "Suddenly we are in the center of a horror movie in our own backyard."

As the disaster grinds on, it becomes clear that everything BP tries in their ongoing Keystone Cops effort to staunch the oil is nothing more than a science experiment. In the midst of corporate PR and government spin, what do we get? More Hail Mary passes. More *what-the-fuck-are-we-gonna-do-next?*

In addition to spraying unprecedented amounts of cancer-inducing Corexit onto the Gulf's surface, they are now spraying it directly on the exploded wellhead. No one knows how the chemical will react at such depths and temperatures.

I watch the spew-cam and Old Horrible's incessant belching and I know with a certainty so solid it has its own genetic code that we are trapped, perhaps forever, in a perfect storm of fuckery.

Amid the unfolding tragedy in the Gulf, *UnspOILed* is finally published. We give readings. We hold rallies. And we feel foolish. None of us saw this simple truth: The Gulf doesn't have state lines; currents don't stop at government mandated boundaries; you drill baby drill in the Gulf of Mexico, a wellhead explodes, and the oil can potentially drift in currents that carry it to all of the landmasses bordering the Gulf and beyond.

Nature is forever on the move and has developed amazing mechanisms that enable plant and animal life to travel along what are essentially maritime super highways.

The Gulf of Mexico has one of the busiest super highways in the world: the Loop Current, a powerful northward moving warm current flowing between Cuba and the Yucatan Peninsula and into the Gulf. It swings north, then east, then south, and finally exits through the Florida Straits where it enters the Atlantic Ocean.

The Loop Current acts as a conveyor belt for all manner of sea life, delivering them to where they need to be at various life stages, including various species of Caribbean and Gulf larvae, turtles, blue fin tuna, and dolphins. It is the path by which sea life enters the world's oceans.

But this maritime super highway has no methods of exclusion. There is nothing to stop it from conveying the oil and dispersant potentially across the globe. So now, in addition to checking the oil spill forecast daily, I also monitor the outlook for the loop current.

The only lucky break I've seen in this entire disaster is that in late May Mother Nature created a giant eddy in the current, thus trapping a large amount of oil, which scientists say might prevent it from entering the Florida Keys and beyond. But the conveyor belt is dynamic, always changing the configuration and speed of its many eddies.

Perhaps Mother Nature, in an unlikely display of incessant wisdom, will keep this particular eddy spinning in place throughout infinity. But isn't infinity, by definition, boundless? Doesn't that figure-eight symbol, ∞, suggest the Now is always and forever? After all, dispersal doesn't mean disappearance.

June 26, 2010, Day 68

Crews begin deploying boom in the waters surrounding Alligator Point. It's as if the Gulf is being adorned with a crimson necklace.

The mouth of the harbor is draped in a different color, cordoned off in a giant smiley face composed of yellow boom.

As I drive, the Alligator Point road and the water all around me becomes jumbled in bright plastic, I think, *Necklaces, smiley faces ... none of this jibes with reality.*

Bill and I photograph the deployment on both the bay and Gulf sides. As I watch more and more boom encircle us, I begin to feel trapped, as if the life is being squeezed right out of me. Large ships carrying boom zip back and forth just offshore. I can find no logic in their comings and goings. Perhaps there is none. Perhaps, as has been the case with this disaster from the beginning, they have no idea what they are doing. With each image I snap, something builds up in me. It's not really rage. It's more like a mushroom cloud of grief and exhaustion. If only BP would come clean and admit they have unleashed Hell on earth. Until they do, those of us living through the apocalypse possess a narrative too easily dismissed. They are on

TV, dominating the twenty-four-hour news cycle and splashing feel-good commercials across the airwaves. Insanely, they have rendered the coastal residents invisible. I want to shout, "See this? This is the empirical truth. Look at what is happening to us. Look at The Truth."

No, I am not a hysterical woman wringing her hands for no reason. But I do remind myself of a friend of my mother's from so, so long ago, in the golden time before my father's death.

Several neighborhood ladies had gathered at our house. It was a weekday morning—or maybe midday—but I clearly remember my father being at work and my sister in school. The women, including my mother, were in full make-up—no self-respecting lady, it seemed, went anywhere, even the mail box, with a bare face—and their starched frocks reminded me of lime sherbet, lemon sherbet, orange sherbet. They stood at our plate glass window, watching the goings on across the street. They were all smoking, pensive.

One of them said, "Maybe he won't do it. Maybe he has changed his mind."

"That bastard is going to do it all right," my mother said.

And then there she was, our neighbor Mrs. Hicks, being led out by a nurse and two men in business suits. Mrs. Hicks also wore a starched sherbet frock but her eyes bore the wild look of a dog being whipped. One of the neighbor ladies, the one in the orange frock, started crying.

I didn't understand what was happening but it seemed really important, so I risked asking.

"They are going to give her electroshock therapy," my mother said. "Mr. Hicks thinks it will cure her menopause."

I didn't know what electroshock therapy or menopause meant. But I wanted the nice lady from across the street, who sometimes brought over lemonade and cookies, to be okay. "Will it? Will Mrs. Hicks be better?"

"No," my mother said, watching her being shoved into the back of a sedan. "She will never be herself again."

I studied the four women. I would be them one day. A lady with a house and a husband and adult responsibilities and freedoms. But at that moment, I didn't know if I ever wanted to grow up because they looked stricken, afraid, like *it could happen to us*, like *when is the other shoe going to drop?*, like *would my husband do that to me?*

Bill and I drive over to the coastal highway and park at the turnabout. We make our way across a pine snag on the northern edge of the harbor and begin photographing the boom floating there. When we're done, we stand at the water's edge, gazing at a dark bay stinking of petroleum. Shorebirds are busy flitting amid the ebbing surf, eating tiny morsels of contaminated life. The yellow boom sloshes back and forth, shimmies and dips.

Bill puts his arm around my shoulders. "We are officially fucked," he says.

I don't respond. I don't want to be the lady who is forced into electroshock therapy for speaking her truth. I lift the camera, bring the boom into focus. Click. Maybe I'm entering The Land Beyond Words. Maybe that's a safer place.

Back at the shack, I flip on the news, check Old Horrible, and search You Tube. I try to avoid videos containing images of suffering, oiled animals because they break apart what's left of me. I understand I over-identify with animals and this is a result of my violent childhood. My mother might have called me despicable names and beat me with everything from hair brushes to leather belts and played a sadistic game of hide-and-seek in the fluorescent glare of grocery stores, but the menagerie of stray dogs and cats I surrounded myself with showed me nothing but what I presumed then and now to be what every child requires: unconditional love.

This is why, I believe, if I see in real life or in a fictional portrayal, suffering or abused animals, I freak. I become that little beat-down girl again, panicked and hurting, totally bewildered by the violence. *I'm so sorry, Mama. I will be better! I swear! Please don't hit me. No, Mama, no!*

I run through several thumbnails on You Tube. Most of them depict oiled birds or dead marine life: More broken bones.

What am I doing? I turn off the computer, flip off the TV, wander into the garden, and sit amid the scent of citrus, herbs, roses, and oil. Bill joins me. We sit, arm-in-arm, silently waiting.

The sun moves through the sky. Birds fly. A mullet jumps. A skink disappears into the labyrinth of rosemary. Waves slap against the boom, creating a hollow echo that ripples from water to land and back to water.

Even the surf song is off-key.

Bill and I dine on linguini and clams in white sauce except I substitute mushrooms for clams. I feel rotten about this. I have good friends in Apalachicola who insist the seafood is safe to eat. They need to say that. Their livelihoods depend on it. But our health might depend on us not eating it.

The loaf of Italian bread I baked is raw in the middle. In silence, we pick at the cooked edges.

Once the dishes are washed and put away, Bill wanders into the twilight to fiddle with his CJ5. The Jeep, because it's old and Bill is a tinkerer-savant, is always in need of a little tender loving care. Plus, the oil gusher has given Bill a new chore: hose down the vehicles to prevent that fine layer of soot from building up. As soon as he's out the door, I decide to venture over to the computer again. I am a crack addict, trying to score my next hit from this calamity. I try YouTube once more.

I'm still hoping, still looking for a narrative larger than myself that I can call The Truth, a truth generated by someone other than me so I can trust myself again, so I can say, "It's not just me. We are legion."

I run across a newly posted video by someone named John L. Wathen. The title, "BP Slick Covers Dolphins and Whales" should be enough to keep me moving onto the next video but for some reason I violate my no-suffering-animal rule.

Wathen, a pilot, and another passenger fly across the Gulf of Mexico, capturing aerial views. In voice-over narration, he explains what they are seeing: a light sheen at the mouth of Mobile Bay, then the first solid mass of oil 1.2 miles offshore of Gulf Shores, Alabama. He comments that on previous flights, there had only been a light sheen. The further they fly toward the Macondo well—what he calls "ground zero"—conditions get predictably worse. He says that at seventeen miles out there is no more clean water and at twenty-three miles out, they find the heaviest oil-swathed water yet, resulting in a rainbow of dark green, purple, and magenta oil spoils. He says, "Some of it looks more like bruised internal organs of the human body than the surface of the ocean."

The screen fills with towering plumes of black smoke from the fires BP has set. By the time the plane has made "a couple of passes," seven fires are consuming sea and sky. I look away from the screen for a moment and out to the Gulf. What about the sea creatures caught in the fires? Sea turtles are out there, swimming in all of that, trying to get to their nesting shorelines, but are they being incinerated alive? My terror level hits a new high. I am trembling. But, still, I return my attention to the video. The addict gets her fix.

Wathen, in a calm, southern voice, intones, "Certainly nothing can live in these rainbows of death that cover the entire horizon."

He goes on to observe, "From 1.2 miles off the shores of Gulf Shores, Alabama to the ground zero site some ninety miles away, we haven't flown over a single square inch of clear water."

I should turn off the video *now*. I know I should. In fact, I should close the spew-cam. I should turn off CNN. I should push myself away from the computer and go outside, see my husband, do ten jumping jacks, play with the dogs. Too late.

Aerial images of dolphins moving through the thick oil "struggling just to breathe," and " ... a sperm whale swimming in the oil had just breached. Along his back we could see red patches of crude as if he'd been basted for broiling," and finally a killing field of dolphins "some already dead, some in their death throes. It seemed to be that they were raising their heads and looking at the fires, wondering why is my world burning down around me? Why would humans do this to me?"

They then fly over the already heavily impacted Chandeleur Islands. Red and yellow boom—a coral snake soaking in oil—floats offshore, just like the ones deployed in my front and back yards today, and he says that if a storm blows through, all that boom will be oil-drenched and onshore along with the oil it rides in on.

I reach for my tissue and clear my mouth, fearing people I love most, even my husband, are beginning to wish I would ignore the ever-widening apocalypse. When does my discomfort, my depression, my mania, become their problem? But what would the world have me do? Go about my business as if nothing is wrong, as if they aren't burning sea turtles alive, as if I never heard the report of whales blowing oil through their blowholes, as if I didn't see images of oil-covered, dying birds in Louisiana, as if I actually believe any of those dolphins in the video made it out alive?

I wander outside. Bill has just put the Jeep's hood down. He wipes his hands on a bandana he whips from his back pocket (he is never without a fresh bandana, a small flashlight slipped onto his belt, and a knife also slipped onto his belt, which means he can clean anything, fix things hidden from the sun, and cut cords that need to be cut) and kisses my cheek. "Hello, lover. What're you doing?"

The first stars are firing the sky. Crepuscular bats and purple martins soar and dive. A heron fishes the shallows. It will fly away soon to wherever its roost is. The two old, lover herons, squawk and settle into the oak. Night birds are taking wing. Nocturnal land animals are waking from secret burrows, testing the air, no doubt wanting and hungry. Diurnal creatures, having made the most of the daylight, are heading home. Twilight and daybreak are busy times on the sandbar. Perhaps if I weren't a person who'd suffered unspeakable losses in her lifetime, I could ignore the apocalypse. I could look out at all this beauty and delude myself into thinking everything will be okay. *Don't worry. Be happy!* But I've been beaten by the one person in all the world who was supposed to love me more than anyone and I've been stripped of my dignity by men who could not control their propensity for physical violence and psychological terror. I know bad things happen to good people. And that boom they put out there today? It will, in the end, do more harm than good. A heavy surf will bring it ashore—oil or no oil—and it will trap baby birds, crush unhatched eggs, booby trap hatchling turtles. It will not stop the oil. My thoughts are not forays into unwarranted negativity. These are facts, facts that rule this new world we find ourselves in.

"Bill?" I slip my hand in his.

"Yes, baby?"

"I don't know how much more I can take."

Two days later, I board a plane that will take me to Vermont. Because it's a low-residency program, I will land in Montpelier twice a year, if they like me, and teach in their ten-day residencies. Between residencies, I will work with a small group of students—some writing fiction, others nonfiction—reading their manuscripts each month, providing copious feedback and suggestions for further reading, helping them establish an aesthetic and strengthen their craft skills, communicating with them through email and phone calls.

I am terrified. I don't know a single soul at the college. Vermont seems so far away. Foreign. Cold. Exotic the way Siberia is exotic. Will they assume I'm stupid or slow because I live in the south? Will I have to pull out my progressive liberal card to prove I am not a racist? What if I'm not smart enough? What if I'm not up to snuff? What if the oil comes ashore and I'm not here? But not here to do what? I am absolutely useless in the face of this tragedy. I flash on the childhood image: my mother standing over my father, beating on his still heart, begging him to live just one more second. She could not save him. And I cannot save the Gulf. I have to get on that plane. I desperately need this job. At the time, I think it's because I need the money. But VCFA and the family I will discover there will ultimately fill deep pockets of loss and longing I wasn't prepared to admit I possessed.

As I tuck my toothbrush, toothpaste, and deodorant into my already overflowing suitcase (I cannot convince myself that Vermont has stores that provide basic necessities so I'm clearing out my medicine cabinet and my underwear drawer), I watch CNN. I drop a bundle of socks onto the couch. "Oh my God, Bill, get in here."

Bill wanders into the living room from the back deck. CNN reports that turtle eggs are going to be dug up throughout the

Florida panhandle and flown by FedEx, *gratis*, to the east coast, probably in the vicinity of the Merritt Island National Wildlife Refuge. It's another Hail Mary pass at saving something. The U.S. Fish and Wildlife Conservation Commission estimates tens of thousands of eggs will be relocated by November.

"But what if scientists are right and their migratory patterns are coded in their DNA? They'll hatch on shores that mean nothing to them. What if their DNA tells them to go south to the Yucatan but they're facing the open waters of the Atlantic? Due east, toward Africa? Not south to the Caribbean?"

"I don't know," Bill says. "They've got to try something."

"Right. That's right. Maybe it will work." Think positively. And even though I'm on a thin crystal edge that only slightly resembles sanity, I can't help but be grateful we have people in the world who do care and act on that caring—the wildlife officer who saved Bond the Bear, the folks who thought up this Hail Mary scheme to save the hatchlings, and, yes, the fishermen who can no longer fish and who are instead in the Gulf trying to contain the oil in whatever way they are allowed. Don't think about the struggling and dying and burning creatures. Just get on that plane, get to Vermont. Find a new way to be.

But before I can, all the false hope I've been baking and freezing has to go. For weeks I have been filling the freezer with loaves of bread. They are stacked like gold bricks dusted in ice crystals, uniform and gleaming and signifying my abject folly.

I march into the kitchen, take out a garbage bag, fling open the freezer door, and start tossing.

"What are you doing?" Bill asks, peering over the freezer door.

"I have to stop. I just have to stop!" The frozen bread burns my skin but I don't care.

"Stop what?"

I grab the last loaf. I don't know if I can say the words.

"What is going on, baby?"

I toss the bread into the bag. It thunks, dull and dead, against the others. "Thinking ... hoping ... I dunno, praying that any of this is going to turn out okay."

Montpelier is situated in Vermont's Green Mountains. Everything about the little town is Florida's polar opposite. I look at the steep hills lined with Victorian homes and wonder how in the world people drive up and down them during the winter. I'm scared to travel on them in the middle of summer. The air is a different kind of fresh, carrying with it the crispness of evergreens at high altitude rather than the salt tinge of life below sea level. Many species of trees and flowers I encounter here are foreign to me. Blossoms are opulent and brightly colored but a little too well behaved to be mistaken as tropical. I find myself frequently stopping people to ask what this or that flower or tree is and, to a person, they look at me like I'm off, like *everyone knows what a lilac is*. I have a lot to learn.

The Victorian homes are painted wild colors—electric lavender, pumpkin, marigold—as if the vibrancy will stave off the oppression of the long winter. I imagine myself living in one of them, bundled up beside a roaring fire while Bill makes us hot buttered rum toddies. If I lived here, I would learn to knit. I would listen to the wind coming off the mountains, not the sea.

The campus is small and stately, with haunted College Hall being the crown jewel. My dorm room is monastic, basic, redolent of a jail cell but in a good way. Given the chaos back home, the austerity is comforting. Simplicity provides the illusion of having control over destiny.

VCFA has made five new hires, which is a lot for a small school. My colleagues, some of whom have taught together for thirty years, are welcoming but some eye us with what I think is a wee bit of suspicion, as though we might be viruses they will never be able to kick. I suppose they feel invaded and as overwhelmed with five new folks as we are at meeting all of them. Will I ever remember their names? If they're poets or prose writers? Academics? Bohemians? Both? This Floridian has been dropped into a foreign land, a place of high peaks and dreadlocked white people.

The VCFA residency proves to be a nearly twenty-four-hour literary boot camp. We are up early for breakfast and we don't stop until deep into evening: workshops, lectures, readings, presentations, discussions, and impromptu conversations filled with insight, hilarity, mind expansions. We eat in what amounts to a mess hall. My mind is starting to fire in ways that were, over the course of seventy-plus days of gushing oil, snuffed out. I rewrite my lecture about unreliable narrators at least twenty times, calibrating it to more sweetly fit this place I will come to think of as my literary home.

I almost never obsess on what is going on at the sandbar simply because I don't have time to concentrate on anything but the residency. Bill and I talk twice a day. He fills me in on the latest disaster news but hesitantly and, I think, only in broad strokes. He knows I need a break, that living amid the dead and dying— seen and unseen—and faced with nothing but uncertainty is pulling me apart, my head from my heart, my heart from my head. *The heads separate from the bodies.* So he just hits the high notes, things I will learn if I check the news: Hurricane Alex is in the Gulf. They've stopped all containment operations and will not resume them until the storm has moved. Old Horrible continues to gush its guts into the Gulf.

I sit in my monastic cell, phone pressed to my ear, staring into a world of green, not blue. "The hurricane will push the oil onshore," I say.

My husband is quiet for a moment and then, with worry and resignation lacing his voice, says, "Yes, baby. Probably so."

I do not pull up the spew-cam. I stay off Facebook, which means I avoid the news, innuendo, and troll fights that define discussions about the tragedy on social media.

But I do give into a weakness I've recently developed. Dan Froomkin of *The Huffington Post* has been writing a series of well-informed environmental stories I've been following since the onset of the disaster. After a long, heady day in book boot camp, before I turn off the light and go to sleep, I decide to see if he has posted anything new. This oil-disaster-aholic needs a fix. Don't do it. Don't take that drink. But I can't help it. I begin reading and with each word, the feeling of being skinned alive returns. I tell myself to turn off the computer. Just look away. Put down the drink. But it's useless. I have to know what he knows. I have to—even if it's through a computer screen—bear witness. To bear witness allows me to hear the martyr, honor the martyr, insist that there is a fucking martyr. In fact, there are thousands upon thousands of martyrs dying thousands of deaths:

"The seemingly endless oil disaster in the Gulf of Mexico is killing countless sea animals and sea birds, large and small. But there is no story as tragic as the plight of the sea turtles. These magnificent, graceful, creatures are particularly vulnerable to the effects of oil in the water, which weakens their eggs, chokes and poisons their young, and leaves adults addled and starving. In the case of the most endangered species, the Kemp's ridley turtle, hatchlings leaving their nests in Mexico this season are swimming right into the heart of the spill area, where their instinct to seek shelter and prey among floating vegetation is betraying them by leading them straight to thick clots of oil and oil-soaked seaweed. There, instead of finding security and food, they are getting poisoned, trapped and asphyxiated. And if that weren't tragic enough, it turns out that shrimp boats hired by BP to corral floating oil with booms and set it on fire have been burning hundreds if not thousands of the young turtles alive."

I muffle my scream by burying my face in my pillow. I will not sleep that night. I will also avoid the Internet for the rest of my time in Vermont.

My mother was an alcoholic, a fact that escaped me until her death. I didn't know she was hitting up everyone in our tenement slum to buy her booze down at the wino liquor store on what was then Tampa's derelict row, Kennedy Boulevard. I was attending University of Tampa on a full scholarship. I was a good girl and a good student … a virgin, almost straight A's (damn math). I rarely drank and never did drugs. I was a dutiful daughter who lived alone with her mother and who, when her mother inexplicably became ever more ill, took care of her with nearly zero help. I don't blame anyone for this. My half-brother lived in Texas where he had a full life—family, job, bills. My sister was married, had a baby, and was in need of not subjecting herself to Mother's mean, mean tongue. So it was just the two of us.

When my mother could no longer walk, I carried her to the bathroom. This was not an easy feat because the booze had turned her into a large woman. She would lean all of her dead weight against me and I'd sort of hurl us from wall to wall, holding on to her, trying to keep us both upright. Once we made it to the bathroom, I'd pull up her nightgown and pull down her panties and wait for her to do her business. When she was done, I'd wiped her ass. And then I'd haul her up off the toilet and our spastic dance would recommence as I tried to ferry her back to bed without injuring either of us. Eventually, she got so ill she could no longer stand. When she shit where she slept (she never slept in a bed again after the night my father died), I cleaned her. I cleaned the sheets. I cleaned the cushions. I cleaned her clothing. I confided in a down-the-hall neighbor who, as grace would have it, once worked as a nurse's assistant. She taught me the proper method of lifting Mother off the couch. When the kind neighbor magically rustled up a wheelchair, gratitude consumed me. At that point, all I had to do was lift Mother into and out of the chair and then onto and off of the toilet. Occasionally, she felt well enough to sit in the chair and stare out at the street two stories below. But when her eyes and skin turned yellow (she must have done her heaviest drinking when I was in class or sleeping), over her growling protests and with the consent of my sister, I called an ambulance.

She was in the hospital for one week. On my second visit on the second day—having caught a city bus to St. Joseph's Hospital—a young, eager, pretty nurse took me aside. In urgent tones, she told me about my mother's condition: the final stages of liver cirrhosis. No chance of survival.

I thanked her but asked no questions. She seemed flummoxed by my lack of hysteria, my calm demeanor. She must have thought I was a horrible daughter or a slow-witted one.

She said, "She is very sick. She is going to die. Do you understand?"

Four days later, I kissed my mother's forehead and told her I loved her.

Her green eyes flashed open, full of hate or anger or maybe both. She said, "You go to hell."

Those were the last words she spoke to me. *You go to hell.*

And now, faced with an apocalyptic disaster, all of this—my father's death, my mother's hide-and-seek cruelty, her final words to me, her death, Rane's death, Katie's death, Atticus' death, Carolyn's death, the deaths of relatives I will never even know existed, the possible death of the Gulf—seems to be part of the same ever-widening bruise. In my mind's eye I tattoo the green, and black, and blue contusion in neon red letters: ABANDON ALL HOPE, YE WHO ENTER HERE.

July 9, 2010, Day 81

I sit against the wall in a Japanese restaurant at JFK, waiting to catch my connector that will take me home. I am drinking a good chenin blanc. I ordered salmon sashimi—two pieces—and miso soup. When the miso arrives, I smell it, taking in the scent of seaweed and salt. For a moment my world tumbles and I am not in a bustling airside in one of the world's busiest airports. I am standing on the beach, gazing at the water. It is full of seaweed and attached to the seaweed are millions of translucent eggs.

Everything is going to be all right.

She is very sick. She is going to die. Do you understand?

No. I don't.

The waitress delivers the sashimi and immediately I am filled with guilt. I should not have ordered salmon. I should stick to carrots and cucumbers. Everything in the sea is embattled. Everything. But, still, I eat it, grateful. *Thank you, Lord, for the food we are about to receive, and for the nourishment to our bodies. For Christ's sake, Amen.* The old prayers never die, only the fish do. *Please, God, thank you for this fish. I hope it did not suffer.* Of course, it suffered, you ninny. *Take care of its spirit, please.* Just stop.

I have a three-hour layover, so I go to a French coffee shop, order *café au lait*, and check my email, which I pretty much ignored while in Vermont. A neighbor on the sandbar sent me a link to a CNN, Anderson Cooper segment. There stands Anderson, the lights of a small Louisiana town aglow behind him, saying the federal government has issued a new rule: No one—private citizens, the press, photographers, homeowners, business owners—are allowed within sixty-five feet of boom, oiled animals, oiled shorelines, and anything else related to the Macondo disaster.

Cooper says, "By now you're probably familiar with cleanup crews stiff-arming the media, private security blocking cameras, ordinary workers clamming up, some not even saying who they're working for because they're afraid of losing their jobs."

He says what those of us who are living through this nightmare have become accustomed to: BP denies time and again that they are anything other than transparent and then time and again block access to oiled sites. But, Cooper adds, the federal government has now joined the effort to make sure as few images as possible—and as little information as possible—reach the public.

He runs an ABC News video of Coast Guard Admiral Thad Allen insisting a mere month ago the media will have "uninhibited access anywhere we're doing operations except for two things: if it's a security or safety problem."

But thanks to the ruling, I can be charged with a Class D felony and hit with a $40,000 fine if I come within sixty-five feet of "any response vessel or booms out on the water or on the beach." Cooper—who appears to barely be keeping his cool—reports that initially the Coast Guard wanted the exclusion zone to be 300 feet. Sixty-five or 300—it doesn't matter to me. I'm in violation of the law simply because of the location of my home.

I'm well ahead of Cooper regarding what this means and the precedents for such an action. Before he can say anything about them denying the public access to what is really going on, I say under my breath, "See no evil, hear no evil, speak no evil."

Now I get it. BP's shenanigans aren't simply about controlling the narrative. I'm shocked that my naiveté prevented me from understanding the situation more fully until this moment. *See no evil, hear no evil, speak no evil.* Make the whole damn thing disappear. That's what the Corexit is all about. That's what the exclusion zones are all about. That's what the BP-generated misinformation is all about. Hell has broken loose, folks, but we're not going to allow you to see it. Because if you can't see it, you won't know The Truth. You won't know what a slip-shod job we're doing. You won't know we don't have a fucking clue how to stop Old Horrible. You won't know how badly we've damaged the environment. You won't know we are burning animals alive. If you don't know what we are doing and how bad it is, you won't be able to say shit. And neither will the courts.

This new policy and the prior behavior of restraining the media is the same card played during the Iraq War: You will not be shown images of the coffins being delivered to Dover Air Force Base so our soldiers' deaths will remain abstractions.

As Cooper points out, this new ruling also echoes what happened after Katrina when the media was denied access to dead bodies rotting in homes in New Orleans. If the images remain hidden and access is curtailed it means, " ... if we can't show what is happening, warts and all, no one will see what is happening and that makes it easy to hide failure and hide incompetence." Cooper sums up the situation with stark simplicity: "We are not the enemy."

I shut down my computer, pay my bill, leave the coffee shop, and stare at the arrivals/departures board. What a great homecoming. I'm going to be arrested.

When Bill picks me up at the Tallahassee airport, I do not ask about Old Horrible. I will be in the midst of it soon enough, might as well side step it while I can. So I chatter about the residency—all the things we did, the new friends I made. The respite was good for me. The immersion in words and books and ideas was healing. Except for the few times I fell off the wagon, I pretty much pretended the nightmare in the Gulf was a figment of my imagination. I run back through my memory bank—snatches of moments when I discussed it with colleagues or students. I think I kept my panic in check. I don't think they saw the real me, the one on the verge of spiritual and mental annihilation.

It's not until we're on Alligator Point Road and about to make the dogleg turn to the west that will lead us to what is always a breathtaking view: the shimmering blue Gulf stretched to our south, beyond the dunes, from here to that eternity we call the horizon, that I'm pulled back into the darkness. As if I'm picking my way through brambles newly sprouted in my mouth, I ask, "What kind of shape are the booms in?"

"It's a fucking mess. The high surf from Alex tangled them up. Half of them are on the shore."

"Crushing bird eggs and …."

"Yes."

My first night home and I am unable to sleep. Bill is snoring with the vigor of a contended, well-fed child. The dogs, too, are sound asleep and snoring. I try counting sheep and only end up wondering who thought up such a silly, ineffectual idea. I grow annoyed with the bleating, the counting, the happy sheep floating through the sky.

I throw back the covers and wander through my tiny shack. Despite The Troubles, as I've taken to calling the disaster, it feels good to be home, surrounded by my books, and bones, and other sweet talismans. I stand at my kitchen window and stare into the night. Heat lightning fires the horizon. It's so beautiful … energy igniting and reigniting, illuminating a thick bank of distant clouds. I think back to the wedding poem Rane wrote for us. What was that line about love? About how love needed you *to talk about thunderstorms, how lightning shines despite its danger?*

In the illuminated darkness, I slip on my flip-flops and grab the walking stick Bill made for me from some of the shack's original timbers. He decorated it with fringed leather and the wood is so fat with turpentine, he says it would burn fast and hard. Like the lightning out there.

I walk down my oyster shell drive and take odd comfort in the familiar sound of the shells crunching against each other and the sand. There is barely a breeze until I crest the dune and then a strong wind, faintly tinged with petroleum, roils in from the south. I walk westward, avoiding ghost crabs and direct contact with the water. Despite my world being contaminated with oil and Corexit, tonight I simply enjoy the moonlight that flickers in and out thanks to the drifting clouds. I enjoy the dark, dark sky and the astonishing blanket of stars that crowds the heavens. I enjoy the way the moonlight shimmers like liquid silver on the water's surface and the way night birds suddenly appear out of the dark only to quickly spiral back into it. I enjoy pretending paradise is not lost.

After about a half mile, I decide to turn back. I'm not anxious, simply cautious because no one knows where I am. But that kernel of rebellion I was born with leads me to know this won't be my last deep night wandering along the edge of the earth.

I turn and head toward the shack, but in my peripheral vision a shadow flashes. Something by the dune line. Probably just that spectral bobcat I forever imagine is haunting the Point. But maybe not. It's loping toward the Gulf with living intention. In this shifting darkness, I can't make out what or who it is. So I stand very still and grip my walking stick.

As it gets closer, the shadows recede and its shape comes into focus. Not a deer. Not a dog. Not a bear. Not a spectral bobcat.

Coyote.

I search the dunes. I don't see any others. No pack. Just a lone animal. This is a quintessential fight-or-flight situation, but I have the good sense to do neither. The coyote comes to within about twenty feet of me before stopping. It stares straight at me, as if sizing me up. I'm oddly calm. Fascinated, actually, I grip my stick tighter and think, *It won't be the worst death in the world,* which in retrospect is a funny, hapless observation. Having your limbs ripped off by a wild animal is by definition a horrible death. I do a free form calculation. Coyotes can run at up to forty-three miles per hour. I'm twenty feet away. If it wants to, the animal will be actively tearing me apart in a matter of seconds.

Its golden-yellow eyes seem to me to reflect a sense of curiosity, not hunger. The plains Indians often depict the coyote as a shape-shifter who takes on the appearance of a man. Without fail, the "man" does not behave well—drinks, cusses, womanizes—and generally wreaks havoc. But what if this is a man who has shape shifted into a coyote? Could this be an ancestor come to tell me something? I listen closely. All I hear is the wind and the surf. The coyote paws the sand. I let out a long, measured sigh. It cocks its head. And then, it runs. Back the way it came: up and over the dunes to I don't know where.

I refuse to skulk or furtively search the shadows. I feel determined, set on this notion: If I am afraid, I dishonor the animal spirit who just visited me.

This walk and all the others I will take in the middle of the night will remain my secret: the last unsullied bond I have with this place.

The rest of the summer drags on in what for me feels like a Corexit haze in which what we witness, what we know to be true, is denied by BP at every turn. Lies are part of our new normal.

Time Magazine reports that on July 7 oil is confirmed present in all five Gulf states. "Tests confirm that tarballs from the spill have washed up on the shores of Texas—meaning that every state in the Gulf region has been touched by the spill. Oil has also been found in Louisiana's Lake Pontchartrain." In the meantime, Tony Hayward—whose days at BP, it will soon become clear, are numbered—continues to deflect responsibility, saying essentially that others are to blame (Transocean most notably) and according to the *New York Times*, he purportedly told London colleagues, "What the hell did we do to deserve this?"

Aerial reconnaissance reveals oil sheen in near-shore waters of Franklin County. BP, without explanation, dismisses the photographic evidence as simply untrue.

Most days when I walk the shore, in addition to dead animals, I come across tarballs and sometimes reddish-brown splats on the sand—like giant bird poop—which I learn is weathered oil. I see a toddler run over to a splat and begin to stick her hand in it. I call out to the parents, "That's oil. She shouldn't be playing with it."

They look confused, as if I'm speaking a lost language, and then turn their backs to me.

I think about the coyote and am flooded by a sense of foreboding bordering on abandonment.

On a startling hot early July day, shortly after returning from Vermont, I ask Bill if any mail from BP or the government arrived while I was gone. He says no. I sift through the pile of envelopes on my desk. Nope. Nothing. So far, my claim has been ignored. I google "BP Claims" and find a recent CNNMoney report that might explain their unresponsiveness: "BP is becoming increasingly stringent with its demands for documentation from victims filing claims for lost wages and income in the Gulf region. Immediately following the spill, many initial payments were distributed in uniform amounts with minimum documentation based on estimates. Now, BP will make payments based on each claimants'3 documented losses."

That afternoon, I drive into Crawfordville to the Winn-Dixie. While standing in line with my cart of groceries, two men ahead of me get in a fistfight. Amid the flurry of well-placed punches, I miss the full gist of what the disagreement is about, but it boils down to one of them is working with BP and the other refuses. I think they're both right.

July 11, 2010, Day 83

I drive to the pint-size post office in Panacea to check my PO box. On the wall are two posters. One looks homemade, printed off a computer. On regular eight-and-a-half-by-eleven-inch paper, it lays out directions and rules for filing a claim with BP. Next to it is a large, full-color, professionally printed poster detailing how to turn in your neighbor or relative if you suspect they have or will make a false claim.

It's not enough to ruin the Gulf and its wildlife, now they are turning neighbor against neighbor, father against son.

When I get back to the shack, Bill and I go for a walk. It's Sunday afternoon and no one else is out here. The visitors have already left, high-tailing it back to their real lives in Tallahassee. Besides, it's not the prettiest of days. Overcast with a strong southerly wind. The stench of oil singes the air. The water is riled up and very dark with odd patches of rust. There are very few birds, just a smattering of sand pipers about twenty yards down the beach. As we stroll along, I tell Bill more of my residency adventures. I'm midway through a blow-by-blow account of the talent show when I stop dead in my tracks.

"What is this?" I look around. It's everywhere, from the shoreline to the high tide line.

"Holy shit." Bill lifts one foot, then the other.

"Is it?"

"Fuck."

We are up past our ankles in the thick, frothy poison.

"We have to get out of it," I say.

Bill points to a vacant house. "Let's go up that way and take the road back."

"We'll need to scrub down."

"Throw away our shoes."

It's a grim trek to the shack. We don't speak. Rather, we sink into our mutual sadness, each of us beyond words.

Why we are surprised is a mystery. The oil has been out here for days, weeks, months. Concentrations change, the form changes—sheen on water, tarballs on sand, and now mousse— but the fact of our situation doesn't change. We are living amid oil and dispersant: toxins all. The oil rages into the Gulf and the dispersant breaks it up into molecules so small, they enter the membranes of oysters, crabs, what have you. They have entered me, thus the glue ropes.

But about our surprise.

Is it a testament to hope that at this point in this calamity we can still be surprised? Perhaps, despite our best efforts and with purpose very much to the contrary, we have fallen victim to their trinity. *Hear no evil. See no evil. Speak no evil.* Maybe on some deep, delusional level, we believed the oil would never wash ashore here.

But now, the evil is covering our shoes, our ankles, our calves, our skin. We are immersed in evil.

Scrubbed clean to the point of redness, there is nothing left to do but wait. How many more hours, days, months, years, will Old Horrible keep spewing? Will The Troubles ever end? How long until the entire Gulf is dead?

I have learned that when waiting for the other shoe to drop, the best thing to do is go on with life.

So we do. I make a tortilla cake, something I create on the spot comprised of black beans and corn and cheese and onions and jalapeños layered between tortillas until it's about six inches tall and baked. We eat dinner in front of the TV. In the sickest of ways, watching the coverage feels nearly delicious. The spew-cam in the right-hand corner of the screen is nothing if not consistent: Old Horrible never takes a break. CNN runs footage of a pristine Florida beach. With calm confidence, without rebuttal or doubt, the talking head reports the government has announced there is no oil on any Florida beach.

"No oil?"

"What!" Bill raises his long arms to the heavens. He looks as if he has just been told his right hand will be amputated simply because.

I grab the remote. Turn off the TV. Tears are useless. Anger has no impact. Hopelessness ferries no light. I think of all that mousse. I reach for my wine. Equilibrium evades.

"Honey," I say, staring into the dark night, "looks like we've just gone down the rabbit hole."

July 12, 2010, Day 84

Come morning, I waste no time. Camera in-hand, I head to the beach to see if the oil mousse has abated or grown worse. In this upside down world, people who want us to believe nothing is wrong dismiss photographic evidence. Half-truths and obfuscations are their choice. My choices are: I'll still document, I'll still witness, I'll still tell the truth of this disaster even if my voice shakes.

I crest the dunes and immediately feel as though the rabbit hole just got weirder, deeper. Workers in white Hazmat suits are scooping up the mousse, the mousse that isn't present on any Florida beach. Some workers struggle to get it into bags. Others simply bury it while another crew spreads straw over it before attempting to rake it up and deposit it in an industrial garbage can. I cross down to the water and head in their direction. I want good, clear photos.

The workers glance up and then quickly look away, as though they are uncomfortable at my approach and are hoping I'll simply saunter on by. Not a chance. I don't want to pay a $40,000 fine, so stealth and speed are paramount. Despite the mousse, I close in fast but hear a commotion and look toward the dunes. A man in khakis and what I think is a company shirt is screaming at me but I cannot make out his words. I maintain my forward motion through the sand, through the mousse, but he takes off at a gallop.

I stop, lift the camera, bring him into focus. And then, just before I click the shutter I hear a voice. It's the same voice from my childhood, the one that maneuvered me to safety: "What the hell do you think you're doing?"

My cool demeanor evaporates. Hesitation is a reaction that in the right circumstance can get you killed. But that's what I do. I lower the camera. I stop thinking with my frontal lobe and instinct turns me towards home.

Do not let them jail you. Do not let them touch you. Do not let them catch you.

And I run.

On July 15, 2010, eighty-seven days after the Deepwater Horizon oil platform exploded in the Gulf of Mexico in an area approximately fifty miles southeast of the Mississippi Delta, BP announces a new containment cap is in place and is effectively staunching the oil flow. I turn on my computer and gaze at the spew-cam. Old Horrible is actually losing steam, gushing with less vigor.

I press my hand against the screen as if I can actually touch the weakening foment, but I jerk away, unable to banish a sensation of being burned. I hear the high cry of an osprey but I do not survey the sky. Rather, I study my palm, search for my lifeline.

I find none.

September 19, 2010

One hundred and fifty-two days after the explosion, I stand on my back porch and apply white paint to a diminutive carved wooden goddess. I feel her round, sturdy head and the holes I drilled where I will insert an array of twigs: a corolla rustic and merry. Using an arsenal of paint pens, I will endow her with red, Betty Boop lips and a proper bob. On the reverse side, I will write, "I want to dance with you inside the delicate heart of the moon."

I set her in the sun to dry her base coat and as I'm reaching for my sketchpad, the top of the hour NPR newscast wavers from the kitchen radio, snagging my attention. BP claims the well is completely sealed. The disaster, they declare, is officially over.

Standing amid a pile of ten unpainted goddesses and their curly detritus of shavings, I feel no joy, no sense of celebration or resolution, because I fear for me the disaster may never be over. And what is more troubling, it may never be over for the Gulf.

I lean on the railing where a hummingbird once tried to feed on my wild head of hair. I study the bay. The water still looks dark, heavy, unnatural. A horrible truth slams into me. The thousands of birds, dolphin, and turtles that washed ashore dead or dying are but a fraction of the true tally. Most of the animals died at sea, to never be seen by the humans who helped create the mess and those who had nothing to do with it. They died in an oil/dispersant hell and drifted to the bottom of a silent sea.

Or, they were burned alive, incinerated in the season of rebirth.

Hear no evil, see no evil, speak no evil.

I watch a white cloud morph into a dragon and then a fat dog. Finally, a bear. I'm surprised that a rare, happy childhood memory pierces my consciousness: my mother and I lying on a madras spread at the beach, watching the sky, naming the ever-changing shapes, their appearance substantial, but in truth clouds are nothing more than a gathering of water droplets.

Today, the dragon, the dog, the bear, break apart, replaced by a pod of dolphins swimming through the heavens. For some reason this fanciful notion provokes a wicked recall. In June, Mac McClelland reported for *Mother Jones* on what he saw at Isle Grande Terre, Louisiana. A BP cleanup contractor warned him to not take any photos. He soon understood why. Approximately sixty dolphins swam nearby, blowing oil out of their blowholes.

Despite my best efforts, I imagine the cloud dolphins doing likewise. *No, no, no.* I close my eyes. When I reopen them, I am left staring into an empty sky.

I return to my sketchpad but I do not give my pencil-scrawled goddess pouty lips or a bob. From her eyes, I draw a tear. My crying goddess. My bereft goddess. My forsaken goddess.

Yet, still, this remains: the moon's delicate heart.

The New Year yields little in the way of hope but rituals, the daily business of living, tethers us to some semblance of sanity.

Bill leaves everyday pre-dawn and drives fifty miles to Tallahassee, swerving to miss bear, bobcat, fox, raccoon, armadillo, and deer. That much hasn't changed.

I get up every morning, feed the dogs, slip into clothes and sunscreen, and walk the beach. That, too, hasn't changed.

But my joy is gone, my sense of wonder pummeled into submission, my religion—the sacred pursuit and immersion in Mother Nature—dead.

As 2011 dawns, the northern Gulf coast is an oiled wasteland where dolphins give birth to dead babies, where a beach stroll becomes a nightmare studded with dead marine life, and where dead turtles are spray painted neon orange as a signal they are to be retrieved as evidence, but in reality, no one comes for them. They fester and rot under the hot sun. No respect in life. No respect in death.

The thick ropes of mucous in my mouth persist, worsen. Sometimes while I'm talking, the build-up is so intense, my words become garbled and I have to excuse myself. Brushing doesn't help. Listerine doesn't help. Drinking copious amounts of water doesn't help. Decongestants don't help. Over the past few months, I've developed a persistent cough. It's just allergies, just allergies, I tell myself. But in the middle of the night I often wake up, gasping for air, feeling as if even in consciousness I'm being pulled into a dark well devoid of redemption, for life is redemption, life is the pulse beat—the proof—that this earth, this universe, this thing we call the cycle of life—is God.

And then I know what I spend much of my waking hours denying. My sandbar is poisoned. My Gulf is poisoned. The life here where all those broken bones of my violent past were healed is poisoned.

It is early March 2011, and an unusually calm spring is dawning. After all, death brokers no sound.

Indeed, we live amid death with the same intensity we once lived amid life abundant, scribbling down that day's losses—*two turtles, three baby dolphin, large fish/species unknown, nothing is eating the corpses, the animals detect the toxins?*—monitoring the Internet and the media for information on what is happening out there in the calamitous Gulf waters. A friend sends me a *Vanity Fair* article that starkly lays out what is known, what is suspected. It was written last August, after the well was capped, and clearly intimates the worst is yet to come. After detailing the horrific effects the disaster has had on marine life, Alex Shoumatoff writes, "So the crisis isn't over, as BP and the government would have you believe. It's only beginning. The biological consequences of this disaster will be felt for years, over generations, like Chernobyl. And we may never know how bad it was."

I wander out to my back deck, four dogs at my heels, perch on top of the picnic table, and gaze at Alligator Bay. I watch and I watch and I watch some more. I know this bay. I know its moods, how it can zip from calm to roiled in an eye blink, how the currents—just like the Gulf's loop current—control what goes where, thus to my amazement delivering to my sandy shore the contents of the overturned kayak, even minutia such as Bill's Chapstick. I know come nightfall, if this disaster had never taken place, the water would be far from silent. Rather, it would scintillate with a large cast of characters invigorated by the night, including spider starfish, shark, and multiple varieties of crabs—horseshoe to stone. I know that by day and night the shallow waters offer relatively safe haven to the newly born. Yes, I sit and I wait and I wait. And what I'm waiting for—what once occurred with the rapidity of popping corn—does not happen. Two hours pass and not a single mullet jumps. This can mean only one thing: They aren't here. The prevailing theory is that mullet jump to clear their gills of mud. From personal observation, I know they almost always jump in sets of three. *Boing, boing, boing!* Are the mullet dead? Have they moved on to untainted water? *We may never know how bad it was* ... I scan the sky. There are no ospreys. No mullet *ergo* no ospreys.

The connections are real, vital. And once a connection is broken, there are consequences all the way down the food chain. Maybe the ospreys have moved on with the mullet. Maybe they're in Tampa or Sarasota or Key West. Maybe they'll be back next year. Maybe. Maybe this situation mirrors in some ways the environmental calamity that unfolded in this country post World War II when chemicals were all the rage and DDT was *de rigueur.* DDT thinned the eggshell walls of ospreys and eagles to the point that when the parent birds—avian incubators—sat on the nests, the eggs cracked under the parental weight. Evil made manifest: A parent nurtures its unborn, does everything right, yet kills its offspring thanks to a poison humans rolled out all in the pursuit of green lawns. Maybe, if I'm right about why birds and coons aren't picking at the beached corpses of oiled animals, the ospreys have flown the coop in search of clean food. Or, maybe, this new absence—this new silence—is the new normal.

Maybe. Maybe. Maybe. Or, *We may never know how bad it was.*

My life has become a puzzle composed of What I Know Because I Observe It With My Eyes, What Scientists Whose Studies Aren't Paid for By BP Say, What BP Says, What Scientists and Universities Funded by BP Say, and What the Government Says. Bitter experience has taught me to trust only what my eyes see and what independent scientists say. As part of my ever-expanding sense of betrayal, I've come to accept an absolute: The petroleum giant never says anything that jibes with What I Know to Be True.

On March 18, 2011, Dave Rainey, a BP executive heading up its Gulf Oil Restoration Organization, conducts a Facebook chat during which he says in reference to the unprecedented number of dolphin stillbirths and dead adult dolphins, burned, oiled, and otherwise, "Everyone in BP is concerned about these media reports …."

Sitting in the stench of the same pajamas I've been wearing for ten days, I scream at the computer screen, "You're concerned about media reports? What about the dolphins?"

My notoriously low blood pressure is on the rise. I can feel my pulse thumping in my right temple.

He refers to the deaths as "stranding incidents" and essentially says they happen all the time, ticking off five years in which he claims there were massive dolphin deaths. He ignores the fact that the numbers are much larger now and are not spread out over an extended period of time. A death toll that might have been spread across a span of twelve months is happening in a week. He also ignores the fact that stillborn dolphin calves are a new, post-Deepwater Horizon phenomenon and are not "strandings." He blames the dolphin deaths on everything except oil and Corexit, even the ones who wash ashore covered in it. He muses viral infections or "naturally occurring neurotoxins in the water."

"If they have infections, it's because you have fucked with their immune systems, you freaking criminal."

How can I still be incredulous after all these months? And what does Corexit and oil do when mixed with naturally occurring neurotoxins?

"We aren't your freaking science experiment," I type into the comment box. And then I delete it. Because that fact is we *are* their science experiment. Every single one of us. Fish of the sea, bird of the sky, and resident of the shore: I believe they view us as unintentional case studies, studies they aim to distort, silence, bury.

I think back to those turtle bones that kept rising through the sand for nearly a year, how day-after-day, more of them appeared, gleaming talismans, hints to a life. It was as if even in death, the turtle wanted its existence recognized, honored. I type into the comment box, then erase it, then pray it: May the truth be known.

On March 27, 2011, I sit at my computer, my hair a mess, my hygiene asunder, obsessing over my destroyed world. Armed with dark chocolate and hot tea, I Google "dead dolphins BP." The ghoulish nature of most of my Internet searches no longer rattles me. I'm resigned to this new reality, hardened on the edge of bitterness.

In an article for *Digital Journal* titled, "Obama administration restricts findings on Gulf's dead dolphins," Lynn Herrman writes, "The Obama administration has issued a gag order on data over the recent spike of dead dolphins, including many stillborn infants ... and scientists say the restriction undermines the scientific process."

One biologist, speaking to Reuters on the condition of anonymity, insists the government's gag order " ... throws accountability right out the window. We are confused and ... we are angry because they claim they want teamwork, but at the same time they are leaving the marine experts out of the loop completely."

But another biologist involved in the testing program claims, "We are treating the evidence, which are the dolphin samples, like a murder case."

Like a murder case ... yes.

I will turn off the computer soon. I will anoint myself in the usual balm of sunscreen and lip-gloss. I will don a wide-brimmed hat, a sheer long sleeve blouse, a peasant skirt, and Jackie O dark glasses. I will look like a scrubbing bubble on the move. I will not take the dogs because the beach is contaminated. I will pause at the arbor covered in star jasmine and will sniff deeply for the blooms are fragrant and alive with the balletic movement of bees and hummingbirds. I will walk over the dunes, noticing the wild flowers are brilliant this year and that the Monarchs, among other butterfly species, are dining on them, gaining sustenance that will gird them for whatever comes next. I will make my way down to the shore and stroll westward. I will whisper to myself everything is okay, nothing is as dire as it seems; my world hasn't become a coffin crowded with death and the deceit of the rich. And that is when I will see it. I will run along the shore, tripping in the folds of my skirt, slogging through the surf, transforming into Woman Who is a Wild Mess and On a Mission. I will drop to my knees. I will think, *I can save it.* This will be redemption. I will save one life. This one life will matter. It will be The Symbol. But no. Instead, I will wail. And the wind will carry my anguish to places I have never been. The baby dolphin will fit in the crook of my arm. It will die there, nearly weightless, as if the lightness of its being reflects the new Truth: Its life, our lives, mean nothing.

Its silver gray body, already violated by greed, which let's be honest, is what caused the oil spill, will be violated again: stained with a spray-painted neon orange X, which will move it from the category of Sacred Creature to Evidence in a Murder Case to Evidence Never Retrieved in a Murder Case.

I will grieve for the baby dolphin with the fierceness of the righteous. I will mutter prayers, incantations, curses. I will see in my mind's eye a mother dolphin give birth to a nearly dead calf. I will watch her watch her baby float away in the current. I will imagine I'm bleeding internally when I think of her somewhere out there, wandering aimlessly in the stained waters of the Gulf.

Bill and I sit on our back deck amid a nearly lifeless and all-suffering spring. The Gulf's deep-sea reefs are dead and no fish are to be found among them. Tuna, shrimp, oyster, and crab populations are decimated. Fishermen routinely haul in various species of fish that are covered in lesions and suffering from fin rot. Scientists are discovering the fish have diseased ovaries and livers. Infections in fish and marine mammals, due to compromised immune systems, are rampant. Rumors whispered in grocery lines, over yard fences, and Internet chat rooms center on the eroding health of fishermen who went out into the Gulf, into the oil, and tried to contain it. The same rumors apply to people who swam in the toxic brew: respiratory problems, lesions, immune systems awry, and in some cases death. There is no central Truth because BP continues to obfuscate, the government continues to shadow box, and scientists need time to study, assess, conclude. This isn't like a disaster movie in which the answers are discovered in two hours and the problems neatly solved. This is real life and the answers will take decades. Recovery? Maybe never.

Bill reaches over and takes my hand in his. I know he is worried and that he doesn't know how to lift me out of what is becoming a persistent fugue state occasionally dotted with beige variations. Today I am a Collapsed Scrubbing Bubble, drinking wine, clearing gluey-stuff out of my mouth, trying to get a full breath, slumped. I haven't taken a shower in twelve days. And my husband hasn't mentioned it. My curly hair is becoming matted, impenetrable. Can dreadlocks be far away? I don't know and don't care.

"We don't want to be twenty-year case studies," he says. There it is. Again. His favorite line. But in this silent twilight, it takes on deeper hues.

"I know."

He rubs my arm and then pets it, like I'm one of the dogs. I don't mind. What I mind is what I know is going to come next.

"I think it's time."

"Probably."

My mind is as lithe as a concrete block. Where is my ability to be a chrysalis? My innate proclivity for reinventing myself in the face of terror? The Collapsed Scrubbing Bubble takes out a tiny chisel and begins to chip away. Flakes of concrete turn to dust, enter my bloodstream ... my home, this place I fled to, this place I dragged the living memory of my father to, is destroyed. I know The Others think differently. They don't see how the water moves more heavily, as if weighted down with fossils. They will say of our current state of decay, "Oh, what a shame!" as they dip their lesion-tatted shrimp into red sauce. They will say, "Look at the beautiful sunset," while they cast no eye on the corpse of the dolphin calf now putrefying on the sand. The Others will do as BP orders: *see no evil, speak no evil, hear no evil.* But it's okay. I suppose everyone has to find their own way to survive.

"I can't sell a book right now," I say.

"I know."

"I can't write fast enough. And even if I could, nothing is selling."

"I know."

"I have two friends whose book contracts were canceled. That's how bad things are now. And the publishers are demanding their advances back."

This time Bill doesn't speak. He squeezes my hand harder than the first time. I feel the swell building. Those tremulous tears. The Collapsed Scrubbing Bubble threatens them with her chisel. *Don't you dare!*

"It's not about books, baby."

I wait until the light has dimmed by a degree or two. The slightest change in light alters the sandbar, recreates this small rise of land into itself and something new. "I know." I look around for the dogs. They are scattered like giant leaves across the length of the deck. Ulysses stands guard at the entrance to the yard. Perhaps he's remembering his awesome encounter with Bond. I call him over. I pet his head. I look into his Ernest Borgnine eyes. I see reflected in them the love I believe my father held for me.

"Sweetheart," I say, cupping his head in my hands. I don't utter the rest of my thought because if I did, the Collapsed Scrubbing Bubble and I would burst. But I don't have to say the words out loud because Ulysses reads minds: *I think it's time to go home.*

St. Augustine shines. The horse carriages bear more flowers. Some are even painted pink in order to raise breast cancer awareness. Castillo de San Marco looks smaller, as if it has shrunk in the salt air. The Bridge of Lions is brand spanking new: an exact replica of the original 1927 bridge. On the hour and half-hour, it draws open and elegant sailing ships glide through. It seems to me the old town is less apologetic about its rich history. *Here we are! We are the oldest city in the United States and proud of it. Take that, Jamestown!*

The intersection where the Klan confronted the civil rights protestors in the 1960s has been renamed Andrew Young Crossing. There is a monument in the *Plaza de la Constitución* honoring The Freedom Riders. That same plaza retains the obelisk honoring St. Augustine's Civil War dead.

St. George Street, a long ago lazy little byway my grandmother and I often strolled down together, threading our way through what my memory tells me were nearly constant archeological digs, is now crowded with tourists seeking bawdy T-shirts and cheap trinkets.

The rivers are still beautiful, as is the Atlantic Ocean. The surfers still surf and the sunbathers still bathe. It's all a little more difficult to see because coastal development did not stop in the twenty years I've been gone. In fact, if it weren't for the state park system, untouched dune systems wouldn't exist.

I walk the ancient streets and admire the old walled Spanish homes. In some ways, it feels as if I've never left. I don't feel my father's presence as strongly as I feel my grandmother's. Some days I feel as if I'm that little pale girl, my hand tucked in her dark-skinned palm, roaming, seeking memories.

In the cool of the day, I go for long walks along the ocean. I kneel down and try to see the coquina with the same wonder I held as a child, but now I need my eyeglasses. I gaze past the breakers to the far horizon and try to imagine African shores. I walk slowly across the raised pathway that takes me over the dunes, making note of gopher holes, snake tracks, wild flowers. I practice careful observation of my known world. It's what I do. I see the color gradations in the white and orange sand. I see the light piercing the apex of a turquoise wave. I see the golden slippers of the snowy egret and the black plume of the great blue heron. I see turtle nests and the signs that mark them. I see that sunlight changes the color of everything, depending on its opacity, its angle, its dance with the clouds.

I see my father hold out his hand to me, and I take it.

I'm not sure how I survived those last few months on the sandbar. In those final days, every morning I opened my eyes, fully cognizant to the new reality, and before I even tossed back my covers, I felt everything break: bones, heart, hope.

It's a miracle, really, that we sold the shack, even if it was for a pittance.

But I knew it was a necessary act, no matter the sale price. I could not continue to live amid the destruction. I did not have the strength of character or the stubbornness of mind to say, "This is my home and even though you have poisoned it beyond repair, you won't take it from me." Nor did I possess the privileged, desperate, blind sight of The Others, the only form of blindness that would make staying on the sandbar a viable option.

I close my eyes in order to see. Gauguin's trick no longer worked for me.

So, yes, we did the unthinkable. We sold my beloved shack by the sea, the place of healed bones and realized dreams. And then I did what I've always done in moments of great crisis: I moved home.

Whisper the magic word: *Whoosh.*

If there is a hero in this part of the tale, it is Bill. He handled the closing of the house—the packing, the getting rid of, the saying goodbye. He took care of everything, shipping me off to St. Augustine to housesit for old friends who once owned St. Augustine's legendary independent bookstore, The Booksmith. They closed the store many years ago and the locals are still mad about, still miss it. But Bob and Diana Smith's lovely house on a salt marsh was a gentle and needed reintegration to the east coast. Alone except for Scout, my aging schipperke, I watched the sun rise, the sun set, the wood storks roost in the pine snag, mullet jump, the tide ebb and flow. I tried to regain my bearings.

I tried not to think about all I had lost. But when I sat on the back deck at bullbat time and gazed at the egret and heron fishing the marsh, I could not cobble together what my future in St. Augustine might look like.

Maybe that's because I never said goodbye to my sacred place. I just got in the car and drove toward the Atlantic. And I suspect I will never say goodbye, that I will stoke my memories of the sandbar and its abundant waters pre-disaster with the same devotion with which my mother recited the rosary long after she had abandoned her vows. Perhaps sanctity does not exist without memory.

My friend Flynn, long returned from his spiritual journey to New Mexico, welcomes me home with the grace and humor of a man who knows when not to ask questions. He simply accepts me back into the fold, into our friendship, as if I had not been gone for twenty years.

Bill and I rent a bungalow Flynn owns in Lincolnville. My neighbors are the Eubanks, a family who were foot soldiers in the civil rights movement. And though they helped shape and drive St. Augustine's struggle for civil rights, their courage came at a great cost. They suffered horrible brutality at the hands of the Klan and their lackeys—beatings, harassment, and false murder charges, which were eventually dropped for lack of evidence. Given the racial climate of the time (Rev. Martin Luther King famously said St. Augustine was "the most lawless city I've ever seen"), the judge's decision to dismiss the trumped up murder charges seems miraculous. Joe and Solomon Eubanks live across the street. We have become friends. I feel as though I live among heroes.

Still, the adjustment from sandbar to city is rocky. While I am grateful to have landed back in the womb, on my feet, still swinging, I feel disconnected. The profundity of the disconnection leaves me wondering about alienation, spiritual and otherwise. What is my life's purpose? Where do I sit down to gaze at the sky? What do I do at low tide? Walk the city streets? Where are the bears? When will the wind shift, carrying with it both the surf song and the scent of the sea?

When I first stepped into the bungalow, I burst into tears. The sea shack was filled with light. I could open all of its windows and doors and there would be no separation from the sky, the sea, the sand. The bungalow, almost by definition, is dark. It's old and cranky, which I like, but most of the windows don't open and there are no screens. It is a precious but borrowed gem. This will always be Flynn's house. Bill and I are its caretakers until the next chapter, which I cannot begin to perceive.

I am unpacking boxes, putting books on shelves. I run across a large, blue hardcover book with mostly blank pages ... an old sketchbook. As I reach up to slide it onto the shelf, a flurry of paper rains down. I pick one up. Then another. And another. My eyes mist and my heart cleaves: one side aglow in reminiscence, the other bloated with grief. My little maps, the ones I sketched twenty years ago during my early days on the sandbar! There's the pathway to the chickee. There's the road with the dogleg turn. There's the beach and Phipp's Preserve. There's the entire property: the Coloney's house and mine. There's the long-gone KOA. They are all here except for the ones I drew on my palms. I remember the horrible ache I felt when I washed them away. Now I know. The aching was a window into my future. I gather up the maps and carry them to the kitchen. I shuffle them into a pleasing order and then crush them into a single ball. I set the ball in the sink. I rummage in the junk drawer until I find a lighter. I set the ball of maps on fire. I am that little girl living in a roach-infested trailer burning her poems and stories. Why? Why? Why now and why these maps?

Things change. And others don't. Flynn remains in his charming, historic wood frame home built in the 1700s. He is still larger than life, parties breaking out spontaneously wherever he goes. He still welcomes friends and strangers with a sweet hug and a glass of brown liquor. New Mexico did, indeed, heal him. He is in a happy, committed relationship with a fine, fine man.

Annie sold her beachfront home and moved to the quiet splendor of the St. John's River. She is older now, with the attendant pains that come with age, but her blue eyes are still bright, still shine with hard earned independence. When I speak to her about the need for isolation, she instinctively understands. Some of us aren't made for cities.

Four years after the disaster, I lose my final human connections to Alligator Point. Anne Coloney passes away in an assisted living facility. Six months later, almost to the day, Wayne Coloney dies of lung cancer, a disease that was diagnosed near the time of his wife's death, his wife of sixty-four years. The official cause of his passing is an empirical fact. But like many empirical facts, it belies a deeper, harder, more mysterious truth. A broken heart can be just as fatal as lung cancer.

It doesn't matter how many hours I spend walking the Atlantic shoreline, studying its moods, its power, its capacity to bear life, I remain unmoved. I see a pod of dolphins and, yes, the sight thrills me, but immediately—like an injection of heroin straight into the vein—I flash on the baby dolphin that dies while resting in the curve of my arm. I worry—knee-bending worry. *How are the Gulf's dolphin now? Can they breathe given whatever damage has been done to their bodies? Do they continue to develop cancers thanks to the toxic waters? Do their unborn continue to die in the womb?*

I cast halting glances at sea turtle nests and only quickly scan news articles about local turtle crawls. I wonder, of course, what is happening to the turtles whose eggs were transferred from the Gulf's oiled sands to these Atlantic shores? Where did those hatchlings go? Were they so confused they swam aimlessly to their deaths, or were their compasses strong, confident, unerring?

We will never know.

I am an environmental refugee. I fled my home in order to reclaim my mental, physical, and spiritual health. I search Ulysses' clouding eyes—yes, my canine protector grows old—looking for some glint of my father's spirit. Rather than being amused at my flight of fancy—*of course this dog is not my father reincarnated*—I feel unhinged, as if the memory of my father is fading, the teardrop in my heart evaporating, and I have to do something to regain the urgency of love.

Western science—from Sigmund Freud to Elisabeth Kübler-Ross—has approached grief analytically, as if grieving is a sterile, quantifiable process. According to Kübler-Ross, the orderly, logical stages an aggrieved person goes through are denial, anger, bargaining, depression, and acceptance. Eastern philosophy, however, sees grief as a narrative process, something that is messy, that ebbs and flows, that contains flashbacks and foreshadowing.

The Eastern view makes much more sense to me. Sometimes my grief over losing my sacred place is omniscient: I experience several Kübler-Ross stages simultaneously. Other times, I fall into a flashback and experience anger over and over again. Sometimes, I project the narrative into the future and I glimpse a life that is hopeful and happy.

I can't stop telling the story of the Gulf tragedy because storytelling is how I work my way through the scary, dark passages of grief. However, there is one stage that will, I suspect, forever escape me: acceptance. Being hopeful and happy doesn't mean I accept what happened in the Gulf. Being hopeful and happy doesn't mean I can't be that old Greek woman the village hires to wail at funerals. Being hopeful and happy doesn't mean all these words that comprise the many pages of this book aren't actually a lamentation for all we lost, for all we might never regain.

Still, I must focus. Believe in the old poem. It is, after all, a psalm:

Hope is that thing with feathers / That perches in the soul.

For the entire twenty years I lived at Alligator Point, I believed the heron lovebirds that made their home in the sentinel oak by the bay were the same pair. They were always there, always taking care of each other, always an immense source of comfort to me, balm to my imagination and heart.

Yesterday, I read that the record for the longest-lived heron is twenty-three years and that their average lifespan is fifteen years. So, in all probability, my love-herons were actually a series of birds that simply had the good sense to roost in the big tree.

But then again, I have witnessed pure enchantment more than once on the sandbar. Maybe they are the same pair: ancient, sacred spirits watching over an ancient, sacred place.

That is what I choose to believe. I see them in my mind's eye. They are standing in the shallows, tranquil and majestic, calm and wise, waiting for this good world to heal.

It's a fine late winter day in St. Augustine. The jasmine blooms redolent and vibrant. Birds are feathering their nests. Baby squirrels chase each other along the canopy of an ancient oak that grows in my front yard. The occasional butterfly wafts by. I take a break from reading student manuscripts and venture out to the mailbox. When I see what looks like official correspondence from a federal court in Louisiana, I tear it open.

The letter says I have been identified as someone who possibly suffered financial losses as a result of the Deepwater Horizon oil spill. It urges me to file a claim by the mid-summer deadline. Tax returns, financial statements, and more will be required.

I stand in the bright light of a strengthening Florida sun and wonder how many people received this same letter. How many people, like me, actually already filed a claim but never received a response? Why me and why now?

I don't want your fucking money. I just want my life back.

A friend who is an attorney urges me to file again. He says he will help me with the paperwork. He says it's important, that BP affected my livelihood and, therefore, should offer recompense. I think it over. If I thought like an accountant, I would realize I lost money when I sold the sea shack. St. Augustine's wages, because this is a tourist town, are abysmal. Teaching is not a lucrative job. Bill and I both need dental work. My old van, essentially, gasps and farts as it chugs down the highway. We are stuck. Yes, we could sure use the money.

So. I try. I open my filing cabinet and retrieve my tax returns. I download forms from the claim center's website. I even begin. Name, address, occupation, social security number. That's about as far as I get before it all comes crashing back, a tsunami of grief.

Filing the claim means reliving the nightmare. It's not worth it. Bill and I will find a way.

When I returned to St. Augustine, I made the same decision I've made every time I've come home: I am never leaving again.

But as I write these words, it is April 20, 2015: the fifth anniversary of the Deepwater Horizon BP disaster. Though I am on the Atlantic coast, clearly I left my heart, my sense of wellbeing, my understanding that God is to be found in nature abundant, on the sandbar, the place where nature enveloped me and I it.

Four months ago, six years into our marriage, Bill and I decided to do something we'd never done before: go on a honeymoon. We decided on a place that worked its way into my heart as I stood on the white, unsullied sands of Alligator Point two decades ago: the Yucatan.

We traveled through lush jungles, picturesque coastal villages, ancient Maya cities painted marigold, and the Spanish colonial jewel of Merida. We made friends. We drank tequila and watched the moon rise over the southern Gulf, a part of the sea that had previously existed for me only in the deep, unknowable blue of the horizon. We saw the beautiful, jewel-toned *motmot* bird with its tail naked except for the celebratory explosions of feathers at its tip. We sat on our balcony at *Hotel Villa de Pescadores* in the biosphere reserve of Rio Lagartos and watched all manner of sea birds soar and glide: osprey, pelican, frigate bird, gull, piper. In the distance, flamingos fed in the shallows.

Sitting there amid the calls of birds on the wing, something happened to me, something that had escaped me for nearly five years: I felt at peace. I felt as if all was not lost, after all. I felt the tug of my ancestors and I knew my mother and father would have loved this place. I knew what Bill meant when he gazed out at the water and said nearly exactly what my nephew said about Alligator Point fifteen years ago: "This is a good world."

Here, in the sweet St. Augustine bungalow we've called home for four years, the disaster remains a daily reality for me. My computer screen is filled with images and news articles about the fifth anniversary. I hound social media, trying to get people to agree to turn off their lights for five minutes at 9:45 p.m. Eastern Standard Time in order to reflect on the disaster five years out and to remember the eleven men who lost their lives. As I convince and cajole, something new takes shape within me … an innate knowledge I cannot shake: We might walk the rest of our days in the shadow of the disaster, but it won't control us.

Soon, Bill and I will return to the Yucatan, not to visit, but to live.

There is a ranch fifty miles from the sea that overlooks the jungle. I dream about it. Bill and I plan what additions we'll make, how we will care for the land, how we will nurture a place that is wholly foreign to us yet feels like home even from this far distance. When I planned our honeymoon trip, I asked the universe to give me just one look at a *motmot*. We saw it in a thick stand of trees at the ranch. The person with us, an expat from England who has lived for many years in the Yucatan, was as excited as I. She said they are very secretive birds, rarely making themselves seen. I know a sign from the universe when it hits me over the head.

Francisco, the ranch's caretaker, told us he had seen only baby rattlesnakes and boa constrictors on the property, as if this should give me confidence that no harm would befall us. But babies don't travel alone. Mamas are always nearby. And if, perchance, while living in the jungle I see a boa or a jaguar or a monkey or an anteater or any of the other animals that make the Yucatan home, I believe my joy will rival what I felt that winter day in 1994 when I first saw the mirage that is the sandbar rising out of cerulean waters.

But the ranch isn't set in stone. We have lots of options. For instance, there is a lovely beach house in a sparsely populated area just outside a village named Chicxulub. There, I could again watch the stars unfurl across a black, black sky. I could swim in water the color of jade, the color of turquoise, the color of light. I could feel the salt air on my skin and breathe deeply again. I could live amid the surf song once more.

Whoosh.

Scientists believe an asteroid struck the Yucatan near the present day site of Chicxulub and that the impact is, in all likelihood, responsible for the extinction of the dinosaurs (yet it spared the ancestors of what would become our present day sea turtles). The Chicxulub crater is 120 miles in diameter. Gravity anomalies exist—both highs and lows—throughout the crater. The asteroid, which was nearly six miles wide, struck the area 65.5 million years ago.

Was this moment, this great impact, the initial event that pushed us down the destructive path of fossil fuel consumption? Undoubtedly. No dead dinosaurs, no oil.

Will my moving to the Yucatan do anything to right a world drunk on fossil fuels, one in which an elite group of people get wealthier and wealthier while the world burns? No.

But I believe it will set my spirit straight.

I have come to the conclusion my business with the Gulf isn't yet finished. Perhaps it's just revving up. In the Yucatan, I can walk along the beaches where the Kemp's ridley sets out on their journey north and I will pray the Gulf has recovered enough health to not poison them. I can visit the monarch forest and see the butterflies gathering there in the *oyamel* firs in great cathedral-winged conclaves. I can feed hummingbirds, fattening them up before their great migration north. By heading south, I complete my circle. I will understand the Gulf, its creatures, it challenges with greater clarity. I am my own sea turtle, finding the right shore.

And, perhaps, I am also entering a global hot spot of environmental destruction and change. But maybe I'm supposed to. Maybe that's my role in this life: witness-bearer, chronicler, storyteller, truthsayer. After all, my time on the Point helped me regain my voice. I'm not going to shut up now.

At a recent literary event, I met a woman who is married to a high-ranking BP executive. I was weirded out but not surprised. *Creatures with wings can end up almost anywhere.* What did surprise me, however, was her response to my reading from this memoir. She reportedly told others in attendance I just needed to get over it. *Get over it.* How does one do that? How does one survive the destruction of her Godhead?

Not by getting over it but by never letting the world forget.

When I wrote my essay for *UnspOILed*, just months prior to the explosion, I typed into my browser the term "oil spill Gulf of Mexico" and got 166,000 hits. Today I did the same thing and got 4,570,000 hits.

Lest we forget.

These are the men who died: Jason Anderson, Aaron Dale "Bubba" Burkeen, Donald Clark, Stephen Ray Curtis, Gordon Jones, Roy Wyatt Kemp, Karl Kleppinger Jr., Keith Blair Manuel, Dewey A. Revette, Shane M. Roshto, Adam Weise. Speak their names out loud.

When I leave St. Augustine it will be for the third time. I've made peace with the leaving. In the wake of the oil disaster, I needed to come home. I needed to walk the ancient cobblestone streets, to feel the Atlantic breeze on my face. I needed to see the big water, even if it was cordoned off from easy view by miles of hotels and condominiums. I needed to come home and rest, lick my wounds.

But I have come to realize St. Augustine is just that for me: a stopover where I regain my bearings. It's not where I stay. Ever.

Bill and I will soon head south. Coastal life, village life, jungle life, ranchero life, or Merida life: We don't know; maybe, eventually, a combination of all five. What we're certain of is our dreams these days are filled with wild birdcalls and *casas* the color of the sea and a sky that looks both tranquil and untamed. Indeed, Bill and I have fallen into a new habit. We take Sunday drives, just like my parents once did, but we take ours on the Internet. We pull up Google maps, randomly choose a Yucatan road, and go for a virtual jaunt, visiting villages, seeing the countryside, window-shopping as we pass houses and huts.

We dream.

Yesterday, Bill asked me where my heart wanted to land in the Yucatan—village, city, jungle, or seaside.

"I don't know," I said. "All the choices sound so good." And then I added, trying to pin down The Truth, "I'm trying to be an adult about it."

Our intentions are firm and our reasons are clear: The move is an attempt to evolve, to learn, to reengage with the natural world, to immerse ourselves in a foreign land so we might grow, to converse with people whose language sounds like a song.

To this extent, our future is knowable: We will pack up the dogs and the cat, Bill will gather his tools, I will box up books and cookery. I will tuck the memory of my father deep inside my heart and carry him with me. I think I will even gather together the tattered images I possess of my mother. I will recreate her into the best version of herself, the one she never had a chance to show the world. I'll do that for my father, too. Yes, I will put them back together. I will, with sacred intention, attempt to forgive them their faults and remember their strengths. I will work hard at understanding their love. By allowing my imagination to complete them, they and their youngest child might heal.

It's inevitable. One day soon I will slip my hand into Bill's. I will look him in the eye. I will not falter ...

Hope is that thing with feathers / That perches in the soul.
I will say, "Honey, it's time to go."

And together, all of us, the living and the dead, the memories and the pain, the imagination and the hope, the wildlife and the water: We will fly.

APPENDIX

BP's Making of a Disaster

The exploratory Macondo well was to be temporarily capped on April 20, 2010, enabling BP to move on to other sites in the Gulf to prepare them for eventual drilling. The faster exploratory wells are put in place and temporarily capped— sort of a *mise en place* approach applied to the oil industry—the more money oil companies make. And BP, by all accounts, was determined to cap Macondo on April 20. What would ensue was a classic case of haste breeding disaster.

There is no doubt BP and the other players in the Macondo Deepwater Horizon disaster took myriad short cuts that led directly to the fatal explosion. The National Commission on The BP Deepwater Horizon Oil Spill and Oil Drilling, whose lead author is former Florida Senator Bob Graham, plainly states, "The explosive loss of the Macondo well could have been prevented. The immediate causes of the Macondo well blowout can be traced to a series of identifiable mistakes made by BP, Halliburton, and Transocean that reveal such systematic failures in risk management that they place in doubt the safety culture of the entire industry. Deepwater energy exploration and production, particularly at the frontiers of experience, involve risks for which neither industry nor government has been adequately prepared, but for which they can and must be prepared in the future."

The Commission's report points out that on the day of the blowout, "BP and the Macondo well were almost six weeks behind schedule and more than $58 million over budget."

Given BP's long history of putting profits over safety, it's unsurprising an avalanche of mistakes and budget-based decisions exacerbated an already tenuous situation. The following information is gleaned from the Commission's report, various news sources, and the Congressional Record.

It is well established that the Macondo project had been beset by problems for some time. In March the blowout-preventer was damaged in an accident. Did BP repair it? We don't know. During exploratory drilling, the well experienced a flurry of strong kickbacks. In the weeks preceding the explosion, an emergency stop work order was put in place because gas had forced its way up the well bore and onto the platform. Natural gas build-up continually plagued the rig, roiling its way into the drill pipes. The government, concerned the gas could ignite an explosion, instructed BP to proceed with caution, something they did not do. Even their partner, Halliburton, concerned with BP's safety-skirting behavior, informed BP they were not following best practice procedures. Their astonishingly bad decisions include:

- Drilling mud is a primary defense against blowouts. It is heavy and dense, helping to prevent oil and gas from spiraling up the bore and exploding. BP elected to replace the mud with seawater, which in weight is essentially the opposite of drilling mud, prior to the cement plug fully hardening. This decision destabilized the well's equilibrium, making the explosion nearly a certainty.

- Halliburton used a different type of chemical cement despite it failing several field tests. Additionally, according to a *Times-Picayune* article written by Richard Thompson, "... the cement pumped into the Macondo well a day before it blew out ... was not allowed time to harden before a negative pressure test was run. That lapse allowed oil and natural gas to travel up the drill pipe to the surface, where it exploded ..."

- The Commissioners' report reveals that on the day of the explosion, a three-man team flew out to the rig to " ... perform a suite of tests to examine the well's new bottom cement seal." BP erroneously believed the cementing had gone well and, therefore, no testing was needed. They sent the testing team home " ... thus saving time and the $128,000 fee."

- Days before the disaster, BP completed drilling the wellbore 5,000 feet below the surface of the sea. The bore required casings to provide redundant barriers. Halliburton followed best practices and recommended four casings. But BP used just a single layer. In doing so, they saved time and about $10 million dollars.

Much has been made of the fact that the blowout-preventer failed. However, this may be the one point in the series of calamities that wasn't the direct fault of BP or its subcontractors. The blowout-preventer used in the United States was never designed correctly. Liz Birnbaum, who directed the Minerals Management Service at the time of the disaster, was the government's top offshore drilling regulator. In early April 2015, the NRDC published an interview they conducted with her for their magazine *onEarth*. Regarding issues with that particular piece of equipment, she said, "It's been more than three years since the National Academy of Engineering told us how inadequate the current blowout-preventers are. The last I heard, draft standards for blowout-preventers had been sent from the Department of the Interior (DOI) to the Office of Management and Budget for review. The final rules won't go into effect for at least another year, and even then they'll have to include a multiyear phase-in period for new blowout-preventers, which are enormous pieces of equipment. Worldwide, there's a limited capacity to build and put them into use."

On April 13, 2015, nearly five years to the day after the Macondo rig blew up, the Federal government finally announced new regulations regarding blowout-preventers.

The Curious Use of Corexit

As I read various reports about litigating BP through the Clean Water Act, I still struggle with the details of BP's response to the disaster. When news of the explosion first unfolded, as it dragged on for months, as the situation—second by second—grew worse, those of us living amid the nightmare descended into survival mode. What can we do? How fast can we stop the oil, save the wildlife, mitigate the damage? BP's public relations campaign contradicted everything we were living. The Gulf was not okay. Wildlife was dying. People were beginning to suffer health impacts. How could BP obfuscate with such willful abandon?

The answer lies in what biologist Riki Ott said: "Disappeared body counts means disappeared damages—and disappeared liability for BP." Under the Clean Water Act, BP would be fined per barrel of oil spilled into the Gulf. When the government put BP in charge of the crime scene, they essentially gave them *carte blanche* to hide and manipulate evidence that would ultimately be tied directly to the amount of damages they would have to pay. So it was very much in BP's self-interest to low-ball and disappear both the dead animals and the oil.

Which leads me back to the unprecedented manner in which BP used Corexit, dumping at least 1.8 million gallons into the Gulf. Turn the oil into droplets so small, they permeate—thus poisoning—the membranes of the living. Make it sink to the Gulf floor, ensuring a dead zone of horrific proportions. No one will be the wiser. *See no evil, hear no evil, speak no evil.*

Corexit's toxicity is not in question except by some BP executives who claim it's just like using Dawn dish liquid. Not quite. According to researcher Susan Shaw of the Marine & Environmental Research Institute, " ... the properties that make it an effective dispersant also enable it to move through cell walls and damage vital organs. For many species, the Corexit-oil mixture is more toxic than oil alone because its toxicity is synergistic. Corexit 9527 alone contains a solvent that ruptures blood vessels and causes internal bleeding and nervous system damage, an effect that was documented in Exxon Valdez spill responders. Banned in the United Kingdom, where BP is headquartered, Corexit dispersants have permanently undermined the health of untold numbers of Americans."

So why was BP so keen on Corexit? Why did the company continue to use it even after the Coast Guard ordered them to use less toxic dispersants, ones that were actually on the EPA's approved list?

My hunch plainly put: good-old-rich-boy nepotism.

I believe Nalco, the maker of Corexit, was BP's go-to company because of the close relationship it had with Nalco's head man, Rodney Chase. According to papers Nalco filed with the Securities and Exchange Commission, in 2005 Chase was appointed Director of the Company. The filing states, "Mr. Chase is a former Deputy Group Chief Executive of BP and served on the board of BP for eleven years. He retired from BP in April 2003 after 38 years of service."

Chase and Hayward's professional alliances are myriad. When Chase resigned from BP, Hayward moved up the ranks, becoming Chief Executive of Exploration and Production. While BP was stockpiling Corexit prior to the spill and then ordering millions of gallons more during the disaster, Chase was Nalco's Lead Independent Director and served on its Board of Directors. When Hayward was forced out of BP in the wake of the Gulf disaster, he formed an investment company, Vallares, and appointed Chase its Non-Executive Chairman. On July 20, 2011, Nalco, which had seen its stock price significantly rise during the disaster (according to a June 2010 *Fortune Magazine* article, Nalco estimated it would "probably sell $40 million worth of Corexit, up from the roughly $2 million in typical annual sales of the product") was sold to EcoLab for $5.4 billion. On September 8, 2011, Vallares bought a Turkish energy company and Genel Energy—focused on drilling in Iraqi Kurdistan—was born. And what is one of the first things Hayward does with his new company? He appoints Chase as Genel's Chairman.

Do I think BP intentionally created the disaster so one of its own could profit financially? Absolutely not. But do I think that once the disaster occurred, BP was determined, to the detriment of the Gulf and its inhabitants, to line the pockets of one of its own? Absolutely yes. I do believe that.

The government's soft-pedaled and subsequently ignored order that BP cease using Corexit is also curious since Corexit's toxicity was well known in this country. Thirty-one years prior to the Macondo disaster, in 1979, the Ixtoc oil spill in the Bay of Campeche flooded the southern Gulf with oil for nearly ten months. Like the Deepwater Horizon disaster, the blowout-preventer failed. Oil found its way as far north as Texas beaches. Pemex, the Mexican government-owned oil company, authorized 493 aerial missions in which Corexit was sprayed, ultimately resulting in an oil mat on the Gulf floor not unlike the mat we see today as a result of the Macondo explosion. The U.S. government, however, was so concerned about the effects of Corexit, they told Mexico not to spray the chemical north of 25°N, which effectively prevented its dispersal across United States waters.

Truth or Consequences

And we may never know how bad it was.
The exact amount of oil that spewed into the Gulf, in fact, will never be known. The government estimates 4.2 million barrels. BP low-balled its estimate, pegging it at 2.45 million barrels. Ultimately, the court ordered BP to pay the largest fine ever levied against a company for environmental damages in U.S. history: $18.7 billion. The ruling allows BP to pay the fine over an eighteen-year-period. So for a billion dollars a year, for eighteen years, BP will toss money at the five affected Gulf states even while the oil giant continues operations in the Gulf. And while $18.7 billion sounds like a great deal of money to most of us, this is a corporation that in the first quarter of 2013 enjoyed a pre-tax profit of $20 billion. Though the company has taken financial hits as a result of Deepwater Horizon-related litigation and lower energy prices globally, a billion dollars a year for one of the planet's largest oil companies is tantamount to a yearly mosquito bite on an elephant's ass. Furthermore, it is likely BP will manage to write off at least part of the fine as a business expense. According to federal law, companies can't write off fines levied for criminal activity, but they can write off damage payments. The *Times-Picayune* reports, "According to the Public Interest Research Group, at least $13.2 billion in the settlement is not defined as a penalty, meaning BP could potentially get tax breaks on that chunk of money. This includes payments to restore natural resources the spill damaged."

As of this writing, despite the magnitude of the disaster and the fact the court found BP to have been grossly negligent, no one involved in the Deepwater Horizon disaster has done one day of jail time. Two well-sight leaders aboard the rig, Donald Vidrine and Robert Kaluza, were charged with eleven counts of involuntary manslaughter, but the federal government dropped the charges. Keith Jones, the father of Gordon Jones who died in the explosion, told news agencies, "As a result of this court proceeding today, no man will ever spend a moment behind bars for killing 11 men for reasons based entirely on greed."

I don't know the name of the BP executive who insisted the drilling mud be replaced with seawater. I don't know who made the call to send home the testing team or who decided to use only one casing, not four. But surely their individual actions contributed directly to the explosion and, therefore, the deaths of the eleven rig workers.

I do know the name of one former BP executive. Tony Hayward. BP's corporate culture of profits before safety didn't begin with Hayward, and I don't know if it ended with him. But he didn't change the culture; indeed, it appears he promoted it. In my view, he has committed a crime against humanity. In a perfect world, which this is not, he would face justice before thinking even once about getting his life back.

The Environmental Impact: What Science Knows

The Deepwater Horizon disaster continues to play out like a dystopian novel crowded with warped looking glasses, hapless victims, and money-gluttonous villains. Given we're over a half-decade from the initial disaster, science is able to begin drawing conclusions, and universally the conclusions contradict BP's *don't worry, be happy, see no evil, hear no evil, speak no evil* public relations spin.

In a 2012 study, coastal geologist James "Kip" Kirby III linked the use of Corexit to the ongoing presence of oil in sand along the northern Gulf coast. He writes, "The presence of

Corexit® brand dispersant in tar product found on beaches in the northern GOM (Gulf of Mexico) is no longer in doubt. Use of Corexit® brand dispersants should be halted immediately for any and all open water applications … their effects on the environment are clearly more widespread in the Gulf of Mexico than previously thought … given the unknown toxicity and potential for dermal absorption of tar product created from crude oil dispersed with Corexit® brand dispersants, it is highly recommended that an immediate examination of this rapid absorption contamination vector through wet skin be started."

In his conclusion, Kirby offers a frightening indictment of Corexit: "Published research confirms that microbial degradation of tar product is inhibited by the presence of Corexit® dispersant still bound to its molecular structure."

So Corexit was effective in making the oil disappear from human eyes, but it's also responsible for the oil remaining in the environment for years. How many, no one knows. And are we, as we stroll along the shore or when our children build sand castles, being exposed to this deadly chemical?

Rapid absorption contamination vector …

Florida State University oceanographer Jeff Canton and a team of researchers discovered a massive oil mat buried in Gulf floor sediment. Estimated to be composed of six to ten million gallons of oil, it is located in the hot zone: sixty-two miles southeast of the Mississippi Delta.

In January of 2015, Chanton told FSU news site *Florida State 24/7*, oil coating the Gulf floor and meshed in its sediment will " … affect the Gulf for years to come. Fish will likely ingest contaminants because worms ingest the sediment, and fish eat the worms. It's a conduit for contamination into the food web."

Contamination of the food web was a central tenet in Rachel Carson's plea for the cessation of agricultural, governmental, and individual use of pesticides. In *Silent Spring*, she elegantly laid out a deadly pathway: Poisons, as they travel up the food chain, become more concentrated. Pesticides flow into the water table and meander through underground streams and rivers, eventually finding their way into open waterways and the tissues of fish that, ultimately, end up on our dinner tables consumed by humans who are the terminus of the food chain.

There is no reason to believe the phenomenon Carson tracked, known as bioconcentration, is not at play in all ecosystems across the planet. She studied DDD, a chemical closely related to DDT, and its application to a body of water known as Clear Lake in California. In an effort to eliminate gnats, authorities began spraying the lake with DDD in 1949. The insecticide was initially sprayed in one part to 70 million parts of water. In 1954, the application was repeated but the rate was increased to one part of insecticide to 50 million parts of water. The western grebe was the first noticeable casualty, dying by the hundreds. The dead birds' fatty tissues were analyzed and "were found to be loaded with DDD in the extraordinary concentration of 1600 parts per million."

As Carson points out, "The maximum concentration applied to the water was 1/50 part per million. How could the chemical have built up to such prodigious levels in the grebes?"

The answer takes us back to the food web. Grebes are fish eaters. Researchers followed the chain and discovered the poison was, writes Carson, "picked up by the smallest organisms, concentrated and passed on to the larger predators ... plant-eating fishes had built-up accumulations ranging from 40 to 300 parts per million; carnivorous species had stored the most of all. One, a brown bullhead, had the astounding concentration of 2500 parts per million. It was a house-that-Jack-built sequence, in which the large carnivores had eaten the smaller carnivores, that had eaten the plankton, that had absorbed the poison from the water."

It's impossible for me to read Carson's findings and not apply them to what is happening in the Gulf. And one must question the motives of any entity who dismisses out of hand the notion that the massive amounts of oil and dispersant dumped into the Gulf do not and will not have lingering effects. Common sense and science tells us otherwise.

In this unending horror show, innumerable fish species continue to develop lesions and fin rot. Shrimp continue to be born with cancerous lesions and no eyes. Crabs are born with no eyes or claws. Sea turtle nests continue to decline. Pelicans and other seabirds remain seriously impacted, both by a poisoned food chain and habitat loss.

Bluefin and yellowfin tuna, species facing multiple challenges prior to the disaster, have been hard hit. According to an ongoing NOAA fisheries study, "Crude oil from the Deepwater Horizon oil spill in the Gulf of Mexico causes severe defects in the developing hearts …"

The primary problem, according to NOAA, is that "Crude oil contains mixtures of polycyclic aromatic hydrocarbons, or PAHs. These PAHs adversely affect heart development in the two species of tuna, and an amberjack species, by slowing the heartbeat or causing an uncoordinated rhythm, which can ultimately lead to heart failure." The thresholds for developmental defects are very low, in the range of approximately 1-15 parts per billion—within the PAH concentration range of water samples collected during the spill.

Fish swim to find food. They swim to find mating partners. They swim to evade predators. If their ability to swim is impeded, they die. And those are the fish that manage to live long enough for the term "life span" to even apply. The NOAA study bleakly observes, "Severely affected fish with heart failure and deformed jaws are likely to have died soon after hatching."

The National Wildlife Federation (NWF), despite ongoing secrecy prompted by unfolding litigation, produced a comprehensive study titled *Five Years & Counting, Gulf Wildlife in The Aftermath of The Deepwater Horizon Disaster*. Its findings are far ranging and disturbing:

Dolphin deaths continue at an alarming rate. In 2014, along the Louisiana coast, dolphins died at four times the historic rate. An estimated 1,500 dolphin and whale deaths have occurred from the Florida panhandle to Louisiana coasts since the disaster. In all likelihood, the actually figure is higher since dolphins (and all other animals) who died at sea and did not float ashore were never counted. In a 2016 report, NWF states, "In the first five years after the disaster, more than three-quarters of pregnant bottlenose dolphins in the oiled areas failed to give birth to a live calf."

In the immediate aftermath of the spill, between 27,000 and 65,000 of the highly endangered Kemp's ridley sea turtles are estimated to have died, and the number of nests has declined in the five years hence. This remarkable little turtle benefited greatly from cooperation between the United States and Mexican governments who worked together to protect nesting sites and prevent by-catch. Their efforts paid off but the disaster has had devastating effects. The NWF report states, "In the period before the spill, the number of nests was increasing at an exponential rate—about 15 to 18 percent annually. In 2010, the number of nests dropped by 35 percent. The number of annual nests recovered to pre-spill levels in 2011 and 2012 but fell again in 2013 and 2014. The recovery of the Kemp's ridley, which once seemed inevitable, may now be in doubt." Because Kemp's ridleys don't reproduce until they are ten to twelve years old, the

NWF concludes with what is becoming a constant refrain: It will be years before the disaster's impact on the turtles are fully known.

The oil spill is responsible for the deaths of an estimated twelve percent of the brown pelicans and 32 percent of the laughing gulls (730,000 birds) residing in the northern Gulf. The impact on brown pelicans seems nearly sinister given the fact their numbers were reduced drastically in the mid-twentieth century due to DDT. Populations began to rebound in 1972 after the DDT ban went into effect. To help ensure the bird's survival, brown pelicans were relocated from the Atlantic coast to Louisiana—exactly where the largest impacts of the disaster were seen in terms of coastal oiling. Their numbers had increased so significantly that just months prior to the disaster the bird was removed from the federal endangered species list. As for laughing gulls, the NWF report states that fatality studies do not include the number of birds who died offshore and that the "National Audubon Society's annual Christmas Bird Count survey revealed laughing gulls in the five Gulf states declined by up to 64 percent between winter 2010 and the winters of 2011, 2012 and 2013."

The effects of the disaster range far beyond the northern Gulf: "Oil and dispersant compounds have been found in the eggs of white pelicans nesting in three states—Minnesota, Iowa and Illinois."

Speckled trout are spawning less frequently in the affected areas and juvenile red snapper populations have been severely impacted.

Large swaths of coral colonies—both deep sea and shallow water—are dead. The NWF states, "Because corals grow very slowly, recovery of dead and damaged corals to pre-spill conditions could take centuries."

In a situation with troubling parallels to Carson's Lake Clear grebes, the migratory common loon offers compelling evidence of an impacted food web. A bird that migrates a thousand miles and more in order to winter along the Gulf coast, loons, according to the NWF report, "eat mostly fish and spend their lives on the water, going onto land only to nest and mate. This leaves loons particularly vulnerable to direct exposure to oil from polluted water as well as to indirect exposure from eating oil-contaminated fish. Long-lived top predators, loons are indicators of overall ecosystem health." The PAH compounds found in oil, among other ills, compromise immune and hormone systems in birds. Researchers have discovered, just like with the grebes, the concentration of PAH in Louisiana loons along Louisiana's Barataria Bay to be steadily increasing: " ... many loons had PAH levels high enough to cause harm. Researchers also found indications of weathered oil, which contains heavier PAHs that are more toxic to wildlife. This increase may indicate that these oil compounds are making their way up the food chain."

The disaster decimated the oyster beds in Apalachicola and elsewhere in the northern Gulf. The NWF study reports, "According to a federal report published in 2013, oyster eggs, sperm and larvae were exposed to oil and dispersants during the 2010 oil spill. PAHs can be lethal to oyster gametes, embryos, larvae, juveniles and adults. They can also have sub-lethal effects, such as reduced reproductive success. Oysters are vulnerable to oil contamination because they are unable to move away from oiled areas."

Foraminifera, microorganisms that are an essential part of the marine food web, are a primary food source for sand dollars, fish, marine worms, and more. In the wake of the BP disaster, these creatures experienced a massive die-off. The NWF study found that, "Deep sea foraminifera had not recovered in diversity a year and a half after the spill. How long the oiled sediments on the Gulf floor will affect these organisms in heavily oiled areas is unknown."

Bull minnow (Gulf killifish) populations continue to decline, suffering the same effects as tuna: reduced heart rates and DNA damage. The NWF states bull minnows "were also used by scientists as a model species to assess the environmental impacts of chemical dispersants. Oil treated with dispersant was consistently more lethal than undispersed oil. Furthermore, they found that Corexit alone could kill fish within a week of exposure." It goes on to observe, "Additional research has found that four common species of marsh fish, including the Gulf killifish, seem to be avoiding oiled areas. These behaviors, even at small scales, could be significant within marsh communities, leading to changes in food-web dynamics."

The Gulf of Mexico is home to approximately 700 sperm whales. This endangered species lives full-time in the Gulf and its preferred range, according to the NWF, "largely overlaps the area of surface oil contamination." Because sperm whales are prodigious divers, in all likelihood these sea mammals' contact with oil and dispersant would not be limited to surface contamination but would include "the entire water column and on the Gulf floor." Citing the ongoing NOAA study, the report states, "Researchers have found higher levels of DNA-damaging metals such as chromium and nickel in sperm whales in the Gulf of Mexico compared to sperm whales elsewhere in the world—two to five times higher than the average globally. These metals are present in oil from the spill and the results suggest exposure, particularly since whales closest to the wellhead showed the highest levels." Thanks to their full-time status in the Gulf, the whales "had higher levels than seasonal migrants." Emphasizing the importance of tracing all possible pathways for contamination, the report adds, "Exposure to oil could have come via direct ingestion of contaminated waters, inhalation of aerosol particles, absorption through the skin, or consumption of contaminated prey." The NWF cites a further study that found Corexit is harming the animals' DNA. "This outcome," the report says, "raises concerns around impacts of Corexit on reproduction, development, and potentially carcinogenesis in marine mammals and other species." Researchers have also discovered that, like the bull minnows, " ... sperm whales are spending less time foraging in the area around the wellhead. Prior to the spill, this general area was thought to have been a preferred sperm whale feeding ground" leading researchers to conclude the " ... whales are being forced into less suitable areas."

Not included in the NWF's study—perhaps because there are so few left—is the plight of Bryde's whales. Just off the Florida panhandle, in a heavily impacted undersea geological feature known as the DeSoto Canyon, a subspecies of Bryde's whale resides as a full-time resident. Recent studies estimate there are fewer than fifteen still in existence. The canyon, itself, is of vital importance to the entire Gulf because it supplies the Continental Shelf with an abundance of nutrient-rich water.

The National Resources Defense Council (NRDC), in its five-year review of the disaster, states that a Bryde's whale biopsied tissue and blubber samples revealed, as with the sperm whales, highly elevated levels of chromium and nickel.

The NRDC states, "Another concern is that Bryde's whales are baleen whales (a.k.a. filter feeders), and research has shown that the calves of other baleen whales may be particularly vulnerable to toxins that build up in their tissues—like nickel and chromium do."

Scientists normally, and should, operate from a base of healthy inquiry and objectivity. Consider this from Yale's

Environment 360 online journal published July 13, 2016: "Six years after the Deepwater Horizon drilling rig spilled nearly three million barrels of crude oil into the Gulf of Mexico, scientists have found that ultraviolet light is transforming the remaining oil into a more toxic substance that hinders the development of heart, eye, and brain function in fish. The research, led by scientists at the University of California, Riverside and the University of Miami, exposed embryos and larvae of mahi-mahi from the Gulf of Mexico to what they called weathered (exposed to years of sunlight) and un-weathered oil (taken from the drilling site) from the Deepwater Horizon spill in 2010. Compared to fish exposed to un-weathered oil, the fish exposed to the weathered oil experienced impaired eye and neurological function, reduced heart rates, and a buildup of excess fluid in the heart.

"'To this day, we remain uncertain of the magnitude of the Deepwater Horizon oil spill effects, particularly in sensitive life stages of fish,' said Daniel Schlenk, a professor of aquatic ecotoxicology, who led the study, published in *Environmental Science and Technology*. 'We are also uncertain of whether biota exposed to the oil can recover, or have recovered, from this event. And we are still uncertain about how compounds present in oil or any other combustion byproduct or fossil fuel cause toxicity.'"

For countless reasons—among them, corporate and governmental obfuscation, the enormity of the disaster, and the limits of present-day science—*we may never know how bad it was.*

But at the end of the day, neither defining an apocalypse by its numbers or understanding consequences through the revelation of personal truths will matter if we don't act on what we learn. The cessation of our fossil fuel addiction is the only way to ensure another apocalypse never happens.

About the Author

Connie May Fowler is the author of seven other books: six critically praised novels and one memoir. Her novels include *How Clarissa Burden Learned to Fly, Sugar Cage, River of Hidden Dreams, The Problem with Murmur Lee, Remembering Blue*—recipient of the Chautauqua South Literary Award—and *Before Women had Wings*—recipient of the 1996 Southern Book Critics Circle Award and the Francis Buck Award from the League of American Pen Women. Three of her novels have been Dublin International Literary Award nominees. Connie adapted *Before Women had Wings* for Oprah Winfrey. The result was an Emmy-winning film starring Ms. Winfrey and Ellen Barkin.

In 2002 she published *When Katie Wakes*, a memoir that explores her descent and escape from an abusive relationship

She teaches at the Vermont College of Fine Arts low residency creative writing MFA program and directs the College's VCFA Novel Retreat held each May in Montpelier, Vermont. Connie, along with her husband Bill Hinson, is founder and director of the newly minted Yucatan Writing Conference. She and Bill reside in Isla Cozumel with their two dogs, Ulysses and Pablo Neruda, and Catalina The Cat.

ACKNOWLGEMENTS

Tanisha Sabine Christie, you were the first one who believed. Robin Hemley, with unfettered enthusiasm, on a windy Vermont porch, you insisted, "Write it all down." That short sentence—four brief words—propelled me forward.

Joy Harris, your unflagging belief in this project, and your insights into structure and focus, helped me discover the book's core truths.

Joan Leggitt, because of your courage and advice, keen eye and boundless tenacity, *A Million Fragile Bones* is more than scattered pages on my desk. It is a reality we hold in our hands. My gratitude is infinite.

To Deidre, and Phil, and Sean: You are always there no matter the distance, giving strength to the connective tissues of life and art.

Bill Hinson, without your encouragement, without you reading my pages over and over, without you feeding the dogs and making dinner and not complaining I had not showered or changed clothes in weeks, without you during the darkest days of the oil spill whispering to me, "Everything is going to be all right," I would be unmoored in sadness. Thank you for taking this journey with me. The sea, once more, abides.

I also owe devout thanks to my colleagues and students at Vermont College of Fine Arts and the VCFA Novel Retreat, my intrepid family from the St. Augustine Writers Conference, and my brilliant Yucatan Writing Conference tribe. You listened to tear-stained readings from the earliest days straight through to the final dotted i.

To all of you, your bountiful words of support and solidarity sustain me in the writing of this book and beyond.

Also by Connie May Fowler

Sugar Cage

River of Hidden Dreams

Before Women had Wings

When Katie Wakes

Remembering Blue

The Problem with Murmur Lee

How Clarissa Burden Learned to Fly